Micéml Tweddle
1896

5V

CHURCH AND PARISH

The Right Honble Arthur Onslow, Esqr Speaker, in his Seat in
St Margaret's Church Westminster, the Parochial Church of the Commons of Great Britain, 1760.

Drawn by B.C. BOULTER 1950 from a contemporary engraving by A. WALKER

THE SPEAKER IN HIS PEW

CHURCH AND PARISH

Studies in Church Problems, illustrated from the Parochial History of St Margaret's, Westminster

THE BISHOP PADDOCK LECTURES FOR 1953–4

by

CHARLES SMYTH

Rector of St Margaret's and Canon of Westminster
Fellow of Corpus Christi College, Cambridge

LONDON

S · P · C · K

1955

First published in 1955
by S.P.C.K.
*Northumberland Avenue, London, W.C.*2

Made and Printed in Great Britain by
The Sidney Press, Bedford

ACKNOWLEDGEMENTS

THE AUTHOR and Publisher wish to make grateful acknowledgement to the following for permission to quote: Miss F. E. Booker, two letters of Bishop Hensley Henson; Rich & Cowan, and John Farquharson, Ltd. (acting on behalf of the author's Estate), *London in My Time*, by Thomas Burke; John Murray (Publishers), Ltd., *My Friend H: John Cam Hobhouse, Baron Broughton*, by M. Joyce, and *My First Eighty Years*, by A. V. Baillie; Faber & Faber, Ltd., *A Dean's Apology*, by C. A. Alington; Martin Secker & Warburg, Ltd., *Tooting Corner*, by Eric Bligh; the Syndics of the University Press, Cambridge, *Education, Religion, Learning and Research*, by J. Burnaby; Hodder & Stoughton, Ltd., *Ad Clerum* and *The Creed in the Pulpit*, by H. Hensley Henson; the Norfolk Record Society, *The Knyvett Letters, 1620-44*, ed. Bertram Schofield; Columbia University Press, *The Rise of Puritanism*, by William Haller; the Proprietors of Hymns Ancient and Modern, the hymn "In our day of thanksgiving one psalm let us offer . . .", by W. H. Draper; Oxford University Press, *Bishoprick Papers, Retrospect of an Unimportant Life*, and *Open Letter to A Young Padre*, all by H. Hensley Henson, *Return Passage*, by Violet Markham, and *Randall Davidson*, by G. K. A. Bell.

CONTENTS

ILLUSTRATIONS

The Speaker in his Pew in the Parish Church of the House
of Commons
(From a drawing by B. C. Boulter after an engraving by
A. Walker in *The Ornaments of Churches Considered*,
1761)   *Frontispiece*

FOREWORD

To Sir John Crowder, M.P.,
and W. J. Chance Quarrell, Esq.

St Margaret's Rectory,
20 Dean's Yard,
Westminster, S.W.1.

MY DEAR CHURCHWARDENS,

I have the honour to present to you the Bishop Paddock Lectures for 1953-4. This Lectureship was established at the General Theological Seminary, New York, in 1880, under the terms of the will of George A. Jarvis, of Brooklyn,

> out of gratitude to God, for the goodness and mercy that have followed me all the days of my life, now far spent, and to His Church, my spiritual mother; and impressed by a deep sense of the good which may, with God's blessing, grow out of an endowment for the encouragement of "the defence and confirmation of the Gospel" by godly and well-learned men.

The founder stipulated that the Lectureship should bear the name of his "former Rector and ever endeared friend, the Right Reverend Benjamin Henry Paddock, D.D., the present Bishop of Massachusetts".

> *The subjects* of the Lectures shall be such as appertain to the defence of the religion of Jesus Christ, as revealed in the *Holy Bible,* and illustrated in the *Book of Common Prayer,* against the varying errors of the day, whether materialistic, rationalistic, or professedly religious, and also to its defence and confirmation in respect of such central truths as the *Trinity,* the *Atonement, Justification,* and the *Inspiration of the Word of God,* and of such central facts as the *Church's Divine Order and Sacraments,* her historical *Reformation,* and her rights and powers as a pure and national Church.

The Lecturer must be an ordained minister in good standing of the Protestant Episcopal Church in the United States of America, or of some Church in communion with it. To mention *The Fellowship of the Mystery* by John Neville Figgis, C.R., *Church and Nation* by William Temple, *Unity and Schism* by T. A. Lacey, and *Authority and Freedom* by A. E. J. Rawlinson —the Paddock Lectures for 1913, 1915, 1917, and 1923 respectively—is to remind you that this Lectureship has previously been held from time to time by other representatives of the Church of England more eminent than your Rector, to whom it is a matter for legitimate pride to be thus associated with them.

The Lectures contained in this volume were delivered in October 1953 in the Chapel of the Good Shepherd at the General Theological Seminary. Founded by the General Convention of 1817 "for the better education of candidates for the Ministry", and expressly intended "to have the united support of the whole Church in the United States, and be under the superintendence and control of the General Convention", this is the oldest and the largest theological college in the Episcopal Church of America, and the oldest in the Anglican Communion with the exception of Codrington College, Barbados (founded in 1710), and the Theological College of the Episcopal Church in Scotland (founded at Edinburgh in 1810). One-fourth of the present clergy and one-third of the present bishops of the Protestant Episcopal Church received their training at the General Theological Seminary. The student body averages 125: the course occupies three years: tuition has always been free. It would be impertinent to say more than that nobody who has had the honour of lecturing at the Seminary can fail to entertain alike for the faculty and for the students a profound and lasting affection and respect.

Archbishop Temple gave to his Paddock Lectures the title, *Church and Nation*. For obvious reasons, I have given to mine the title, *Church and Parish*: and I would gladly have dedicated this book to the staff and to the congregation of St Margaret's, Westminster, in whose service I have been privileged to spend eight of the happiest years of my life. Alternatively, I should have been happy to have inscribed it to my friends at the General Theological Seminary by whom these Lectures were so generously received, and particularly to Dean Lawrence Rose and Professor Powel M. Dawley. But the book seems to have taken the choice out of my hands by effectually dedicating itself to the memory of one of the most outstanding of my predecessors, Hensley Henson, Rector of St Margaret's from 1900 to 1912 and afterwards Bishop of Durham, to whose genius my work is, both directly and indirectly, so much indebted.

My own views on many questions (and particularly on the issue of Disestablishment) were, and are, very different from those with which he had identified himself: but I had the greatest admiration for him, and he had always been extremely kind to me; and of all the letters of congratulation that I received on my preferment, there was none that I valued more than his. You will forgive me for quoting it.

Hyntle Place, Hintlesham, Ipswich.

July 23, 1946.

MY DEAR CANON,

I have just read in the *Times* the announcement of your appointment to the Canonry of Westminster which carries with it the Rectory of St Margaret's, and I make no delay in sending you the assurance of the pleasure which that announcement has brought to me. Indeed, if I had been charged with the responsibility of choosing a successor to the present Dean of Westminster [Dr A. C. Don, Rector of St Margaret's, Westminster, 1941-6], I should have chosen *you*. May God give you wisdom and courage for the right fulfilment of your task in a position, *than which there is hardly any more potentially important!*

I am so greatly handicapped by failure of eyesight, and other enfeebling concomitants of Senectitude, that I have had to make an end of any public exercize of my ministry....

But I am cheered by the assurance that St Margaret's will be in good hands.

Please convey my best regards and felicitations to Mrs Smyth and believe me to be

Affectionately yours

H. HENSLEY HENSON,

Bishop.

The Revd. Canon Charles Smyth
Corpus Christi College, Cambridge.

In writing to thank him for this most generous letter, I ventured to ask him not only for his prayers, but for his counsel: and I mentioned that a friend of mine had told me that as a boy in 1906 he remembered being very much impressed by the number of Members of Parliament who attended the Parish Church of the House of Commons on Sundays during Dr Henson's incumbency. To this, however, he demurred: the attendance of M.P.s, he wrote (15 August 1946),

was *never* so considerable as your friend's transfiguring memory has suggested. *Indeed, 1906 was the year in which a rather noticeable diminution in the number of worshipping M.P.s was observable.* The General Election, which placed Campbell Bannerman in power, removed an appreciable body of normal worshippers. His great majority was generally either Non-conformist or Secularist, very rarely Anglican. *Archie Fleming's* ardently national ministry in S. Columba's tended to withdraw the body of Scottish Members, who had generally resorted to S. Margaret's, the church in which the Solemn League and Covenant had been subscribed; and, above all, the *week-ending habit,* which was lessening attendance in all the West-end churches, did not leave S. Margaret's unaffected. All the local conditions were changing, and all the changes were unhelpful. When I came to Westminster at the end of 1900, there were still a number of *residents* in Richmond Terrace, Queen Anne's Gate, and

xiv

Victoria Street, but they were being rapidly edged out by public buildings and offices. The "House of Commons seats" were still full, but their occupants were by no means all M.P.s. You must remember that the ever increasing strain of Parliament disinclined even devout Anglican M.P.s to make the journey to Westminster on *Sundays,* when they had to do so *during the week.*

I write all this to re-assure you. There is no reason why you should not (and I think you will) build up a congregation entirely worthy of the church's tradition. But it will be, as all London congregations tend to become, *personal.* People will come because they desire to "see light in the preacher's light". I made a rule of being in my place, and refusing to accept invitations to desert my own pulpit in order to occupy others. And I believe this is a sound rule. *If the preacher is often not in his church, the solidarity of his congregation will fail, and his ministry lose much of its effectiveness.*

Forgive all this, and believe me always to be

Affectly yours

H. Hensley Henson,

Bishop.

Although, as you know, I and our friend, the Reverend A. J. Wilcox, assistant priest since 1945, have consistently endeavoured to make the attachment of our congregation to St Margaret's as *impersonal* as possible, yet I can never be sufficiently thankful for that "rule of *being in my place*" whether I was preaching or not, which I accepted from the outset as one of the conditions of my work as Rector. I have also emulated Dr Henson in making the history of this church and parish the favourite study of my leisure hours. Of that study, recommended by his example and illuminated by his published writings, this book is to a large extent the product. To no other of my venerated predecessors do I stand so much indebted. The least that I can do in gratitude is to dedicate these Lectures to his memory. I wish that I could think that my ministry at St Margaret's has been as effective as he hoped it might be: but I am profoundly happy to have been given this church and congregation, above all others, to love and to serve.

There are other acknowledgements to be made: and although it is impossible for me to enumerate all who, in one way or another, have helped me with this book, yet I am very grateful to all my friends who have encouraged me to discuss it with them, especially Dr G. M. Trevelyan, Dr Kitson Clark, and Professor Butterfield; or who have advised me on particular topics, especially Professor J. E. Neale, Dr Wallace Notestein, Dr W. K. Jordan, Professor William Haller, Mr Roger Fulford, Mr John Saltmarsh, and the Very Reverend the Provost of Bradford; or who have furnished me with valuable material, especially Dr Albert E. J. Hollaender, the Reverend R. D. Middleton, Mr Lawrence Tanner, the Reverend J. S. Reynolds, the Reverend Dr N. W. Rightmyer, and Mr Peter Winckworth.

Here then (with my compliments) is this book. It is the kind of book that I have always longed to write, though I could never have anticipated that St Margaret's would play so large a part in it. I hope that it may encourage others to investigate more thoroughly the rich material contained in our parochial records. You will find that I have made very little use of unpublished documents: but what I have written is based upon fairly wide and miscellaneous reading over a long period of years, and I venture to think that any reader who has the hardihood to explore the appendices and notes will find himself rewarded.

Finally I must testify my gratitude to those who did me the honour to nominate me to this Lectureship, and thereby occasioned the writing of this book. I have taken the opportunity to expand some passages of the lectures, but otherwise I have left them substantially as they were delivered: and in so doing I am reminded of the concluding words of F. D. Maurice's preface to his *Lectures on the Ecclesiastical History of the First and Second Centuries,* published exactly a hundred years ago:

I will only add, that I have not attempted to exchange the

familiarity of the lecture-room for the solemnity of an historical style. The latter might be more agreeable and respectful to the reader, but the former is more natural to me. I have been too long in the habit of addressing young men to be able to divest myself of the feeling that I am still speaking to them when I am writing down words for some unknown reader. Nor can I pretend that I wish to lose these associations, or any by which we are bound to those from whom we are separated on earth. The responsibilities which we have incurred by our intercourse with them we cannot cast off: may it not help us, to think that they are still listening to us?

With my dutiful and affectionate remembrance to all who work and worship at St Margaret's, Westminster, believe me, my dear Churchwardens,

Your Rector and friend,

CHARLES SMYTH

St Margaret's Day
20 July 1954.

CITIZEN AND CHURCHMAN

"HOME", as one of your own poets has said (both yours and ours), "is where one starts from":[1] and it is a commonplace that a knowledge of the history of a particular region or locality can be immensely valuable, not so much as a basis for, but rather a criterion of, generalizations about the history of the nation as a whole. For the outlook of the historian of a parish does not require to be parochial: moreover, the questions that start up at him in the course of his investigations may not merely throw new light—or, what is sometimes equally valuable, new obscurity—upon national history in the period with which he is engaged, but may even serve to raise issues of greater magnitude in Church and State, and to open up new vistas of problems which are timeless and oecumenical in their significance.

That, as you will have guessed, is my apology for the line of treatment adopted in these lectures. In the course of the past hundred years, the study of history has become increasingly specialized, but here is specialization in reverse: the movement of thought is from the microcosm to the macrocosm; from what is local, particular, and concrete, to abstract principles of universal reference.

"Home is where one starts from": and, although I would emphasize that these lectures are conceived as a contribution from, rather than as a contribution to, parochial history, yet "home" for me is naturally the parish which it is my privilege to serve. Some of you when in London may have visited—for it has many associations with your country—the beautiful and historic church, dedicated in honour of St Margaret of Antioch, Virgin and Martyr, which stands in its own churchyard (disused since 1853), alongside and a few yards to the south of the Abbey church, and directly opposite Westminster Hall, which is the oldest part of the Palace of Westminster, more commonly known as the Houses of Parliament.

You will forgive me if I say a few words about this church, by way of introduction.

The great Benedictine Abbey of Westminster, refounded by King Edward the Confessor, and dedicated to St Peter, was never intended for more than seventy-five monks, and in fact seldom had as many as fifty (with their servants) on the establishment. The point is that the Abbey and its church were built for a monastic community, and not for the use of the general public: and although for a time the laity were allowed to worship in the north aisle of the Abbey church, this could not be more than a temporary arrangement, and, from the monks' point of view, it was far better that the local inhabitants —a few folk living in the vicinity of the Royal Palace[2]— should have a parish church of their own, which could be served from the Abbey, like a mission church, by the monastic clergy or their deputies. This is the explanation of the proximity of St Margaret's to the Abbey: in the Middle Ages, they were not in competition.

Tradition relates that a church dedicated to St Margaret of Antioch, Virgin and Martyr, was built by King Edward about the year 1064, "without the Abby church of Westminster, for the ease & commodity of the Monks".[3] The date is certainly conjectural: but the tradition that the church was founded by the Confessor is probable, and has not been disproved.[4] Abbot Herebert (1121-40) some time before his death made a grant of sixty shillings from the profits of the parish church "towards the service of the high altar [of the Abbey] and the needs of the entire church of Westminster": this is the earliest documentary reference to St Margaret's that survives. In 1189, the Abbot and Convent of Westminster procured from Pope Clement III a bull (dated 20 July, which is St Margaret's Day) confirming their claim that the church of St Margaret was outside the jurisdiction of the Bishop: this claim had recently been challenged by Gilbert Folliot, who was Bishop of London from 1161 to 1176, and it was challenged again during the primacy of Archbishop Stephen Langton, who with other papal judges delegate in 1222 gave judgement in favour of Westminster Abbey against the Bishop of London and the Chapter of St Paul's, recognizing the exempt status of the Abbey and the parish church, and describing the boundaries of the parish, which then comprised an area of some forty-four square miles.[5] The association between St Margaret's and the Abbey has always been maintained, and even now the Rector of the parish church is always a Canon of Westminster: but, in distinction from his colleagues on the Chapter, who have no parochial responsibilities, he is primarily a parish priest, and (in the words of Dean Armitage Robinson, himself a former Rector of St Margaret's) parochial duties claim the chief part of his time and strength.[6] Nor is the parish any longer exempt from episcopal jurisdiction. By the reforming initiative of Sir Robert Peel,[7] St Margaret's was made independent of the Dean and Chapter of Westminster and was incorporated in the diocese of London in 1840: the first Rector was Canon H. H. Milman, the ecclesiastical historian, afterwards Dean of St Paul's.

The original church of St Margaret, built by St Edward the Confessor, became ruinous in the course of time, and was largely rebuilt in the reign of King Edward III,[8] "at what time the Wool Staple was at Westminster": "the parishioners and several of the wool merchants built the aforesaid church of St Margaret anew from the foundations, except the great chancel which had been repaired in previous years by the Abbot and Convent of Westminster." The second St Margaret's has no recorded history, except that one of the sessions of the celebrated Court of Chivalry convened to settle the dispute between Sir Richard le Scrope and Sir Robert Grosvenor as to the right to bear the coat *Azure a bend or* was held "en lesglise de Seint Margaret a Westm'" on 12 October 1386, when three knights—Sir Maurice de Bruyn, Sir John Eynesford, and Sir Stephen de Hales—gave evidence on behalf of Sir Richard Scrope before Sir John de Derwentwater, Commissioner for the Lord Constable. Among the other deponents in favour of Scrope

3

was "Geffray Chaucere Esquier", of the age of forty years and more, armed for twenty-seven years: but Chaucer's deposition was not taken (as is sometimes stated) in St Margaret's church, but at the next session which was held in the Refectory of the Abbey of Westminster on 15 October.[9] A hundred years later, the second St Margaret's "stood in need of great repairs", and had in turn to be rebuilt.

The present church—the third St Margaret's—dates from this period (c. 1486-1523), although an eighteenth-century exterior in portland stone (1735) masks one of the few Perpendicular interiors in London, and architecturally one of the most beautiful in the whole of England. As described in Edward Hatton's *A New View of London* (1708), "It is (tho ancient) an Ornamental Church": and it may be claimed without any fear of contradiction that there is not a parish church in Britain so rich in literary and historical associations. Some of these will be noted later in these lectures, although, since it is not my object to produce a history of the Mother Church of the City of Westminster but only to draw upon that material in order to illustrate those wider problems to which I have alluded, the treatment must necessarily be selective. Here it must suffice to mention that within the church or churchyard are buried the printer, William Caxton (1491), John Skelton, Laureate (1529), Nicholas Udall, dramatist and headmaster (1556), Sir Walter Ralegh, founder of Virginia (1618), Admiral Blake (1661), John Pym, the great Parliamentarian (1661), James Harrington, author of *Oceana* (1677), Wenzel Hollar, the engraver (1677), George Hickes, Non-juring Bishop of Thetford and pioneer in the field of Old English scholarship (1715), Elizabeth Elstob, "the learned Saxonist" (1756), James Rumsey, whom the State of West Virginia honours as the inventor of the steam-boat (1792), and a cousin of Lord Byron, Captain Sir Peter Parker, Bt., R.N., killed in a commando raid on the coast of America (1814). Our Registers record the marriages of Samuel Pepys (1655), John Milton (1656), and Sir Winston Churchill (1908), and the baptisms of Lady Castlemaine (1640), Lord Liverpool (1770), and Beau Brummell (1778). One of the earliest instances of pew-rents (1460) is to be found in our Churchwardens' Accounts: [10] and it is believed that the last occasion on which a Bishop officiated at an ordination in an episcopal wig was at St Margaret's in 1848.[11] (In the days when Bishops were still sufficiently opulent to maintain London houses, St Margaret's, by reason of its convenient proximity to the House of Lords, was not infrequently used for ordinations: Robert Gray, the first Bishop of Cape Town, was ordained in this church in 1833, and Dr John Mason Neale, the hymn-writer and founder of St Margaret's Sisterhood, East Grinstead, in 1841.)

But, in addition to these matters of more than ordinary interest, St Margaret's, Westminster, possesses one distinction that is certainly unique. It is the Parish Church of the House of Commons. Territorially, indeed, the entire Palace of Westminster lies within the parochial boundaries, and although the Crypt Chapel, being the chapel of a Royal Palace, falls under the control of the Lord Great Chamberlain, yet, because it is not licensed for marriages, therefore, whenever a marriage is solemnized there, it has to be entered in the Registers of the parish church. But the official place of worship of the House of Lords is, and has always been, the Abbey church: whereas the official place of worship of the Commons is specifically the parish church of St Margaret, adjacent to, but independent of, the Abbey. This is so well known that it is often popularly supposed that the Rector of St Margaret's is automatically Chaplain to the House of Commons, or, to be more accurate, Chaplain to The Speaker: yet in fact, in the past hundred years, only three Rectors during any part of their incumbency have combined both offices, in addition to their full share of duty at the Abbey in their capacity as Canons of Westminster; and, in these strenuous and short-handed days, it is improbable that this arrangement will ever be repeated, although the present Rector is privileged to act as an unofficial deputy for The Speaker's Chaplain and to read Prayers in the Chamber of the House of Commons from time to time. But every Member of the House of Commons is automatically a parishioner of

St Margaret's, with the rights and privileges thereto appertaining: moreover, since 1681 a special pew—it is now the front pew on the lectern side—has always been allocated to Mr Speaker (and, by a tradition probably dating from the eighteenth century, whenever he is present at a service, it is the duty of the senior chorister to bring him a copy of the anthem, regardless of whether he is musical or not), while the pews immediately behind are known officially as the House of Commons pews. Furthermore, it was in the Parish Church of the House of Commons that on Sunday 22 October 1950 a special service in connection with the opening of the New Chamber (to replace the Chamber destroyed by German bombs in 1941) was attended by Speakers from the Empire and Dominions' Parliaments.

These are details: but they signify that St Margaret's stands in an unique relation to our Legislature. In the words of an eighteenth-century *History of London:* "This Church, in the Year 1735, was not only beautifully repaired, but the Tower thereof cased and mostly rebuilt, at the Charge of three thousand five hundred Pounds, given by Parliament, in consideration of its being, as it were, a national Church, for the Use of the House of Commons."[12] The connection indicated in that concluding phrase—*"a national Church, for the Use of the House of Commons"*—is, I believe, without parallel in any other country in the world: and I would ask you to consider its wider implications.

It dates from Palm Sunday, 17 April 1614, when for the first time the Members of the House of Commons came to St Margaret's for what would now be called a Corporate Communion on the occasion of the opening of a new Parliament. (As we shall see, however, their intention was not so purely edifying as this might suggest: it was not until the Oxford Movement that the Anglican piety became refined.)

Parliament was still a lay synod, supposed to be composed exclusively of members of the Church of England, and it may be noted that almost from the very outset of the reign of

6

Elizabeth I each day's business in the House of Commons began with the Litany, followed by prayers: from 1571 to 1597 The Speaker personally led the House in prayer. (This duty has long since been assigned to The Speaker's Chaplain; and since 1580 the Litany has been omitted.[13]) In St Stephen's Chapel, where the Commons sat, The Speaker's Chair occupied the site of the altar.[14] The religious temper of the House was a curious blend of spiritual earnestness, erastianism, and anti-Romanism: the latter element was reinvigorated by the Gunpowder Plot, discovered on 5 November 1605, which finds an echo in an item of 10s. in the accounts of the Churchwardens of St Margaret's for that year, paid to the bell-ringers "for ringing at the tyme when the Parlement howse should have been blown upp". The erastianism of the Commons may be calculated from a passing reference in the *De Republica Anglorum* (1583) of Sir Thomas Smith, where the learned author—*"Doctor of both the lawes, and one of the principal Secretaries unto the two most worthy Princes, King Edward the sixt, and Queene Elizabeth"*—is illustrating the omnicompetence of the English Legislature: ". . . The Parliament abrogateth old lawes, maketh newe, giveth orders for thinges past, and for things hereafter to be followed, changeth rightes, and possessions of private men, legittimateth bastards, establisheth formes of religion, altereth weights and measures. . . ."[15]

The Parliaments of Elizabeth (to go no farther back) opened with a service and sermon in the Abbey church, attended by the Queen and her Court, including virtually the entire House of Lords. Meanwhile, the Commons met in their own Chamber, and, while across the road the service was proceeding, the Lord Steward saw to the roll-call of Members and to the administration of the Oath of Supremacy. The Commons then waited until the Queen and the Lords arrived, when they were summoned to the Upper House.[16]

The corporate Communion of the House of Commons in 1614 was an entirely new departure, for which the *locus classicus* is a letter (dated "from London this 14th of Aprill") written by John Chamberlain to Sir Dudley Carleton, who was then Ambassador at Venice.[17]

> ... Upon the motion of Sir James Parrat, Duncombe, and Master Fuller yt is resolved the whole house shall receve the communion together on Sonday next. The place was once agreed to be Westminster church, but for feare of copes and wafer-cakes, and such other important reasons yt is now altered to St Margets and those three appointed sextans or overseers to note who be absent. ...

"Westminster church" is, of course, the Abbey; and the reference to the "feare of copes and wafer-cakes" is both significant and ominous.

For, although the Speech from the Throne expressed the pious aspiration that the new Parliament which met in April 1614 might be a Parliament of Love, yet, in the circumstances of the time, this was unduly sanguine: and it has in fact gone down to history as the Addled Parliament. Suspicion of recusancy, and of the Government's intention to relax the laws against it, was in the air. Consider, for example, the contribution of Mr Thomas Wentworth, M.P. for Oxford, to the debate on the King's Speech on 12 April, or rather the somewhat disjointed precis of it in the Journals of the House of Commons:

> The general Offer good ...
> Four Heads:
> 1. Religion.—1. Truth of Religion, which established.
> No Cross upon the Bread at the Communion.
> 2. Growth of Religion.—Resteth much upon the Ministers.—Ability, Fidelity,—Ability two parts: Learning, Diligence.—No Proceedings against Non-residents sithence 26 *H*. VIII.—
> Moveth for a Committee, for the growth of Religion, and the Causes of the Hindrances thereof.
> Religion the Root of Justice.—Judges, Sheriffs, Wit-

nesses. No Danger to the Peace of the Land, but for want of Religion.—Great Men in Danger this Way, or those that lie in their Bosoms.—The Root of the Powder Treason not dead.

So for Plenty: For Hope of that, when we at Peace with God.—

Moveth for a Message of a Declaration of the Thanks of the House, for his Majesty's Choice of the Match of his Daughter, for Religion, and for the Writing of his Books against the Pope . . .—Provision for Fish, &c. . . . .

We have no means of judging whether Mr Wentworth's speech was in fact as rambling and as incoherent as the reporter's notes of it: but the latter give us a very clear idea of what was in the speaker's mind, and in the minds of a majority of his fellow-Members. This is the clue to the resolution of the House of Commons to have a corporate Communion, and (on second thoughts) to have it at St Margaret's. The original proposal was mooted on 9 April by Sir James Perrott, Knight, who sat for the Welsh borough of Haverfordwest.

Despite, or possibly because of, his anti-Spanish prejudices and his Puritan sympathies, the Member for Haverfordwest was an interesting and attractive personality, and one of the most popular and experienced debaters in the House of Commons.[18] Born at Harroldston in Pembrokeshire in 1571, the illegitimate son of an illegitimate son of Henry VIII (or so reputed)—his father, Sir John Perrott, a former Lord Deputy of Ireland, ended his life in the Tower of London in 1592, having been convicted of high treason—James Perrott matriculated at Jesus College, Oxford, in 1586, but left the University without taking a degree, entered the Middle Temple in 1590, and "afterwards travelling, returned an accomplish'd gentleman" and settled down upon the estate at Harroldston which had been given to him by his father. There he devoted himself to literary pursuits: his first book, *A Discovery of Discontented Minds, wherein their several sorts and purposes are described, especially such as are gone beyond ye Seas*, was published at

Oxford in 1596, with a dedication to the Earl of Essex: it was designed to "restrain those dangerous malecontents who, whether as scholars or soldiers, turned fugitives or renegades, and settled in foreign countries, especially under the umbrage of the King of Spain, to negociate conspiracies and invasions." In the following year, Perrott entered Parliament. In 1603 he was knighted by the new King.

Before him lay a career of varied activity and usefulness. Like other politicians of the reign of James I, Perrott was in many respects a typical Elizabethan. As deputy vice-admiral for the Earl of Pembroke, we find him writing to the government to report Turkish pirates in the Bristol Channel, or urging the necessity of fortifying Milford Haven and restraining the predatory habits of the Welsh wreckers. He was a member of the Virginia Company, to which he subscribed £37 10s. He was also a lessee of the royal mines in Pembrokeshire. In the Parliament of 1621, he urged military aid for the Elector Palatine, and spoke in favour of a war of diversion and attack on Spain in the Indies. He forfeited the approbation of the King by the warmth of his denunciation of the Spanish Match, and by his insistence upon fresh guarantees against Popery. In the Parliament of 1628, he made a powerful speech against Laud. He also wrote a life of Sir Philip Sidney, which was never printed. He contributed some commendatory verses to *The Golden Grove* of his friend, Henry Vaughan. His last literary publication was *Certaine Short Prayers and Meditations upon the Lords Prayer and the Ten Commandements: with other particular Prayers for severall purposes* (London, 1630: dedicated to the Earl of Pembroke). The "particular Prayers" included "A Prayer for our afflicted Brethren the Protestants beyond the Seas"; and this section of the work was prefaced by a short essay on "The differences in Devotion and exercises of Religion betwixt the Protestants and the Roman Catholiques". Perrott died at his house of Harroldston on 4 February 1637, and was buried in the chancel of St Mary's Church, Haverfordwest.

Such was the man who on Sunday 9 April 1614 opened

the debate which is thus recorded in the Journals of the House of Commons:

> Sir *James Perrott* moveth, that all the Members may, before a certain Day, receive the Communion.—The King's Motion, that this Parliament is to be a Parliament of Love between the King and us: Next, to free those that shall take it, from unjust Suspicion: Thirdly, to keep the *Trojan* Horse out of the House.—Allowed a good Motion.
>
> Sir *Jo. Sammes, accordant;*—and for Good Friday.
>
> Mr *Fuller:*—This the best Means for Love.—Difference in Faces, but Unity in Faith.
>
> The Day, upon Palme Sunday, at the *Abbey,* at Nine of the Clock in the Forenoon.
>
> Mr *Duncombe* concurreth, for the Day, and Place.
>
> Sir Dudley D[*igges*].—
>
> *Ordered,* That the Clerk, with Three of the House, attend, to take the Names of all. The Three; Sir *James Perrott,* Mr *Fuller,* and Mr *Duncombe.* And every Man to bring his Name, and of what County or Borough they are, and deliver it to these Persons: These Persons to take their Names, as they communicate.
>
> Sir *Edw. Gyles:*—That whosoever shall not then receive, shall not after be admitted into the House, till he have received, whether he be now in Town, or no—and ordered accordingly.

But the prevailing temper of the House was puritan, and over the week-end it must have occurred, or have been represented, to some of the Members that the Abbey was High Church: and therefore on Wednesday 13 April the matter was brought up again.

> The Communion to be received at the Parish Church: Not at the *Abbey,* but at the Parish Church.—
>
> That, in the *Abbey,* they administer not with common Bread, contrary [to the] 20th Canon, and the Book of Common Prayer.

Question, Whether at the Parish Church:—*Resolved,* Yea.

Mr *Rolles* and Mr *Heale* to be added for Supervisors.— Eight of the Clock.—

Mr Speaker to bespeak a Preacher.—

The preacher has not been identified, although we know that neither he nor the ministers would accept any remuneration for their services, and, by order of Monday 18 April, "the Distribution of the Collection" was referred to Mr Speaker and four other Members. The supervisors were happily in a position to report that not one Member had refused the Sacrament according to the Anglican rite.

That is the full story, so far as we know it. The methods and principles involved are recognizably other than those of our own day and age. Yet it may be conceded that, in their honest muddled fashion, these Jacobean knights and burgesses were seeking to achieve a variety of ends of which some were highly laudable and none completely indefensible: to hallow their deliberations, to promote a godly union and concord among themselves, to prevent the secret enemies of the English Church and State from infiltrating into the citadel of government (a problem which has its modern counterpart), and to clear the innocent of unjust suspicions of their loyalty. Their error consisted in supposing that for all these diverse purposes the Sacrament of Holy Communion is equally appropriate and efficacious. That this was in fact what they supposed is made even clearer by another speech of the pertinacious Member for Haverfordwest in the new Parliament which met in January 1621.

Sir *James Perrott* moveth for a Communion of all the Members of the House.—Out of many Parts of the Kingdom.—A Means of Reconciliation, and so of Concord in Counsel, of those, who dwell near; and, of those more remote, to know their Religion.—This a Touchstone to try their Faith.—*A Jove Principium,* according to His Majesty's Speech in Star Chamber.—A Blessing by it upon all other Consultations.—All then to take it.—

Six supervisors were again appointed:

> Four [*sic*] Gentlemen; Sir *Francis Barrington*, Sir *James Perrott*, Sir *Jerome Horsey*, Sir *Edw. Gyles*, Sir *Wm. Pitt;* and the Clerk.—*St. Margarett's* Church, *Westmynster*, on *Sunday* next. Doctor *Usher* to preach, upon Question: The Clerk to give him Knowledge.
>
> Every Man, in writing, his Name, and the Place, for which [he] serveth. The former Order, last Session, to be observed.

On this occasion, however, there was trouble with the Dean and Chapter of the Collegiate Church of St Peter, who objected that, since St Margaret's was within their jurisdiction, the House of Commons had no business to nominate a preacher. Their protest is summarized in the Belasyse Diary:

> The parishe church at Westminster was appointed for the receivinge of the communion and Doctor Usher to preache; but the Deane and prebends willed us by our Speaker not to infringe their rights by appointinge the church without ther consents nor to dishonour them by makinge choise of a strainger, ther beinge a Deane and 12 learned prebends who would be readye to do ther best service. . . .

But, in the words of another Parliamentary diarist—John Pym himself—

> This put the House into some heate, and thereupon it was resolved to change the place of the Communion from Westminster to the Temple

—that is, the Temple Church in the Inns of Court, the stronghold of the legal fraternity, who were formidably if not numerously represented in this Parliament. On second thoughts, however, the Commons decided to appeal to the King, who supported them against Dean Williams and his Chapter, but advised Dr Ussher in private audience that he "had charge of an unruly flock to look to next Sunday". The wily monarch also suggested that Ussher might work into his sermon something about the importance of voting money for the support of

the Elector Palatine: and it is to the credit of the Bishop-
designate of Meath and future Primate of All Ireland that
he neglected to take the hint.

So the Commons had their way: and on Sunday 18 February,
as John Chamberlain reported to Sir Dudley Carleton, "all the
nether house communicated ... at St Margerets where Dr Usher
(newly made bishop of Meath in Ireland) made as I heare but
a drie sermon and kept them so long, that yt was neere two a
clocke before they had all don." A vote of thanks was subsequently accorded to the Dean and Prebendaries, and another
to Dr Ussher, who was requested to print his sermon, which
the great majority of the Members (whatever John Chamberlain might have heard to the contrary) had very much enjoyed.[19]

The character of the Commons' corporate Communion as a
sacramental test (which was precisely what the old Queen had
been most anxious to avoid and most determined to prevent)
was even more transparent in 1621 than it had been in 1614.
On Monday 19 February it was "ordered that none should be
admitted to the House that did not receive the communion on
the day appointed, before he receive it in the presence of some
of the committees [or supervisors] appointed for the ordering
thereof." On 27 February "Sir James Perrot, one of the committees [or supervisors] for ordering the communion, reported
who had not received it." (The names of nine defaulters are
recorded in the Journals of the House.) "Some were sick and
some absent, and some who had received it were ordered to
receive it again before one of the committees. There was
gathered at the communion 31 *li*. 15*s*. and odd money which
was to be bestowed to such charitable and fit purposes as the
committees shall think fit."

What may perhaps be difficult for us fully to appreciate is
that the Members who were so active and vigilant in this matter
were strongly religious men. They did not consider the corporate Communion simply as a trap for the detection of
Papists: and when Sir James Perrott moved for a third time in
1623 that the House "receive the holy Sacrament, as a Sign
and Symbol of our Unity and Charity", he took for granted that

there could be no real unity except among those who were able to communicate together at the Lord's Table, and therefore what would appear to us to have been primarily a sacramental test was to him primarily a bond of concord, as in religion, so in counsel.

It is always perilously easy to undervalue the piety of a generation that is dead and gone, and to suspect that, because their religion was more coarse-fibred or at some points less sensitive than that in which we have ourselves been nurtured, it cannot have been very genuine nor gone very deep. It is therefore valuable that we should observe, in the report of the debate on 10 February 1621, the distress felt by the Members that, at a time when they were preparing to receive the holy Sacrament, they should find themselves involved in an irritating and incongruous dispute with the Abbey authorities. It will be remembered that they had invited Dr Ussher to preach at their corporate Communion at St Margaret's; the invitation had been vetoed by Dean Williams; and, since neither side was willing to give way, the only method of resolving the deadlock was to appeal to Cæsar. But the temper of the House was ruffled, and the Members were not, and knew that they were not, in love and charity with all men. Accordingly, Sir *Thomas Hobby* moved

—To put off the receiving the Communion till *Sunday* come-sevennight.

Sir *Edw. Mountague:*—Not so fitted now for receiving the Communion, in respect of these Crosses.—To put it off till *Sunday* come-sevennight.

Mr Treasurer:—That, in respect of better Preparation, to be deferred.

There is no suspicion of hypocrisy here: which goes to show that a genuine sacramental piety was, at that time, compatible with a sacramental test. Indeed, the underlying principle of the latter was simply that a Christian nation should be governed by loyal members of the national Church as by law established. We may think of analogies in humbler walks of life. It is desirable that in a Church school all the teachers should be convinced and practising Churchmen. It is desirable that in a College which is, by definition, a religious foundation, all the undergraduates (and all the dons) should attend a number of services in the College Chapel every week during Term. It is desirable that a boy who belongs to a Scout troop or other Youth organization attached to a particular church should worship in that church at least once every Sunday. But what is unexceptionable in theory may be difficult to apply in practice. The spirit of a regulation may be admirable, but the letter of it may be odious.

It was inevitable, for example, that the regulations governing the administration of the corporate Communion of the House of Commons in the seventeenth century should be developed by a kind of case-law. Each several Member was to deliver to the appointed supervisors "a little note of his name and of the place for which hee served . . . immeadyatlye after the receavinge of the wine". Any Member who had failed to communicate on the appointed day "shall not, after that Day, come into the House, until he shall have received the Communion, in the Presence of some, or One, of the Persons hereafter appointed to that Purpose, and the same be certified, and the Certificate thereof be allowed by this House". In the summer of 1625, when, on account of an outbreak of plague in the capital, Parliament was adjourned to Oxford, it was ordered that any Member who had not yet received the Communion should receive it the next Sunday in Exeter College Chapel. In February 1626, a Member (Sir Robert Howard) who had been excommunicated by the Court of High Commission was dispensed by order of the House from receiving the Communion on the appointed day, and was allowed to sit in the House until other Order be taken. Most disquieting of all is an entry in the Commons Journals under the date 1 April 1624: "Mr Recorder:—A Gentleman of the House before, returned again.—Whether to receive the Communion again.— *Resolved*, No."

The nature of the problem is already visible, and to multiply illustrations of it would be superfluous. It may suffice to note that in November 1640 particularly stringent precautions were adopted "to prevent Profanation, and Rejection of the Sacrament: and for the securing of this House, that no Papist sit here amongst them". After that date, and until the Restoration, the corporate Communions appear to have been discontinued, although the Sermons were retained and indeed multiplied. As Professor Haller has written in his *Liberty and Reformation in the Puritan Revolution*: "The fixing of the custom of regular fast days, with special services at St Margaret's for the House of Commons, gave to the preachers recognition and responsibility such as they had never known. They now found themselves the prime exponents of the religious and moral sanctions of a revolution moving forward at a quickening pace to conclusions they had not foreseen and were not likely to approve."[20] Then, at long last, in May 1661, as recorded in the Commons Journals, it was explicitly

> *Resolved,* upon the Question, That the Sacrament of the Lord's Supper shall, upon *Sunday* next come Sevennight, being the Twenty-sixth of this Instant *May,* in the Forenoon, be administered at *St* Margaret's Church in *Westminster,* according to the Form prescribed in the Liturgy of the Church of *England*; and that all the Members of this House shall then and there receive the said Sacrament; and that whosoever shall not then and there receive the said Sacrament, shall not, after that Day, come into the House, until he shall have received the said Sacrament in the Presence of Two or more of the Parties hereafter appointed to that Purpose, and the same be certified, and the Certificate thereof allowed by this House. . . . Mr Dr *Gunning,* and Mr *Carpenter,* the Chaplain of this House, are desired to officiate at that Time, and to preach, one of them in the Morning, and the other in the Afternoon.

But a good deal of water had flowed beneath the broken bridges of the Established Church in the past twenty years, and the traditional Order was no longer capable of strict enforcement.

On 30 May Andrew Newport wrote to Sir Richard Leveson:
"There were so many Members absent of both parties from
St Margarets on Sunday last, when they were appointed to
receive the Communion, that neither party thought fit to take
notice of it in the House next day. Mr Prynne and some few
others refus'd to take it kneeling. 'Twas moved the next day
that Dr Gunneing might have the thanks of the House for his
pains, and be desired to print his sermon; Secretary Maurice
and Mr Prynne oppos'd it; the former said it was a scandalous
sermon, but the House order'd thanks, and in waggery some
desir'd that those two opposers should be the persons to carry
them, but not so order'd."[21] Nor had the unedifying incident
in St Margaret's failed to be noted, with circumstantial detail,
in the diary of Mr Samuel Pepys:

> May 26th. (Lord's Day.) This day the Parliament received
> the Communion of Dr Gunning at St Margaret's, West-
> minster. Sir W. Batten told me how Mr Prin (among the
> two or three that did refuse to-day to receive the sacrament
> upon their knees) was offered by a mistake the drinke after-
> wards; which he did receive, being denied the drinke by Dr
> Gunning, unless he would take it on his knees; and after
> that, by another the bread was brought him, and he did take
> it sitting, which is thought very preposterous.

Other Members also, if less truculent than Mr Prynne, had
conscientious scruples, and were prepared to justify them. The
Member for Clitheroe in Lancashire, Sir Ralph Assheton, Bt.,
whose father, the first Baronet, had fallen foul of Archbishop
Laud in the days before the Great Rebellion, "desir'd he might
be admitted to Shew his Reason why he could not (as his
particular Case was) with a good Conscience receive the Communion", but the House agreed by a majority vote that the
Order should not be debated. Although Assheton himself was
allowed a tacit dispensation, the House was "much unsatisfied
both with the Matter and Manner" of the excuse given by
another Member, and resolved "That the said Mr Love be
suspended from sitting in this House, until he shall communi-

cate, and bring Certificate thereof." What had originally been intended as a religious test to exclude only Roman Catholics, because their loyalty was suspect, was now beginning to operate also against Protestant Dissenters. In 1666 leave was again asked "for speaking against the orders to receive the sacrament": it was refused by 98 votes to 54, but by 1672 such orders cease to appear in the Commons Journals.

It is significant that in 1672, and again in 1673, Bills to exclude "Dissenters in matters of religion from the Church of England" from sitting in the House of Commons were defeated, and that the Test Act of 1673 (which excluded Nonconformists from municipal corporations until 1828) was not made applicable to Members of Parliament. The Relief Act of 1829 finally admitted Roman Catholics. Parliament had ceased to be a lay synod of the Established Church: yet, inasmuch as Jews and avowed infidels were ineligible, it was still exclusively a Christian legislature. By 1888 these barriers had also been removed. All that remained was a moral certainty that any Member of the House of Commons who had been involved in divorce proceedings would be defeated if he stood again at the next General Election: and even this vanished into limbo in the interval between the two World Wars.

Thus ended what may not unfairly be described as an experiment in theocracy. That word is normally reserved for more self-conscious disciplines, notably the polity established by Calvin at Geneva, which moved John Knox to describe that city as "the maist perfyt schoole of Chryst that ever was in the erth since the dayis of the apostellis"; or the left-wing Puritan ideal of the Rule of the Saints, which caused so much embarrassment to Oliver Cromwell; or the regime of the Jesuits in Paraguay. But it is applicable also to any constitutional embodiment of the principle that the government of a Christian nation should be exclusively composed of Christian men and should frame its policy exclusively by Christian standards. This principle, which the medieval Church had constantly endeavoured to enforce by the spiritual weapons of interdict and excommuni-

cation, was reasserted by the Protestant Reformers. Furthermore, the Church of England at the Reformation retained,
within the altered context of a National Church outside the
Papal obedience, the axiom that Church and State comprise
the same men regarded in two distinct capacities, as citizens
and Churchmen: and this assumption was fundamental to the
thought of such eminent and representative divines as Stephen
Gardiner, Richard Hooker, and William Laud, while Thomas
Hobbes himself, "the Atheist of Malmesbury", was able with
perverted ingenuity to make a quite unwarrantable use of it
in his *Leviathan*. It is more surprising to find it reiterated by
Edmund Burke, for by that time it had ceased to be even a legal
fiction. But the Establishment remained: the ecclesiastical
superstructure had outlasted the political foundation upon
which it was traditionally based: and this tended to disguise
the ineluctable necessity of recasting the theoretical assumptions which had always been associated with it. Thus, at the
time of the struggle for Catholic Emancipation, Robert Southey
could write to Grosvenor Bedford (23 February 1823): "Our
constitution consists of Church and State, and it is an absurdity
in politics to give those persons power in the *State*, whose duty
it is to subvert the *Church*. This argument is unanswerable."
Or, still more recently, in the debate in the House of Commons
on the Revised Prayer Book of 1928, it was possible for Sir
Thomas Inskip, M.P., a staunch Low Churchman, to declare
that if our English Church "is to be the Church of England it
must teach the faith of the people of England" and must "bring
the doctrines of the Church of England into accord with the
doctrines of the people": phrases which inadvertently recall
the classic statement of George Harwood in his *Disestablishment: or, a Defence of the Principle of a National Church*
(1876)—"A National Church means a Church teaching the
religion which the nation holds, not that which it ought to
hold."

In point of fact, Church and State were never literally co-
extensive, and it was always possible to point to certain
anomalies in practice, such as the grudging but unavoidable

establishment of Presbyterianism in the Channel Islands (which are part of the diocese of Winchester) in the reign of Elizabeth I.[22] Yet until the Glorious Revolution, which conferred on Protestant Dissent a legal status under the Toleration Act, the old ideal of a single national Church with no nonconformity permitted remained a workable hypothesis. Superficially—and perhaps not only superficially—it may be argued that this hypothesis found its noblest expression in the corporate Communion of the House of Commons in St Margaret's, Westminster, from 1614 to 1640, and from 1661 to 1666. To any priest who celebrates the divine mysteries at the altar of the Commons' Church, it must always be a moving thought that in this very chancel the protagonists in the tragic conflict between Crown and Parliament that issued in our Civil War —Wentworth and Pym, Hampden and Falkland, Cromwell and Vane and Hyde—knelt, in a sacred fellowship transcending all personal and public animosities, to receive the most comfortable Sacrament of the Body and Blood of Christ.

Unhappily there was one public animosity which was rather asserted than transcended by this sacred ordinance. The corporate Communion served a dual purpose: not only to unite, but also to exclude. It was not only a corporate Communion: it was at the same time a sacramental test. For the sense of identity between Church and State was intensified by the consciousness of a common danger from the forces of the Counter-Reformation militant and, over the greater part of Europe, alarmingly triumphant. Those who associated Roman Catholicism with Antichrist, and those who associated it with foreign despotism, were not regarding the problem from precisely the same angle: but they were natural allies.

The indecency of using the Sacrament of Unity for a negative and extraneous purpose which was, moreover, as much political as religious, is to us the fundamental point of criticism. Hardly less obvious is the objection that a religious test places a premium on insincerity (which no external criterion can ever infallibly detect), and that to employ the Sacrament of the Lord's Supper for this purpose is to invite profane and sacrilegious communions. We should do well to remind ourselves that the seventeenth-century Ecclesia Anglicana has no monopoly of blame in this respect: to mention only one example, the First Communion in the parish church of St Roch in Paris on Christmas Day 1719, of the notorious wizard of finance, John Law of Lauriston, who had required to be received into the Church of Rome in order to qualify for a government appointment under the French Crown, was not a particularly edifying incident.[23] But two blacks do not make a white: and it is even more important that we should recall the scathing *Expostulation* (1782) of the Evangelical poet, William Cowper, against the Test Act:

> *Hast thou by statute shov'd from its design*
> *The Saviour's feast, his own blest bread and wine,*
> *And made the symbols of atoning grace*
> *An office-key, a pick-lock to a place,*
> *That infidels may prove their title good*
> *By an oath dipp'd in sacramental blood?*
> *A blot that will be still a blot, in spite*
> *Of all that grave apologists may write.*

And that indictment is unanswerable.

Alluding to the Donation of Constantine—the legendary archetype of the alliance between Church and State—Cardinal Pole in his *De Concilio* congratulated Pope Sylvester on having landed a bigger fish than St Peter ever caught. Yet the saying of the Lord, "Render unto Cæsar the things which are Cæsar's; and unto God the things that are God's" (which von Ranke called "historically the most important text in the Gospels"), remains enigmatic, not in principle, but in application: and there has always been considerable variety in the relations between Church and State.[24] It is of course possible for the State to persecute the Church, although the modern State will seldom, if ever, adopt religious persecution as an article of official policy: even the Constitution of the U.S.S.R. confines itself to separating the Church from the State, and the school from the Church, in order to ensure to citizens freedom of conscience, while recognizing for all citizens freedom of religious worship and freedom of anti-religious propaganda. Or it is possible for the State, at least on paper, to ignore the Church, and to adopt a policy of religious neutrality: thus it is stated in the Treaty of Peace and Friendship with Tripoli (1796) that "the government of the United States of America is not, in any sense, founded on the Christian religion", and the U.S. Supreme Court declared, in Everson *versus* the Board of Education (1947), that "We have staked the very existence of our country on the faith that a complete separation between the State and religion is best for the State and best for religion." Or the State may qualify its neutrality by regarding itself as "a spiritual society": the Fascist State, as defined by Mussolini, "has no theology, but it has an ethic": the Nazi Party, as conceived by Hitler, "stands for a positive Christianity, but does not bind itself in the matter of creed to any particular confession", while it "demands liberty for all religious denominations in the State, in so far as they are not a danger to it and do not militate against the moral sense of the German race."

In a State that is genuinely neutral or nominally Christian, the Church may organize or support a political party (such as the old German *Centrum*), or it may operate as a pressure group in defence of its own interests whether broadly or narrowly conceived. Again, the Church may claim, in the words of the Encyclical *Immortale Dei* (1885), that "the State . . . is clearly bound to satisfy its many and great duties towards God by the public profession of religion". Where this claim is admitted, the State may identify itself with the Church, as in England under the Tudors and the early Stuarts: or it may ally itself with the Church, more or less on the terms and with the objects stated by Bishop Warburton in his *Divine Legation* (1738), however these may be disguised as a concession to modern taste. A particularly interesting variant is afforded by the Constitution of the State of Eire, which acknowledges that the homage of worship is due to Almighty God, and recognizes the special position of the Holy Catholic Apostolic and Roman Church as the guardian of the Faith professed by the great

23

majority of its citizens, but at the same time recognizes the Church of Ireland and the other religious denominations, Christian and non-Christian, existing within its borders.

All these various solutions of the problem, however theoretically simple, are attended by administrative complications: in the phrase of Burke, their theoretical perfection is their practical defect. In my judgement, at once the most superficially attractive and the most indefensible in practice is that which postulates in a nation organized as a State the ethical standards and ideals of a Church, and applies in the interests of the latter the coercive methods appropriate to the former. We have seen what this led to in the perverted State religions of Fascist Italy and Nazi Germany. In a completely different context, we may also recognize in this description the nemesis of English Puritanism in the Interregnum. The Church can never be identical with the State because it is not co-extensive with the Nation. Nor is there any specifically Christian system or form of government prescribed by Holy Scripture: and where the Church identifies itself with a particular polity— which means, in practice, with a particular regime—it thereby places its eternal interests at the mercy of temporal vicissitudes and the hazards of political catastrophe.

We may confess that, on a superficial view, there has been a good deal in our history to foster the illusion (which lingers faintly yet among the politically ignorant) that "the Church of England is as much a department of the State as the Civil Service, or the Army, or the Navy". In 1826 there was a certain novelty in the thesis of Hugh James Rose's sermons in the University Church at Cambridge on *The Commission and Consequent Duties of the Clergy*, that the Church is not a social institution to be judged like other social institutions, but a Divine Society possessed of a Divine Commission. This was to be the thesis of the Oxford Movement, which in the providence of God revitalized for the Church of England as by law established that article of the Creed, "the holy Catholick Church". How startling it appeared to contemporaries may be inferred from a letter written in 1848 by a devout Churchman

24

and Member of Parliament for Oxford, Page Wood, afterwards Lord Chancellor Hatherley. The writer had approved of the Repeal of the Test Act and of the Roman Catholic Relief Bill, and had lately made his maiden speech in the House of Commons in support of the admission of Jews to Parliament. "Only yesterday," he wrote to his friend W. F. Hook, the famous Vicar of Leeds, "when I said in the presence of several sensible men, calling themselves Churchmen, but really Conservatives, 'How did the Church first make its way?—Not by political enactments', they said, 'Oh! you cannot compare the times when there was supernatural assistance'. I replied, 'That is just what I complain of; you rely on Acts of Parliament because you have lost your faith in your own Church.' They seemed quite amazed when I told them I believed we are supernaturally assisted now."[25]

As we look back across the intervening centuries, we have no reason to regret the breakdown of the English experiment in constitutional theocracy of which the corporate Communion of the House of Commons in St Margaret's, Westminster, was so notable an expression. But at the same time we have every reason to be thankful that the withering away of the State connection in the form which it had assumed under the Elizabethan Settlement did not involve any repudiation of the underlying principle, which Burke defined as "the consecration of the state by a state religious establishment", signifying the acknowledgement by the State of the Sovereignty of God in the affairs of men, and incidentally (as Professor Leonard Hodgson has pointed out) conferring upon the Church the right and the duty "to exercise a prophetic ministry, and to seek to perform the function of a conscience for the whole community" in regard to social, economic, and political affairs. Indeed, a healthy appetite for episcopal pronouncements on miscellaneous topics of current interest is one of the distinctive attributes of English life. But that is a digression.

After the Restoration of the Monarchy in 1660, St Margaret's continued as before to be "as it were, a national Church, for the

Use of the House of Commons", which the House attended officially upon official occasions, as (when in session) for the State Services on 5 November, 30 January, and 29 May, and on General Fast Days and Thanksgiving Days appointed by Royal Proclamation. The attendance fluctuated a good deal: but the House continued to appoint preachers, to thank them, and to desire them to print their sermons.

This was largely a formality: [26] only the Thirtieth of January —the sombre but controversial anniversary of the Decollation of the Royal Martyr—introduced an uncertain element into the ceremonial religious exercises of the Commons. In 1750 the Reverend William Stephens, Rector of Sutton, Surrey, "told them that the observation of that day was not intended out of any detestation of his murder, but to be a lesson to other Kings and Rulers, how they ought to behave themselves towards their subjects, lest they should come to the same end."[27] On the following day, the customary motion that the thanks of the House be given to the preacher was negatived without a division: and it was *"Resolved,* That, for the future, no Person be recommended to preach before this House, who is under the Dignity of a Dean in the Church, or hath not taken his Degree of Doctor in Divinity."

In the ensuing year, Parliament was not in session until 10 February: but, having occasion to invite a preacher for 4 April 1701, being "the Day appointed by his Majesty's Royal Proclamation for publick Fasting and Humiliation", the Commons played for safety and asked the Dean of Canterbury. They were, however, subsequently to discover that no such security against exceptionable sentiments was afforded merely by a Doctorate in Divinity. The preacher on 30 January 1710 was Dr West, a Prebendary of Winchester: and, for the first and last time in its history, the House divided on the motion that he be given a vote of thanks and desired to print his sermon, although the motion was in fact carried by 124 votes to 105.

But in 1772 the House was placed in an even more embarrassing position. The preacher was the Reverend Dr Thomas

Nowell, Regius Professor of Modern History and Public Orator in the University of Oxford, and Principal of St Mary Hall. The sequel is described in a letter, dated 21 February, from Edward Gibbon, the historian, to his friend Holroyd:

> To-day the House of Commons was employed in a very odd way. Tommy Townshend moved, that the sermon of Dr Knowell, who preached before the House on the 30th of January, (*id est*, before the Speaker and four members,) should be burnt by the common hangman, as containing arbitrary, tory, high-flown doctrines. The House was nearly agreeing to this motion, till they recollected that they had already thanked the Preacher for his excellent discourse, and ordered it to be printed. Knowell's bookseller is much obliged to the Right Honourable Tommy Townshend.[28]

One Member proposed "That for the future, the Thanks of this House be not given for any Sermon preached before this House, until such Sermon shall have been printed and delivered at the door of this House". On 25 February, the subject was resumed upon a formal motion to expunge from the Votes of the House the vote of thanks to Dr Nowell for his sermon, and this was eventually agreed without a division: but the account in the *Parliamentary History* makes it transparently clear that the House was not at its best in this debate, which was tinged throughout with a strong element of farce. The Member who had seconded the vote of thanks explained that he had done so against his better judgement, having been over-persuaded by the Member who proposed it. The Speaker said that he himself had highly disapproved of Dr Nowell's sermon, and had taken care to mention the disgust it gave him to a gentleman who, he was sure, would convey his sentiments to the preacher, from which The Speaker had presumed that the offensive passages would be omitted from the printed text. Sir Roger Newdigate "with extreme violence and heat" justified both the preacher and King Charles I. Mr Frederick Montague said, "The clergy of this country are in a very disagreeable situation when they are obliged to preach on the 30th of January. I remember when a clergyman was refused the thanks of the House because he preached in the opposite extreme to Dr Nowell." He gave notice of his intention to bring in a Bill to repeal the statute (12 Car. II, c. 30) by which the religious observance of the anniversary was appointed.

This was debated on 2 March. Sir Roger Newdigate opposed the Bill. Mr Stephen Fox "said, he was against abolishing the ceremony of the day; that he thought it did no harm, unless (addressing himself to the Speaker) the obliging you, Sir, to go to church once a year; that the day was almost forgot as a fast; that for his part he never fasted; and, that he looked upon the motion as not very material." After a somewhat frivolous discussion, the House divided, and the motion was lost by 125 votes to 97. But there does not appear to have been any marked improvement in the attendance of the Commons at their parish church on the Thirtieth of January, for Spencer Perceval at the beginning of the nineteenth century was distressed to find it "discreditably thin".[29]

By 1859, when the State Services were finally abolished, the official attendance of the House of Commons at St Margaret's had already ceased, apart from these and certain special occasions, of which almost the last were in connection with the Crimean War—the General Fast on Wednesday 21 March 1855, and the General Thanksgiving Day (for Peace with Russia) on Sunday 4 May 1856. The preacher on 21 March 1855, was the silver-tongued Henry Melvill, and a newly elected Member, Stafford Northcote, went to St Margaret's

> with the House—that is to say, about 150 members and the Speaker. Oddly enough, I was placed next to Disraeli, who entered into conversation with me very amicably afterwards, and agreed with me that the sermon was exceedingly "flash". Every now and then the preacher paused at the end of a flowery sentence, and the whole congregation coughed and sneezed approvingly, exactly as if they were cheering. I was a good deal disgusted.[30]

Very different was the scene on the next occasion when the

House of Commons attended St Margaret's in state, on Sunday 22 May 1887, "to offer thanksgivings on the jubilee of the reign of the Sovereign. Such an event had never occurred before, and it was one which demanded and received some observance of stately though simple ceremonial." The circumstance that Archdeacon Farrar was now Rector of St Margaret's was itself a guarantee not only that the opportunity would not be missed, but also that it would be exploited to full advantage.

Members met in their places in the House before eleven o'clock in the morning, and the arrival of the Speaker at the Clerks' table signified the time for attending the service.

Just before the clock struck a quarter to eleven the Speaker, Mr Peel, arose and walked down the Chamber to the door, the Members forming behind him in order, four abreast . . . altogether about four hundred. . . .

On the procession passing out of Palace Yard into Parliament Square, it was joined by the band of the Queen's Westminster Volunteers, who, playing an appropriate march, led the way with slow and measured pace, as befitted the dignity and character of the participants and the function. It was nearly five minutes after the hour appointed for the commencement of the service when the west door of St Margaret's was reached and the procession entered the church, their progress having been awaited by a great crowd of six or seven thousand well-dressed persons. . . .

. . . The scene in the church was exceedingly animated, though, of course, it was marked by a fitting solemnity and quietude of demeanour. The seats in the nave were reserved for Members, those in the two aisles being set apart for their ladies. . . . Meanwhile the Archbishops of Canterbury and York had taken their places on either side of the altar table, which was slightly decorated with flowers, while in front of it stood some splendid specimens of the azalea in full bloom. . . . The Speaker, who wore his full-bottomed wig, and his state robes richly embroidered with gold, took his seat in the front pew with his predecessors, Viscounts Eversley and

Hampden. Mr Erskine, the Serjeant-at-Arms, who had borne the Mace thus far, placed it on rests constructed specially for the purpose in front of the Speaker. . . . The service opened with the singing of the national anthem; and, as the choirs of Westminster Abbey and St Margaret's were combined for the occasion, and the congregation joined heartily in the singing, the effect was very grand. . . . Archdeacon Farrar . . . read the second lesson from Rom. xiii., the first (1 Kings iii. 5-14) having been read by the Hon. and Rev. T. Byng, the Speaker's Chaplain. The absolution was pronounced by the Archbishop of York, and the benediction at the close of the service by the Archbishop of Canterbury. After the third collect Handel's well-known Coronation Anthem was sung with much effect, and then followed a fine hymn composed expressly for her Majesty's Jubilee by the Bishop of Ripon, and set to music by Dr Bridge, who had introduced into the tune the melody known as "Gotha" composed by Prince Albert. This hymn of praise and worship was entitled "For the priceless gifts", and at its conclusion the sermon was preached by its author, the Bishop of Ripon, whose discourse, remarkable for its power, brilliant illustration, and sustained eloquence, was listened to with intense interest.

. . . During the singing [of the final hymn] a collection was made on behalf of the funds of Westminster Hospital. . . . The amount collected was one hundred and eighty-seven pounds. The service closed with the Hallelujah Chorus. . . .[31]

The last time that the House of Commons had occasion to thank a preacher in the traditional form was ten years later, in respect of the sermon preached in St Margaret's on Sunday 20 June 1897, "at their Public Thanksgiving for the completion of the sixtieth year of the reign of Her Majesty, Queen Victoria". For this office they had very appropriately invited Dr Farrar, formerly Rector of St Margaret's and (from 1891 to 1896) Chaplain to The Speaker, who had lately been promoted to the Deanery of Canterbury. Because this is the last entry of its kind in the Commons Journals, it may be quoted in full: [32]

Friday, 2nd July 1897

Commemoration Service in St Margaret's Church.

RESOLVED, *Nemine Contradicente.*
THAT the Thanks of this House be given to the Very Reverend FREDERIC WILLIAM FARRAR, D.D., Dean of Canterbury, for the Sermon preached by him on Sunday the 20th day of June last before this House in St Margaret's Church, Westminster, and that he be desired to print the same; and that Mr Balfour and Secretary Sir Matthew White Ridley do acquaint him therewith.

REGINALD F. D. PALGRAVE
Cl. Dom. Com.

Yet that is not quite the end of the story of the traditional association between the House of Commons and St Margaret's, Westminster. It is not a mere relic of the past that, in accordance with immemorial custom,

> *St Margaret's bells,*
> *Quiring their innocent, old-world canticles,*
> *Sing in the storied air* [33]

when, at the beginning of a new Parliament, Mr Speaker assumes, or resumes, his tenure of the Chair; or that the annual parochial Vestry Meeting is always held upon the Thursday before Whitsun—an exceptional date, but chosen in order to avoid the Easter Parliamentary recess, when the Members will be out of Town. All Members of the House of Commons are *ex officio* parishioners of St Margaret's, which, deviating from the pattern laid up in the Enabling Act of 1921, has only a Parliamentary Electoral Roll and a Parliamentary Church Council: and at the statutory services on Sundays, pews are officially reserved for Members and Officers of the House. It is true that, under modern conditions, these are more sparsely occupied than they used to be before 7 May 1902, when the Parliamentary half-day was altered from Wednesday to Friday, for the convenience of Members who wished to go home for the week-end. But from time to time the country is signally reminded that it is not in name alone that St Margaret's, Westminster, is, "as it were, a national Church, for the Use of the House of Commons".

Thus, at the end of the First World War, within these venerable walls was held one of the most historic services in the annals of the English Church and Nation. On 11 November 1918, wrote Archbishop Davidson,

I went to the House of Commons and heard Lloyd George announce the signing of the Armistice and recount the terms it contained. After reading them, he moved that the House should adjourn to St Margaret's to pray. They were joined on the way by the House of Lords walking in procession with the Lord Chancellor. I myself went across before them, and robed in St Margaret's, and took part in the service—simple, sober, and intensely moving. To say it was managed well, is not at all the right way to put it. It managed itself because everybody was in earnest.... I do not suppose there has ever been in our history a more significant recognition of the Divine Presence and aid than in this sudden attendance of the Houses at Divine Service in lieu of a Commons debate.[34]

This precedent was followed on 8 May 1945, and again on 15 August, except that on these occasions (which were less impromptu) the House of Lords correctly went, not to St Margaret's with the Commons, but to the Abbey church. Nor can I omit to mention an even more remarkable and indeed unique occasion on 4 August 1918, when, at a very critical juncture in our military fortunes, the King and Queen themselves came to St Margaret's to join with the Members of both Houses of Parliament in a Service of Intercession on the fourth anniversary of the declaration of war.

Now it is not my business, as a priest of the only Established Church in all the Anglican Communion, to advocate a National Establishment of Religion: but it is perhaps my duty to explain it. What it means, in the contemporary setting, is not that the Church is identified with the State, nor that the Church is a department of the State, but (as I understand it) that the Church is formally accredited by the State to bear the *persona* of the Nation considered in its religious aspect, and to lead the Nation in prayer. Archbishop Lang once remarked to the present Dean of St Paul's, "Always remember that the Archbishop of Canterbury has great responsibility but no power": and the same may be said of the Established Church of England. It receives no payment from the State: but it has received a pastoral commission, which is recognized by the State, to pray for all, to care for all, and to instruct and, in a sense, to keep, the conscience of the Nation. The nature of its relation to the State is seen most clearly in the Form and Order of the Coronation of the Sovereign: "The Church blesses the State, prays for its welfare, and helps its people on the way to life eternal. The State protects the Church, administers justice, cares for the weak, and preserves peace."[35]

But even this is not the whole matter. For it is arguable that the fundamental principle for which Sir James Perrott and his friends so earnestly contended—the public identification of this realm as a Christian realm acknowledging obedience to Christ the King—the pledge that the law and government of our country shall be Christian, and shall be administered on Christian principles and to Christian ends—is secured, not by the dubious and fallible device of a Sacramental Test for Members of the House of Commons, but by the inescapable fact that the greater part of the English Coronation Order takes place within the very framework of the Communion Service, between the Creed and the Offertory, and that the climax of the ceremony is not the Crowning, but the Communion of the Sovereign. As the Head Master of Rugby, Dr Thomas Arnold, said in the sermon that he preached in the parish church of Ambleside on the day of Queen Victoria's Coronation (28 June

1838)[36]—a sermon which Dean Stanley, one of his old pupils, was subsequently to describe as "the best expression which has perhaps ever been given of the full religious aspect of an English Coronation"—

> . . . We are met here to celebrate the coronation of our sovereign. Now, let us remember where the coronation takes place, and with what rites it is accompanied. It takes place not in the Queen's palace, nor in one of the great squares of the capital, nor in the supreme court of justice, not even in the house of the great council of the nation—the parliament. Our sovereigns receive their crown in that place where all the most solemn acts of our individual life are commonly solemnized—in the church of God and of Christ. And with what rites is the coronation accompanied? Immediately, and as an essential part of the ceremony, it is followed by the Communion, the Sacrament of the Lord's Supper—the most solemn bond which binds Christians to one another and to Christ. Thus, on the very face of it, our sovereign's coronation is essentially a Christian act. . . . Her coronation pledges her to her people, and her people to her; but both in Christ, and to Christ. . . .

APPENDIX A

THE FOUNDATION OF ST MARGARET'S, WESTMINSTER

THE FOLLOWING is a translation from the *Liber Niger Quaternus* (Westminster Abbey Muniments, Book 1, f. lxxvj.*b*). This is a large quarto, parchment, ff. 1-151, incorporating documents mainly of the fourteenth and fifteenth centuries, and appears from the description in the title to be a copy made at some time between 1474 and 1485 at the charges of Thomas Clifford, who was a Monk of Westminster from 1462 to 1485, while Thomas Estney was Abbot (1474-98).

OF THE PARISH CHURCH OF SAINT MARGARET FIRST FOUNDED BY SAINT EDWARD THE CONFESSOR.

A certain senior of this Church [i.e., Westminster Abbey], a monk named John Tothale, who was present at, and assisted in, the coronation of King Edward the third after the Conquest, was frequently wont to say that he himself saw a certain monk of the monastery who assumed the habit in the same place in the time of King Henry the third. The latter was accustomed to relate that he heard his seniors asserting that in the time of Saint Edward, who renovated this Church anew from the foundations, the same saint of God for the greater honour and peace as well of the monks as of the parishioners founded the first Church of Saint Margaret in the place where it is now situated, which formerly had been constituted in the Nave of the old Church, that is to say from the north part, where also the parishioners were bound to congregate and were accustomed to attend divine worship and receive the sacraments of the church. And so this same church lasted until the times of King Edward son of King Henry the third, at what time the wool staple was at Westminster. Then indeed the parishioners and several wool merchants built anew from the foundations the aforesaid church of Saint Margaret except the great chancel, which great chancel to wit had been repaired in previous years by the Abbot and Convent of Westminster, but which at the present time is undoubtedly in great need of repair: and this the Almoner for the time being of the monastery of Westminster is required to do, because he is Rector of the said parish church and has been accustomed to receive tithes of corn and hay throughout the whole parish of Saint Margaret.

APPENDIX B

PRAYERS FOR THE PARLIAMENT

AT THE beginning of each day's sitting, Prayers are read in the Chamber of the House of Commons by The Speaker's Chaplain (or his deputy), all strangers being excluded. "The devotions of the House are private: after the Speaker and Chaplain have taken their respective places, the doors of the Chamber are closed, and no member can enter until, with the cry 'Prayers are over', the doorkeepers throw them open. Each day's sitting commences formally from the time that prayers begin." The Prayers follow a set form dating from 1661 (and printed in the article, "Parliament at Prayer", by Sir Arnold Wilson, M.P., in the *Nineteenth Century and after,* April 1937, pp. 1-37), including the following prayer, of which the authorship is unknown:

Almighty God, by whom alone Kings reign, and Princes decree justice; and from whom alone cometh all counsel, wisdom, and understanding; We thine unworthy servants, here gathered together in thy Name, do most humbly beseech thee to send down thy Heavenly Wisdom from above, to direct and guide us in all our consultations: And grant that, we having thy fear always before our eyes, and laying aside all private interests, prejudices, and partial affections, the result of all our counsels may be to the glory of thy blessed Name, the maintenance of true Religion and Justice, the safety, honour, and happiness of the Queen, the publick wealth, peace, and tranquillity of the Realm, and the uniting and knitting together of the hearts of all persons and estates within the same, in true Christian Love and Charity one towards another, through Jesus Christ our Lord and Saviour. *Amen.*

It was to the language of this prayer that Sir Robert Peel so eloquently appealed when introducing the Bill for the Relief of Roman Catholic Disabilities in 1829.

2

THE CHURCH UNDER PERSECUTION

IN THE Preface to his classic sally into the field of textual criticism of the New Testament—the *Letters to Mr Archdeacon Travis, in answer to his Defence of the Three Heavenly Witnesses* (1790)—Richard Porson wrote: [1]

> An impartial judge, I think, must allow that Mr Gibbon's History is one of the ablest performances of its kind that has ever appeared. His industry is indefatigable; his accuracy scrupulous; his reading, which indeed is sometimes ostentatiously displayed, immense; his attention always awake; his memory retentive; his style emphatic and expressive; his periods harmonious. His reflections are often just and profound; he pleads eloquently for the rights of mankind, and the duty of toleration; nor does his humanity ever slumber, unless when women* are ravished, or the Christians† persecuted.

That the persecution of Christians was a topic of purely academic interest in the late autumn of our Augustan Age can readily be understood. Soon enough, the Reign of Terror was to engulf the Church in France and to precipitate the emigration of Catholic priests to Protestant but charitable England: it was to them, and to the Irish potato famine in the 1840s, that the revival of Roman Catholicism in this country is, in the judgement of a Roman Catholic historian, Hilaire Belloc, principally due. [2] But the last occasion on which the shadow of impending persecution fell across the Church of England was during the Second Counter-Reformation—the age of James II and Louis XIV. There were then advantages, both social and pecuniary, to be gained by conversion, and many careerists were added to the Roman fold:

---

* Chapter LVII, note 54.   † In the whole sixteenth Chapter.

although when in 1687 the Earl of Peterborough, having changed his religious allegiance, was asked by the Church-wardens of St Margaret's, Westminster, for permission to dispose of his pew, he replied cautiously: "No, no. One doth not know what may happen."[3] With rare and discreditable exceptions, the clergy exhibited an admirable resolution. Dr Simon Patrick, a Prebendary of Westminster and Rector of St Paul's, Covent Garden, noted in his *Auto-Biography* that the Declaration of Indulgence, appointed to be read in all the London churches on Sunday 20 May 1688, "was not read by any considerable person; but our Dean [Dr Sprat] sent it to one of the petty Canons to read in the Abbey. But at St Margaret's and the new [Broadway] Chapel it was refused."[4] Before the year was out, the threatening cloud was providentially lifted by the Protestant wind that brought William of Orange to Torbay.

I imagine that nothing that has happened in our generation, except the breakdown of liberal democratic governments and the revival of torture in Europe, would have seemed more incredible to our Late Victorian ancestors than the recrudescence of religious persecution. Often in the past a Church has paid the penalty of its loyalty to a losing cause, like the Church of England in the seventeenth century, the Episcopal Church of Scotland after the '45, and the Protestant Episcopal Church in North America at the time of the War of Independence: and this is also in part the explanation of the persecution of the Orthodox Church in Russia after the Bolshevik Revolution. But what is new in our own time is religious persecution which is not essentially political (like the sporadic persecution of Recusants in England under Elizabeth I), but is in fact primarily ideological. And one of the problems which this raises for the dispassionate historian—a problem which it is difficult to answer—is whether, under modern conditions, a Church can survive a sustained and systematic persecution over a long period of years unless its resistance is fortified and stiffened by a considerable element of superstition in the piety of its adherents. There is the further question whether, in the long run, this element of superstition will prove an asset or a liability. I cannot pretend to answer these obscure and highly complicated questions, and it would be impertinent for me to attempt to do so: but I would venture to propose them for your speculation.

Because this is so largely a new problem, the testimony of the past is only indirectly relevant, but it is suggestive: and indeed we have little else to go upon. There is also this additional point to be considered. We must read history with our imagination, but it is difficult for us to imagine what it meant to live under a religious persecution: our imaginative faculty is paralysed between Scylla and Charybdis—between the artificial impersonality of the historian, and the esoteric or at least eclectic personalities of the martyrologist. The historian fails to see the trees for the wood: the hagiographer fails to see the wood for the trees. The annals of a single parish may therefore offer a cross-section which is more truly representative, and consequently more revealing: for it illustrates not only the personal tragedies involved, but also the variety of those tragedies (a point which is sometimes overlooked), and the sombre and enigmatic quality of the circumstances that produced them. Moreover, it is easy enough to say that the blood of the martyrs is the seed of the Church, but that is not the end of the question: for the soil in which that seed persists is often fertilized by the obtuse, insensitive, unorthodox, but stubborn and intractable conservatism of mental habit which is wholly alien from the spirit of the martyr and devoid of any tincture of fanaticism.

Although disguised externally by an eighteenth-century façade of portland stone (for which it is indebted to a grant from the House of Commons in 1735), the existing church of St Margaret, Westminster, was in fact completed on the eve of the Reformation. It had been thirty-five years in building, and was consecrated in 1523. Wolsey was then in power, and his royal master had but recently received from Pope Leo X the title of *Fidei Defensor* in recognition of a theological work which he had written in reply to Luther. This was the lull before the storm: for the times were pregnant with dramatic and momentous changes, and the third St Margaret's, by reason of its situation and of the increasing importance of Westminster in the political life of England, was soon to find itself at the centre of the maelstrom of events.

Six years later, a turbulent and somewhat disreputable cleric, who was also Orator Royal, poet laureate, and Rector (non-resident since 1513) of Diss in Norfolk, was buried with no little ceremony before the high altar of St Margaret's. An epitaph on alabaster marked his grave: *Joannes Skeltonus vates pierius hic situs est. Animam egit xxj. die Junii, A.D. 1529.* (Bishop Bale, in his *Scriptorum illustrium majoris Britanniæ catalogus*, adds the words *relictis liberis*, "having left children": but this, however truthful, can hardly have formed part of the inscription.) Skelton's satires against Wolsey, culminating in the unrestrained invective of *Why Come Ye Nat to Courte?* (written in sanctuary within the Abbey precincts), doubtless contributed something to the element of anti-clericalism in the English Reformation. The Cardinal, however, had long since come to terms with him, and in the winter of 1527 Skelton wrote his last satire, which he dedicated in almost fulsome terms to his new patron, by whom apparently the work had been commissioned: it was levelled against two of the Cambridge Reformers, the saintly Thomas Bilney (whom Foxe calls "the first framer of that University in the knowledge of Christ"), and his companion in tribulation, Thomas Arthur. Nor was this Skelton's sole appearance as a champion of orthodoxy, for in May 1528 we find him giving evidence at the trial in London of a very frightened heretic from Colchester. It is to be inferred that the theology of the "Pierian bard", unlike his morals, was above suspicion. Indeed, he was almost certainly a member of the Our Lady Brotherhood of St Margaret's, the parish Guild of the Assumption: for when he died, a special knell was rung for him at their expense.[5] In 1531 "little Bilney" was burned at Norwich as a relapsed heretic. But it was very soon apparent that the spread of

Protestant heresy was not so easily to be restrained.

In 1555, Mr Henry Machyn, citizen of London, made the following entries in his *Diary*:

> The xiiij day of Aprell, the wyche was Ester day, at sant Margatt parryche at Westmynster, after masse was done, one of the menysters a prest of the abbay dyd helpe hym that was the menyster to the pepull who wher reseyvyng of the blessyd sacrement of the lord Jhesus Cryst, ther cam in-to the chyrche a man that was a monke of Elly, the wyche was marryed to a wyff: the sam day ther that sam man sayd to the menyster, What doyst thow gyff them? and as sone as he had spokyn he druw his wod-knyffe, and hyt the prest on the hed and struck hym a grett blowe, and after ran after hym and struck hym on the hand, and cloyffe ys hand a grett way, and after on the harme a grett wond; and ther was syche a cry and showtt as has not byne; and after he was taken and cared to presun, and after examynyd wher-for he dyd ytt.

> The xx day of Aprell was [ar]raynyd at Powlles a-for the bysshope of London and many odur and my lord cheyffe justys and my lord mayre and the shreyffes; ys name was (master Flower, alias Branch); he was a monke of Ely; and ther was a goodly sermon, and after he was cast and con-demnyd to have ys hand that hurt the prest cut off or [=ere] he shuld suffer, and after dysgracyd, and after cared to Nuwgatt.

> The xxiiij day of Aprell was the sam man cared to Westmynster that dyd hurt the prest, and had ys hand stryken of at the post, and after he was bornyd aganst sant Margett chyrche with-owt the cherche-yerde.

The incident created no small stir, and there is a picture of the burning of William Flower in Foxe's *Book of Martyrs*. Foxe does not attempt to defend the act of sacrilege: he says plainly that Flower therein "did not well or Evangelically"; and whereas Flower pleaded the example of Moses, Joshua, Zimri, Jehu, Judith, and other Old Testament heroes, Foxe comments that "extraordinary zeales are no generall rules to be followed".

He calls Flower a martyr, not because he struck the priest, but because, when arraigned for his crime before Bishop Bonner, he refused to purchase his life by recanting his Protestant beliefs.[6]

It was an age of violence, and there is evidence that in the sixteenth century the parishioners were sometimes turbulent in their behaviour in church. Our Churchwardens' Accounts for 1548-50 contain the curious item: "payd to William Curlewe for mendynge of dyvers pewes that were brokyn when Doctor Lattymer dyd preache .. xviij^d."

But these somewhat primitive demonstrations of religious fervour were trivial in comparison with the deeper issue between Prerogative and Prelacy on the one hand, and Parliament and Puritanism on the other, which was already beginning to take shape on a more adult plane as the inexorable logic of events moved forward sombrely to the Great Rebellion.

In the small hours of the morning of Tuesday 23 November 1641, after a long and angry debate, the Grand Petition and Remonstrance of the Commons was carried by a majority of eleven votes. It was remembered that the chimes of St Margaret's across the road were serenely striking two o'clock as the Members left the House. From that moment, the situation deteriorated very rapidly.

It had been visibly deteriorating since 3 November 1640, when the Long Parliament assembled. On 11 November, Strafford was impeached; and Laud on 18 December. On 1 March 1641, the Archbishop was taken from Lambeth Palace to the Tower of London, from which his hated rival, the Bishop of Lincoln and Dean of Westminster, John Williams, whom Laud himself had sent there in 1637, had lately been delivered. To be precise, it was on 16 November 1640 that the Peers, "after they had look'd about them a little while", sent Black Rod to the Tower with an order to the Lieutenant to release the Bishop. He was conducted to his seat in the House of Lords: and on the following day he was reinstalled as Dean of Westminster. One of the Prebendaries, Dr Peter Heylyn—a protégé of Laud, and therefore an enemy of Williams—did not fail to observe a notable coincidence, which he afterwards recorded in his *Cyprianus Anglicus* (1668):

> The first Assault against the Church, was made at St *Margarets* Church in *Westminster*, on a day of Publick Humiliation, *November* 17, the same on which the Bishop of *Lincoln* was re-stated with such Triumph in the *Abby*-Church: At what time the Minister Officiating the Second Service at the Communion-Table, according to the ancient Custom, was unexpectedly interrupted by the naming and singing of a Psalm, to the great amazement of all sober and well-minded men.[7]

Meanwhile on 9 November the Commons, following the precedent established in 1614, had resolved to come to St Margaret's for their corporate Communion on 22 November, being the Sunday after the Fast, and had invited Mr Gawdy [=Gauden] to preach to them in the Forenoon, and Mr Morley in the Afternoon. A Select Committee (which included Pym, Hampden, St John, and Sir Harry Vane) was appointed "to take some Course, to prevent Profanation and Rejection of the Sacrament; and for the Securing of this House, that no Papist sit here amongst them; and to take into Consideration some Way for the Members of this House to bring, with convenient Speed, Certificates when, and where, they received the Sacrament last. . . ". This report was presented on 20 November by Sir Robert Harley. "The Committee took into Consideration, that none should sit in this House, after the Communion Day, but those that had first received the Sacrament; and this was intended for the Discovery of Papists amongst us. The Committee conceived fit, that some Confession of Faith, and Renunciation of the Pope, &c., be made, by such as are suspected; as by those that were Papists, and now go to Church; or have their Wives Papists; or bring up their Children in Popery; or keep a considerable Number of Papists to their Servants. And if any here know any such, to give notice of their Names." In addition, the House had developed an anti-Laudian scruple regarding the position of the Holy Table in St Margaret's, and

44

opportunity was taken to refer this to the Dean of Westminster, the Dean and Chapter being the Ordinary of the Church. Twenty years earlier, as has already been described, Dean Williams and the House of Commons had been at loggerheads over the question whether the Commons were entitled to nominate a preacher for their corporate Communion without reference to him: but on this occasion they rightly counted on a more conciliatory attitude from the episcopal author of *The Holy Table: Name and Thing* (1637). Accordingly (the report continued), "Two Members of this House were required to repair to the Reverend Dean of *Westminster*, to give him an Intimation from this House, that it was desired the Elements might be consecrated upon a Communion-Table, standing in the Middle of the Church, according to the Rubrick; and to have the Table removed from the Altar; he gave this Answer, to One of the Members, that was intreated to go unto him, That it should be removed, as it was desired by this House; with this further Respect to the House, that, though he would do greater Service to the House of Commons than this, yet he would do as much as this for any Parish in his Diocese, that should desire it."

But on the very day after this report was presented—Saturday 21 November—there occurred an unexpected hitch. The story is told in a letter from Thomas Knyvett, a Norfolk squire, who three years later was to be taken prisoner by the Parliamentary forces under the command of Colonel Cromwell. On 24 November he wrote to a friend: [8]

And now reformation goes on again as hot as a toast. I pray God the violent turning of the tide do not make an inundation; if thou didst but hear what sermons are preached to the Parliament men, thou wouldest bless thyself, and I go to Church now to learn the old way to heaven. The Parliament men would not receive the communion at St Margaret's Church in Westminster, which they should have done on Sunday last, before the Rails were pulled down and the communion table was removed into the middle of the chancel, which the Bishop of Lincoln was very ready to yield to, yet for all this the communion did not hold by reason of an accident which befel on Saturday in the afternoon. Justice Howard [Peter Heywood] of Westminster, being employed by the Parliament to make a list of all the recusants in Westminster, which he had done, and shewing of it to Sir John Strangg[wayes] and some other Parliament men, one Robert James, a recusant, having an old rusty dagger under his cloak, stabbed the poor old Justice into the body, whereof 'tis thought he will die. This made such a disturbance among the Parliament men that they have deferred the communion, I think till their minds be better quieted. This James is a man of four or five hundred *per annum*. He could not have devised to have done the Catholic cause a greater injury, for this act hath exasperated all men's hearts against them, the King most extremely.

The Communion was only postponed until the following Sunday, 29 November, when Mr Gauden preached a sermon to which we shall have occasion to recur. But the honeymoon between the House of Commons and Bishop Williams (who on 7 December 1641 was advanced by Charles I to the Archbishopric of York) was not of long duration: for, before that year was out, his hot temper and impetuosity had again landed him in the Tower of London and nine of his episcopal brethren with him, while the Bill for excluding the bishops from sitting in Parliament, which had been hanging fire for the past two months, passed through the House of Lords, and the King reluctantly gave it his assent.

It is clear however that already, before the end of 1640, everyone's nerves were very much on edge, and it is perhaps surprising that hostilities did not break out until August 1642. One consequence of the appeal to arms was that Parliament no longer needed to disguise or to restrain its animosity against the Church of England. Hitherto it had confined itself to infiltrating Lecturers into parishes: now it began to eject incumbents.

This can be illustrated from the annals of St Margaret's,

Westminster. The House of Commons may indeed be credited with a genuine desire to remedy "the great scarcity of preaching ministers throughout the whole kingdom",[9] which had been one of the matters specially entrusted to the consideration of the Committee for Preaching Ministers on 19 December 1640: a beginning was made with the Cathedrals (14 June 1641), and, three months later (8 September), upon a petition from the parishioners of Stepney for leave to set up a Sunday lecture at 7 a.m. and 2 p.m., the Commons made a general order which empowered the parishioners of any parish in the kingdom to make similar provision, if they required it, at their own expense. Accordingly, in the Journals of the House, under the date 18 February 1642, the following entry may be noted:

The humble Petition of the Inhabitants of the Parish of *St Margarett's, Westminster,* read.

Ordered, That Mr *Stephen Marshall* be recommended, by this House, to the Parishioners of *St Margarett's, Westminster,* to be made Choice of as their Lecturer; the House holding the said Mr *Marshall* a Person fit and able for the Discharge of that Place.

There is a corresponding entry in our Churchwardens' Accounts:

27th Feb., 1641 [o.s.].

MEMORAND. That the day and yeare above written, Mr Stephen Marshall was chosen by ye p'ishioners of the p'ish of St Margarett's, Westmr., to bee theire lecturer beeing recommended to them by the Honoble House of Commons to take his place ye next Lord's day after ye feast of the Annunciacon next ensueing. This election was made in the presence of Mr Dr Wimberley the present lecturer of the said p'ish who voluntarily resigned his place and consented to the choice of Mr Marshall.

This is signed by 42 parishioners, beginning with Sir Robert Pye and Mr Emery Hill, of whom we shall hear more in another chapter.

It would be extremely interesting to discover whether the humble petition of the parishioners of the Parish Church of the House of Commons was entirely spontaneous. This we have no means of knowing: for nothing can be deduced from the mere fact that the minister of St Margaret's, unlike some other parsons, offered no resistance. But the appointment of a lecturer who was so much *persona grata* with the Parliament men, and the promptness with which he was to enter upon the duties of his office, are certainly suspicious.

A graduate of Emmanuel College, Cambridge, the Reverend Stephen Marshall, B.D., had begun his ministry in 1618 as the successor of Richard Rogers as Lecturer at Wethersfield in Essex. In 1625 he was presented by a private patron to the neighbouring vicarage of Finchingfield, a valuable benefice worth £200 a year. In 1636 he was reported for "irregularities and want of conformity", and in the following year the Archbishop's Vicar-General, Sir Nathaniel Brent, warned Laud against him as "a dangerous man, but exceeding cunning. . . . He governeth the consciences of all the rich puritans in those parts and in may places far remote, and is grown very rich."

In the spring of 1640, the eleven years of Personal Government came to an end, and a Parliament was summoned. It was dissolved after three weeks: but, before the year was out, the Long Parliament had been returned. At the previous election, Marshall had been one of those who "preached often out of their own parishes" in the interest of the Puritan Opposition, and his services were not forgotten. Repeated invitations to preach Fast Day sermons before the House of Commons in St Margaret's attested and enhanced his credit with the Parliament men. The preachers were normally desired to print their sermons: but when Marshall preached, his auditory signified their admiration by voting, in addition, a sum of money with which he was requested to buy himself a piece of silver plate. That the House should expressly recommend him to the parishioners of St Margaret's to be their Lecturer is therefore not surprising. In vain his own parishioners in Essex, headed by the patron of the living, petitioned Parliament against the appointment, and expressed their "desire to retain Mr Marshall their Pastor among them". The petition was rejected, except in so far as Marshall was permitted to retain his benefice. Before him lay a meteoric career in the affairs of Church and State. In the admiring words of his most recent biographer, for the next few years "Finchingfield saw little, if anything, of its now famous vicar . . . Stephen might continue to hold his country living, but his gifted tongue was needed elsewhere." As Thomas Fuller wrote of him in our first Dictionary of National Biography, *The History of the Worthies of England* (1662):

> In the late *long lasting Parliament,* no man was more gracious with the principal Members thereof. He was their *Trumpet,* by whom they sounded their solemn *Fasts,* preaching more *publick Sermons* on that occasion, than any *foure* of his Function. In their *Sickness* he was their *Confessor,* in their *Assembly* their *Councellour,* in their *Treaties* their *Chaplain,* in their *Disputations* their *Champion.*

He was a leading figure in the Westminster Assembly of Divines. But for seven years there was no administration of the Holy Communion at Finchingfield: and when, in the spring of 1650, "he bade farewell to the scenes of his brilliant public life, and returned to take up again the simple duties of a village pastor", he was received with unexpected coldness. In 1651 he resigned Finchingfield to become Town Preacher at Ipswich, where he remained until his death on 19 November 1655. He is said to have died worth £10,000. He was buried in the south aisle of Westminster Abbey, with great solemnity.[10]

When Marshall was appointed Lecturer of St Margaret's in February 1642—an office which his other avocations cannot have enabled him to discharge for very long—the Minister, Dr Gilbert Wimberley, was not otherwise molested or disturbed. But after the Civil War had broken out, his fate was sealed by three successive Orders of the House of Commons.

Wednesday, Oct. 25, 1643. Day of Public Humiliation. "*Ordered,* That Mr Recorder, Mr *Wheeler* and Mr *Bell,* do take some Course that *St Margaret's, Westminster,* may be furnished with godly Preachers on the Lord's-days, in the Afternoon."

Wednesday, Nov. 29, 1643. Day of Public Humiliation. *"Ordered,* That Mr Recorder and Mr *Wheeler* do bring in an Ordinance for sequestring the Profits of the Vicarage of *St Margaret's, Westminster,* and the Tythes belonging unto it, to make Provision for an able Minister to preach there."

Monday, Feb. 12, 1644. "An Order for sequestring of the Rents and Profits of the Curateship of the Parish Church of *Saint Margaret's, Westminster,* whereof Dr *Wimberley* is now Curate, to the Use of *Samuel Gibson,* Batchelor in Divinity, a learned and orthodox Divine; who is hereby appointed and required to preach every Lord's Day there; and to take care for Discharge of the Cure of that Place, in all the Duties thereof; and shall have, and enjoy, for his Pains therein, paying all Duties that shall be due to his Majesty out of the said Church, the Vicarage House, together with all Tythes, Oblations, Emoluments, Fees, Stipends, and Profits whatsoever, belonging to the said Vicarage, or to the Curateship of the said Church, until further Order shall be taken by this House; was this Day read; and, by Vote, upon the Question, assented unto."

It is, however, noteworthy that the evidence as to the fate of Dr Wimberley is not so clear as could be wished. Walker, in his *Sufferings of the Clergy,* has this entry, under the Collegiate Church of Westminster: "GILBERT WIMBERLY, D.D., *Prebend* of the 9th *Stall,* And [Minister of] St *Margaret's Westminster.* This Worthy Person was at that time also *Chaplain* to his Majesty, and had this Prebend conferred upon him (as far as I can guess by the Account which I have received of him) by his Majesty, *after* the Parliament had *Turned out* the *Prebendaries* of this Church. . . . At the same time that he was *Sequestred,* his House which stood in St *Margaret's* Church-yard, was *Plundered* of his *Plate* and *all his other Goods,* and a *Library,* which was valu'd at 1000 *l.* The Confusions never permitted him to Enjoy this *Prebend*; which is all that I know of him."

A good deal more about him has since come to light. He was born in 1594: educated at Trinity College, Cambridge, where he became a Fellow in 1618: Rector of Stansfield, Suffolk, 1621-35: Minister of St Margaret's, Westminster, 1630-44: Prebendary of Wells, 1632: Rector of Englefield, Berkshire, from 1635: Prebendary of Westminster, 1643: Chaplain to Charles I. He was the friend of Laud and Strafford, and when they were prisoners in the Tower was himself imprisoned there for six weeks. It is related that the Archbishop and Dr Wimberley dined together the day after Black Tom Tyrant's execution (12 May 1641). Referring to the fact that he had fainted after giving the Earl his blessing in farewell, His Grace of Canterbury said pathetically that it might perhaps be thought an effeminacy or unbecoming weakness in him to be cast down, but that he hoped by God's assistance and his own innocency that when he came to his own execution (which he daily longed for), Dr Wimberley would perceive that he had been more sensible of the Lord Strafford's loss than of his own: "And good reason it should be so (said he) for that Gentleman was more serviceable to the Church (he would not mention the State) than either himself or any of all the Church-men of England had ever been." It is not known when Dr Wimberley was released. As the situation became more menacing, he consigned his wife to the protection of his patron, the Marquis of Winchester, at Basing House, not far from Englefield, where others, including the Reverend Dr Thomas Fuller, Inigo Jones, and Wenzel Hollar, also took refuge: but this Royalist stronghold was besieged and stormed by Oliver Cromwell in October 1645, and although Mrs Wimberley escaped, she died shortly after, on 5 December, as a result of the horrors which she had experienced, and was buried in Englefield church. She was 43.

Bishop White Kennett states that Dr Wimberley was "sequestered, plundered, imprisoned, and, dying under persecution, was buried in the middle chancel of St Margaret's Church, Nov. 29th, 1653". In *An Abstract of all the Inventories of the goods of delinquents and Papists seized in Westminster and the liberties thereof, which have been sold and the money received by John Jackson, Collector of the same moneys,* between 3 February 1643, and 23 May 1643, the price of Dr Wimberley's goods is recorded as £89 7s. 11d. Mackenzie Walcott adds that he was "reduced to great poverty". As against this, however, are the facts that he was not apparently deprived of his country living (though he may not, of course, have enjoyed the income of the benefice): that in July 1648 he was married to his third wife: that the Churchwardens of St Margaret's appear to have paid him rent for his house in the churchyard, which was the old Anchorite's House, adjoining the Vestry; and that his will, dated 3 October 1651, and proved 31 December 1653, disposed of considerable property, including houses and lands in London and in his native Lincolnshire, as well as jewellery and silver plate. Be that as it may, Dr Gilbert Wimberley assuredly deserves to be recorded among those who suffered for their loyalty to Church and King: and against the entry in our Burials Register, a later hand has added: *"Once Minister of this Church and Prebendary: was outed sequestered imprisoned and plundred by the Rebells."* It is pleasant to record that when the Dean and Chapter came into their own again at the Restoration, one of their first acts was to order the making of a lease of "the Tythes belonging to the Parsonage of St Margarett's and the Benefitt of the Chancell and all Benefits belonging to the p'sonage lands . . . in trust for Dr Wimberley's Children."

Another sufferer was the Very Reverend Dr Isaac Bargrave,[12] Dean of Canterbury and Rector of Chartham in Kent, formerly "of great esteem with the Parliament . . . who took the Sacrament constantly at his hands at St *Margarets Westminster,* where he was for many years [1621-8] a faithful Minister, and advice from his mouth often at Convocation, whereof he was several times an eminent and active Member. . .". In February 1624 Bargrave had preached before the House of Commons in their Parish Church a sermon on the text, "I will wash mine hands in innocency: so will I compass thine altar, O Lord", in which he washed his hands of Popery, evil counsellors, and political corruption, with a vehemence that offended James I. He was at that time Chaplain to Prince Charles, who on his accession to the throne promoted him to the Deanery of Canterbury, where he habitually quarrelled with his Chapter and made himself generally disliked. At the very outset of the Civil War, in August 1642, a parliamentary Colonel named Sandys, whom (according to *Mercurius Rusticus*) Bargrave "had been a *special Means* of saving from the *Gallows* not many Years before, when he was *Indicted for a Rape* at *Maidstone Assizes*", broke into the Deanery late at night, when the Dean was absent, and brutally intimidated his wife and children. Shortly after, on hearing that the Dean was to be found at an inn at Gravesend, Colonel Sandys and his men proceeded thither, rushed into his chamber with swords drawn, and carried him away prisoner to the Fleet. After three weeks' imprisonment, Dr Bargrave was released without having been brought to trial. He returned to Canterbury broken in health, to find his Cathedral despoiled and desecrated. Sinking under his misfortunes, he died in January 1643, at the age of 56.

Even more tragic was the case of Dr Wimberley's assistant curate, William Rowland. A graduate of Oxford, of humble origin, he fled to Paris, where he joined the Church of Rome, and took to drink. In *Legenda Lignea* (London: 1653), he is pilloried, with an invective as squalid as the condition it describes,[13] among the "*Romish* Converts . . . who (undutifully scorning their own Mother, clad in a torn and tatter'd habit, and poor persecuted dresse) have made choice of a rich cunning Stepdame, and have strained their Consciences to supply their Conveniences. . .". Anthony Wood points out that this savage characterization of William Rowland as a confirmed inebriate should be received with considerable caution; but adds a few touches of his own, which are almost equally depressing. The ex-curate of St Margaret's was (he says) "a boon Droll, a jolly Companion, and was generally called Doctor, having had that degree conferr'd on him, (as I have heard) at *Paris* . . . where by the name of *Rolandus Palingenius* he made a shift to get a livelihood by his mendicant scribbles, his lepid vein, and art of Poetry among the *English* Gentlemen, and other Grandees of *France.* . .". He died of a consumption about the year 1659.

In the words of that "impartiall" (but anonymous) "honorer of truth, *D.Y.*", who compiled the *Legenda Lignea: with* . . . *a Character of some hopefull Saints Revolted to the Church of Rome* in reply to Mr Birchley's *The Christian Moderator*: "Poverty hath a terrible face, and pincheth shrewdly; the fear of the loss of Liberty hath alarum'd some out of their quarters, & driven them timrously to comply with the *Roman* interest, not so much out of Conscience, as Complyance; to get Pensions and Portions from Strangers hands." The attribution of motive is always dangerous: but the pressure deliberately and relent-lessly brought to bear upon the Anglicans in exile deserves to be remembered, and what is remarkable is that the conversions to Popery did not reach more serious proportions. Very few of the clergy fell away.

With that reservation, we may accept these three case-histories, drawn from a single parish, as representative of the trials and temptations of the Anglican clergy under persecu-tion. Dr Bosher has indeed reminded us that not all the Anglican clergy were called upon to suffer, and that in fact two-thirds of those who were beneficed remained in their cures more or less undisturbed.[14] But we should do well to remark that the demoralizing influence of persecution is not simple, but manifold; and that not all confessors have the grace of sanctity. Persecution, like pain and poverty, degrades as well as exalts: it may bring out the best in human nature, but it can also bring out the worst: as is indeed observable not only in the case of the Reverend William Rowland, but also in the case of the author of *Legenda Lignea*.

It has also to be noted that the analogy with modern religious persecution is imperfect: for the persecution of the Church of England between 1642 and 1660 was neither systematic nor sustained. No doubt in remote country parishes life went on very much as before: only in Wales, under the Act of 1650 "for the Propagation and better Preaching of the Gospel in Wales, and redress of some Grievances", did the Church undergo an extreme degree of disestablishment and disendowment.[15] But, for obvious reasons, the situation in London was particularly tense: and there is no period so full of incident in the annals of St Margaret's, Westminster.

The occurrence on the Day of Public Humiliation, 17 November 1640—"the first Assault against the Church"—has already been described. The next item is an entry in the Journals of the House of Lords (Monday 5 July 1641):

> Upon Complaint made this day unto the House, "That several Ministers have of late preached dangerous and seditious Doctrine, in *St Margeret's Church*, in *Westm.*, by the Oversight or Neglect of the Lord Bishop of *Lincolne*, Dean of *Westm.* and Ordinary of the said Parish;" it is thought fit, and so ORDERED by this House, That the said Lord Bishop of *Lincolne* is, by virtue of this Order, to take more Care and Diligence hereof; and to receive Information every *Thursday*, who are to preach in the said Parish Church of *St Margerett's* on the next *Sunday* following; and they are to be allowed of by his Lordship before they preach unto the said Congregation.

It is not clear what lay behind this, or why the Lords (whose place of worship was the Abbey) should have taken it upon themselves to interfere in the concerns of the Parish Church of the House of Commons. At all events, it stung the Commons into action, for on 23 July they ordered the Committee for Printing to be revived, added more Members to it, referred to its attention an anonymous pamphlet entitled *The Order and Form for Church Government by Bishops and the Clergy of this Kingdom*, and "all others of the like nature", and ordered it to

> send for one Mr *Hollingworth*, that preached a Sermon on Sunday last at *St Margerett's*, *Westminster*; and for a Copy of that Sermon; and to consider of it; and to report it to the House: And that a Copy of an Order, informed to be made

in the House of Peers concerning the Bishop of *Lincolne*'s appointing such as shall preach there, be brought to that Committee; and to be considered by them, whether there be any such Order; and to inform this House thereof: And that the Information given to this House concerning Two Orations made in the Two Universities of *Oxon* and *Cambridge*, touching the Decay of Learning, by the Vice-Chancellors of the said several Universities; and the Sermons preached by Mr *Burton*, and one Mr *Blackwell*, at *St Margarett*'s, *Westminster*, be referred to the Consideration of that Committee. . . . And they are to meet To-morrow *post meridiem* at Two of Clock. . . .

The outbreak of the Civil War gave Parliament (or what remained of it at Westminster) a freer hand, and intimidation was succeeded by destruction. On 24 April 1643, the House of Commons appointed a Committee of nine "to receive Information, from time to time, of any Monuments of Superstition or Idolatry in the Abbey Church at *Westminster*, or the Windows thereof, or in any other Church or Chapel, in or about *London*: And they have Power to demolish the same, where any such superstitious or idolatrous Monuments are informed to be: And all Churchwardens, and other Officers, are hereby required to be aiding and assisting in the Execution of this Order." On the following day, an additional six Members, including "the Burgesses that serve for the City of *Westminster*", were added to this Committee for demolishing superstitious monuments. The Parish Church of the House of Commons was the first to suffer at the hands of the Parliamentary iconoclasts. The Royalist newspaper, *Mercurius Aulicus*, published at Oxford, reported "that upon *Tuesday* April 25, a *Committee* thereto authorized by the House of *Commons*, and guarded by a band of Souldiers, purged Saint *Margarets* Church in *Westminster* of all the scandalous pictures (that is to say all painted glasse) in the windowes, and of the *statua's* or images in the tombs and monuments, and that the like was to be done in the *Abby* also. . . ".[16]

But even in London the Parliamentary party was not yet unquestionably secure: for on the ensuing monthly Fast Day, when the Members were listening to the sermon in St Margaret's, a messenger entered, who went up to John Pym and whispered in his ear the news of the detection of Waller's Conspiracy. Pym "whispered it to others that were placed near him, and then went out of the church, leaving the rest in solicitude and amazement".[17] The plotters were easily apprehended.

Four months later, there followed an even more historic occasion in the annals of the Commons Church, when the Solemn League and Covenant was ratified within its walls by both Houses of Parliament and the Westminster Assembly of Divines together with the Scottish Commissioners. The procedure is described in Dr John Lightfoot's *Journal of the Proceedings of the Assembly of Divines, convened for the work of Reformation in the Church, by the authority of both Houses of Parliament*: [18]

Monday, Sep. 25.]—This morning being met, we had word presently, after our sitting into Assembly, that the House of Commons was gone to St Margaret's church, and so we went after them. And after a psalm given by Mr *Wilson*, picking several verses, to suit the present occasion, out of several psalms, Mr *White* prayed near upon an hour. Then he came down out of the pulpit, and Mr *Nye* went up, and made another exhortation of another hour long. After he had done, Mr *Henderson*, out of the seat where he sat, did the like; and all tended to forward the covenant. Then Mr *Nye* being in the pulpit still, read the covenant; and at every clause of it, the House of Commons, and we of the Assembly lift up our hands, and gave our consent thereby to it, and then went all into the chancel, and subscribed our hands: and afterward we had a prayer by Dr *Gouge*, and another psalm by Mr *Wilson*, and departed into the Assembly again; and after prayer, adjourned till Thursday morning, because of the fast.

Our ancestors, it should be remembered, were more inured than we to these devotional marathons: for example, in 1625, when the plague was raging in London—it carried off at least one-sixth of the total population, and the horrors of it left a lasting impression upon the minds of Londoners—"there was a solemn fast celebrated by the parliament. The King, and Lords of the upper house of parliament, had their exercise in the cathedral church of Westminster, which continued six hours with the sermons: viz., one in the forenoon, and th' other in the afternoon. The lower house had three sermons; the first sermon being three hours, and each of the others two hours a-piece. Their exercise was performed" in St Margaret's church, " and continued full nine hours, during all which time it was observed that not any one man of their company fainted."[19]

In the months that followed after the signing of the Covenant, the sermons at St Margaret's must have attracted unprecedented congregations. The mother of Philip Henry, who entered Westminster School in 1643, used (by the kind permission, if not with the approval, of the Head Master, the Reverend Richard Busby) to take her boy with her "every monthly Fast to St Margt's Westr. which was our Parish church where preacht the ablest men of Engld. before the then H. of Commons":[20] and there must have been very many like her, in all ranks and conditions of life. Indeed, on 4 November 1644, the House of Commons was obliged to order that the Gallery at St Margaret's (which had been added in 1641) "shall on every Day of Humiliation or Thanksgiving, be preserved for the Members of both Houses: And that no other Persons besides the said Members be admitted to come thither on those Days, except the Prince Elector [=Charles Ludovick, the Elector Palatine], and the *Scotts* Commissioners."

Shortly before this date, the Westminster Assembly of Divines (to whose labours the Church of Scotland is indebted for the Shorter Catechism) had been thrown into some commotion by a most untoward incident. *The Glasse of Gods Providence towards his Faithfull Ones, held forth in a Sermon preached to the two Houses of Parliament, at Margarets,*

Westminster, Aug. 13, 1644, by the Reverend Herbert Palmer, B.D., contained a sensational passage denouncing John Milton's *The Doctrine & Discipline of Divorce,* of which the second edition had actually been dedicated "To the Parliament of England with the Assembly". Indignantly Mr Palmer sounded the tocsin of alarm from the pulpit of the Parish Church of the House of Commons. "If any plead Conscience for the Lawfulnesse of *Polygamy;* (or for divorce for other causes than Christ and His Apostles mention; Of which a *wicked booke* is abroad and *uncensured,* though *deserving to be burnt,* whose Author hath been so *impudent* as to *set his Name* to it, and *dedicate it to yourselves,)* or for Liberty to *marry incestuously,* will you grant a *Toleration* for all *this?"* The Assembly, who were not prepared to tolerate Popery or even Anglicanism, were certainly not prepared to tolerate this kind of thing when it was brought to their official notice, and they caused the author of the offensive work to be summoned before the House of Lords for examination: but the House of Lords refused to be co-operative. Meanwhile Milton, highly incensed by Palmer's "calumnious digression" (as he called it), had retorted by publishing, on 23 November, *Areopagitica; A Speech of Mr John Milton For the Liberty of Unlicens'd Printing, To the Parliament of England.*[21]

Revolutions are seldom unanimous throughout their course: and the situation was plainly getting out of hand. Nor was it noticeably eased when, in January 1649, "Charles Stuart, the Man of Blood"—whom Hugh Peter had recently[22] denounced from the pulpit of St Margaret's as "the great Barabbas, murderer, tyrant, traitor"—was tried and executed within the boundaries of this very parish. "That event", says Dr Bosher, "marked the nadir of Anglican fortunes": yet "paradoxically, the renewal of Laudian activity dates roughly" from this very year. And, between 1650 and 1655, in the country at large, "Puritan rigour . . . against the Anglican clergy was slowly but progressively relaxed."[23] Indeed, in the summer of 1653, that episcopal innocent, Dr Godfrey Goodman, the deprived Bishop of Gloucester, called Cromwell's attention to this interesting circumstance in the preface to his *The Two Great Mysteries of Christian Religion*, in which he expressed his joy

> in some things which have lately hapned; for living here in the Church-yard of St *Margarets* in *Westminster*, which was the Church proper to the Parliament . . . when as in their time the Font was pulled down, and so continued demolished and in ruines, it is now set up again in a most decent and comely manner; and I hope it will be an example for other churches to follow; so like wise they had a very solemn perambulation in Rogation week, according to the old manner; which had been omitted during the sitting of Parliament: and Holy Dayes began to be kept; thus with joy and alacrity, not without hope of good times to succeed, I thought fit to publish this Treatise, as containing the grounds of Christian Religion. . .

What Oliver thought of all this (if he ever read it) may be conjectured. But it is gratifying to record that when Bishop Goodman died in January 1656—"a Member of God's holy Catholick Church", though whether in the Anglican or the Roman communion remains an enigma—he bequeathed to the Churchwardens of St Margaret's the sum of 20s. for the adorning, either by painting or otherwise, of the Font, near which he desired his body to be buried "in the meanest manner, according to the due deserts of my sins".[24]

There was a sharp and sudden recrudescence of persecution after 1655, and in June 1657 the House of Commons desired the Lord Protector to remove "a notorious delinquent" who had been insinuated into the lectureship at St Margaret's which had once been occupied by Stephen Marshall. Then Cromwell died, and the shaky edifice of the Protectorate rapidly disintegrated.

Humanly speaking, the factors making for the survival of the Church of England during the years of persecution and of exile are anybody's guess. Across the Channel, the Anglican position acquired a more positive, a more precise, and a more coherent intellectual content than it had previously been obliged, or able, to provide: and the Prayer Book of 1662, which was in part the work of men who had returned from exile, may be said to have placed the coping-stone upon the doctrinal Reformation in the Church of England. But why did the people cling so stubbornly to "the proscribed and persecuted Church" at home? And what class of people?

There is no short and simple answer to these questions. But it is possible to point to two measures of anti-Anglican policy which most conspicuously outraged popular sentiment and prejudice.

The first was the attempt to suppress the observance of Christmas. The Puritan objection to this festival had two roots, which require to be distinguished. In the first place, the Puritans objected that it was tainted with paganism. This was perfectly true: the Church in the Middle Ages had been well aware of the fact, and so is the Church of England in the twentieth century, although modern paganism and medieval paganism are not one and the same thing. In the second place, the Puritans objected that the observance of Christmas was tainted with Popery. The Reformed Church at Geneva under John Calvin might observe the Festival of our Lord's Nativity and the other major Festivals of the Christian Year: but the Reformed Church at Edinburgh under John Knox regarded such laxity as a deviation from the true Protestant party line. Indeed, the Book of Discipline (1560) enumerated among the things to be utterly suppressed as "damnable to man's salvation" the "keeping of holy days of certain saints commanded by men, such as be all those that the Papists have invented & the feasts, as they term them, of Apostles, Martyrs, Virgins, of Christmas, Circumcision, Epiphany, Purification and other fond feasts of our Lady". It is surprising to find Christmas thus included among the feasts of our Lady: it is perhaps almost more surprising to find the Blessed Virgin thus described in so Protestant a document.

Such was the double background of the Puritan attack on Christmas. But the main objection was that

The generality of Christmas-keepers observe that Festival after such a manner as is highly dishonourable to the name of Christ. How few there are comparatively that spend those *Holidays* (as they are called) after an *Holy manner.* But they are consumed in Compotations, in Interludes, in playing at Cards, in Revellings, in excess of Wine, in mad Mirth. . . Nor is it to be wondred at if that Festival be accompanied with much Profaneness and Vanity, when the chief Pleaders for them (yea Dr *Hammond* himself) are not ashamed to justifie the playing at Cards as lawful for a Divertisement on Christmas Holy-days. And is that the way to honour *Christ*? The *Love-Feasts* (though in themselves lawful) which began in the Apostles times, were wholly laid aside amongst Christians because they had been an occasion of Riotous Abuses. There is much more reason to omit the Observation of Christmas Festivities, which have brought a Deluge of Profaneness on the world. The Scandal of them calls for their Abolition. The School Doctors affirm rightly, *Etiam Spiritualia non-necessaria sunt fugienda, si ex iis Scandalum oritur.* Things of an indifferent nature, when they become an occasion of Sin, should not at all be used.

Thus, with erudite and public-spirited disapprobation, the Reverend Increase Mather ("Teacher of a Church in *Boston,* and Rector of *Harvard* College at *Cambridge* in *New-England*"), in *A Testimony against several Prophane and Superstitious Customs now practised by some in New-England, The Evil whereof is evinced from the Holy Scriptures, and from the Writings both of Ancient and Modern Divines* (1687)[25], echoed the same thesis that had been stated with more brevity and less scholarship a century before by the Elizabethan Puritan, Philip Stubbes, in his *Anatomie of Abuses* (1583): "in Christmas tyme, there is nothing els vsed but cards, dice, tables, masking, mumming, bowling, & such like fooleries. . . . But the holier the time is (if one time were holier than another, as it is not) the holier ought their exercises to be." That is the typical Puritan case against popular Christmas festivities, and there is something to be said for it, including the fact that it has distinct affinities with medieval puritanism.

The first overt trial of strength occurred in 1644, when Christmas Day happened to fall on the last Wednesday of the month, a day always reserved and sanctified by Parliament as a Day of Fasting and Humiliation. The following "Ordinance for the better observation of the Feast of the Nativity of Christ" was therefore promulgated:

> Whereas some doubts have been raised whether the next Fast shall be celebrated, because it falleth on the day which heretofore was usually called the Feast of the Nativity of our Saviour; the Lords and Commons do order and ordain that public notice be given, that the Fast appointed to be kept on the last Wednesday in every month, ought to be observed until it be otherwise ordered by both Houses; and that this day particularly is to be kept with the more solemn humiliation because it may call to remembrance our sins and the sins of our forefathers, who have turned this Feast, pretending the memory of Christ, into an extreme forgetfulness of him, by giving liberty to carnal and sensual delights; being contrary to the life which Christ himself led here upon earth, and to the spiritual life of Christ in our souls; for the sanctifying and saving whereof Christ was pleased both to take a human life, and to lay it down again.

This edict was not at all popular: and though Parliament sat on every 25 December from 1644 to 1656, yet in 1644 the shops in London were all closed on Christmas Day, and in 1646 the shop-keepers who opened their shops upon that day were so roughly used that they petitioned Parliament to protect them in the future.

The following Christmas, 1647, was again critical. The shops indeed were open: but evergreen decorations were put up in the City, and the Lord Mayor of London and the City Marshal had to ride about setting fire to them. At Canterbury, where the Mayor had ordered a market to be held, there was extensive rioting; and there were disturbances elsewhere in the provinces, notably at Ipswich. The occasion is marked in the Accounts of the Churchwardens of St Margaret's, Westminster, by two justly celebrated entries:

> Paid for Rosemarie and Baies that was stuck about the Church at Christmas   xviijd
>
> Paid in ffees unto Mr ffriend and Mr Denham twoe of the Messengers unto the Sergeant att Armes attending the Commons howse of Parliament, when theis Accomptants were Committed for permitting Ministers to preach upon Christmas day, and for Adorning the Church   iijl.

The resistance was successfully broken, by physical force. But the resentment remained. And at Christmas in St Margaret's, by tradition—a tradition which I am modestly proud to have invented—we always decorate the church with rosemary and bay-trees, The Speaker's Pew being especially distinguished by a large bunch of rosemary ("that's for remembrance").

The other measure that antagonized public opinion was the Act of Parliament of 24 August 1653, which declared no marriages to be lawful but those solemnized before a Justice of the Peace. For several centuries—at least since the Council of Winchester in 1076—the Church had been at pains to drum into the heads of the English people that they must be married in church: and so well had they learnt their lesson that they were not now to be persuaded that they must *not* be married in church. Cromwell's own daughters themselves jibbed at a civil marriage (his womenfolk had always been attached to the Church of England): and Clarendon records that in 1657 the weddings of his two unmarried daughters, Frances and Mary,

> were celebrated at *White-Hall* with all imaginable Pomp and Lustre; and it was observ'd, that though the Marriages were performed in publick View according to the Rites and Ceremonies then in use, they were presently [=immediately] afterwards in private Married by Ministers Ordain'd by Bishops, and according to the form in the Book of Common Prayer; and this with the privity of *Cromwell*;

Paid for Rosemarie and Baies that was stuck about the
Church att Christmas

Paid for a little window for the Belfrie

Paid m.r fidd and m.r Dunham two of
the Messengers vnto the Sergeant att Armes attending the
Comons house of Parliament w.ch then Attempting w.th
others devisitted for permitting Ministers to preach vpon
Christmas day and for Adorning the Church

iijs

xijd

CHRISTMAS 1647

from the Churchwarden's Accounts of St Margaret's, Westminster
see p. 64

who pretended to yield to it in compliance with the importunity, and folly of his Daughters.

Actually, Mary Cromwell, who was privately married to Lord Falconbridge at Hampton Court by the Reverend Dr Hewitt (subsequently executed for high treason as a Royalist conspirator), does not appear to have gone through any previous civil ceremony whatsoever.

It is clear that women who were married before a magistrate without the blessing of the Church did not feel at all convinced that they were properly married: and this bore most hardly on the poor and simple, who obviously had not the resources of the gentry to enable them to evade the law. The two most interesting civil marriages recorded in the registers of St Margaret's, Westminster, during the period of the Commonwealth are the marriage of John Milton to Katherine Woodcock, his second wife (their banns were published on 22 and 27 October and 3 November 1656), and the marriage of "Samuell Peps of this parish Gent & Elizabeth Marchant De Snt. Michell of Martins in the ffields Spinster": their banns were published on 19, 22, and 29 October 1655, and they "were married by Richard Sherwyn Esqr. one of the Justices of the peace for the Cyttie and Lyberties of Westm. December 1st": the entry is signed "Ri: Sherwyn". It is, however, a highly interesting and significant fact that Samuel Pepys always observed the anniversary of his wedding not on 1 December, but on 10 October; from which it is to be inferred that he and his bride had already been married secretly by a priest of the Church of England before going through the formalities of a civil ceremony before a Justice of the Peace, in accordance with the requirements of the law.[26]

Now, the conservatism that clung so obstinately to established custom in respect of the observance of the Feast (and the festivities) of Christmas, and in respect of marriage in church, may not have been theologically well-instructed, and may sometimes have contained a large ingredient of superstition;

although we should always remember that "the word super-stition is not to be used too easily in describing other people's beliefs".[27] It was at least more rational, and better grounded, than number 19 of the thirty-two "common opinions of the poor ignorant people" as enumerated by "that famous and worthy Minister of Christ in the Vniversitie of Cambridge, Mr William Perkins", namely, "That it was a good world, when the olde Religion was, because all things were cheape"; or than the settled conviction of Addison's Tory fox-hunter, that "there had been no good weather since the Revolution".[28] It was a conservatism that, however mixed and even muddled may have been the motives underlying it, did at least instinctively hold fast to that which is good, within the somewhat limited area of its own experience. The teachings of the Church may have been imperfectly apprehended: but they had undeniably left their mark.

Have you ever considered the peculiar character and quality of English anti-clericalism? It has been a constant force, and sometimes a decisive factor in English history: in combination with the power of the Crown it carried through the Reforma-tion, in combination with Puritanism it broke the erastian prelacy of Laud, in combination with Anglicanism it effected the Restoration, in combination with Protestantism it turned out James II. Its outbreaks have generally been fomented by specific grievances against the Church and its officers: but it has never been implacably hostile to the clergy as human beings, and it has never been essentially anti-Christian, like anti-clericalism abroad. It has produced only one literary classic, *Hudibras* (1663); which, if not exactly a work of Angli-can piety, was indirectly an extremely effective piece of Anglican propaganda.

As this last reference may suggest, English anti-clericalism has habitually been resentful and suspicious of those who are righteous overmuch: yet it has always moved within the orbit of a diffused Christianity. And it was this kind of anti-clericalism, which had its roots in a diffused Christianity, that joined with a more instructed Anglicanism in sabotaging the Rule of the Saints when the Saints took it upon themselves to outlaw Christmas and to prohibit marriages in church.

Of recent years, "diffused Christianity" has been having a bad press among us, or at least a bad religious press: and the issue has shown signs of coming to a head over the question of "indiscriminate baptism", although we are not in a position to decide that question until the Church of England has reconsidered its theology in regard to the sacrament of Holy Baptism, on which it has done no serious work since the Gorham Judgement (1850).[29] The context of this problem is essentially pastoral: and the Church of England, partly because it is the Established Church of the English nation (an historic circumstance which has influenced profoundly its conception of its pastoral duty), has always known in its bones that it can never retreat to the catacombs, and that it must never become a sect.

The Church of God is, by its very nature, a missionary society, which exists to win souls for Christ, and to edify them within the fellowship of his mystical Body. It is not its business to make itself popular: in the words of Archbishop Magee, "The Church has not always failed in her mission when she has failed to attract and conciliate." But neither is it the business of the Church to make itself unpopular: and when it has done so, this has seldom been purely and exclusively for righteousness' sake. It is the duty of the Church, in each succeeding generation, and by example as well as by precept, to make its Gospel intelligible: and it is equally its duty not to be too exclusive or superior in its attitude to those who do not perfectly understand. The parish priest must never expect too much, though neither must he attempt too little. There is, of course, a real pastoral dilemma here: although it is as old as the antithesis—the superficial antithesis—in the Gospel, between the two sayings of our Lord: "He that is not with me is against me" (Matt. 12. 30), and "He that is not against us is for us" (Luke 9. 50). But, when all is said and done, a diffused Christianity is a better thing, and a more hopeful soil for the authentic Gospel, than the alternative of a diffused materialism. The Church cannot be broadminded, but it must be tolerant, and, above all, it must be patient—and intellectually patient. A diffused Christianity falls very far short of the real thing, but it is of the real thing that it does fall short (as indeed we all do, in our different ways): and perhaps it is not altogether cynical to conclude, from this brief and restricted study of the Church under Persecution, that although the Church must never cheat, must never compromise its intellectual integrity, yet it never knows when it may not need friends, and it never knows where it may not find them when it needs them.

RELIGIOUS EDUCATION

ON THE night of Thursday 16 October 1834, the Houses of Parliament were almost totally destroyed by fire. There is an eye-witness account of the disaster in the private journals of Sir John Cam Hobhouse, M.P., the First Commissioner of Woods and Forests, whose Department (with that illogicality which is so exasperating to a foreigner) was responsible for the care of Ancient Buildings. He writes as follows: [1]

> The whole building in front of Old Palace-yard was in flames, and the fire was gaining ground. . . I assisted in breaking open the entrance to Bennett's Cloak-room, and then, with several others, rushed upstairs to the Libraries above, next to Bellamy's Eating-rooms. There I directed the men with me to bring down the books from the Libraries, and sent for cabriolets and coaches to carry them over the way to St Margaret's church. Shortly afterwards a large body of troops marched down, and more fire-engines came. . . The soldiers worked admirably; so did the police. I ordered liquor for them and the firemen, who now worked very earnestly, and did great service. The crowd behaved very well; only one man was taken up for huzzaing when the flames increased. . . .
>
> [Westminster] Hall was quite safe by two o'clock; but the fire was still raging in many places; and when I went down the next day at eleven o'clock, was still burning. . . . I went to St Margaret's Church, to look over the books and manuscripts which had been removed from the Libraries. The Rolls had suffered more from water than from fire, and, as it turns out, they would have been less injured if they had not been removed at all.

It was a minor consequence of this catastrophe that on

Sunday 19 October, the Parish Church of the House of Commons was still so cluttered with confused heaps of salvaged books and papers that no services could be held there, and the Charity Sermon which was to have been preached that morning on behalf of the Westminster Blue Coat School had of necessity to be transferred to the neighbouring church of St John the Evangelist, Smith Square.[2]

To citizens of the Welfare State of modern times, there is something incongruous in the connection between Charity Sermons and elementary education.[3] Apart from the public schools (which of course are private), our educational system is financed out of rates and taxes, and not by church collections and charitable subscriptions: it is supported by public authority, and not by pulpit eloquence: and this has now come to be so far taken for granted that it is by no means easy for us to appreciate that until comparatively recently the provision of schooling for the children of the lower orders of society was essentially a work of charity, and was so regarded.

Thus, for example, when on 20 December 1594—three months after the death of her husband, Gregory Fiennes, Lord Dacre of the South—the Lady Dacre, of Stourton House, in the parish of St Margaret, Westminster, made a will in which she provided for the building and endowment of "an hospitall" (or what would now be called "a Home"), to be "called *Emanuell Hospitall in Westminster* or suche like good name", for "ye reliefe of aged people, and bringing up of children in vertue and good and laudable artes in ye same hospitall, whereby they mighte ye better live in tyme to come by their honest laboure", she was following an established pattern of philanthropy which can be traced back into the Middle Ages. A conspicuous instance is "the King's College of our Lady of Eton beside Windsor", founded and established by King Henry VI in 1440 "to endure to all tyme, to the praise, glory and honour of our Crucified Lord, to the exaltation of the most glorious Virgin Mary, His Mother, and the support of the Holy Church, His Bride": this combined the features of a College of secular priests (such as Westminster Abbey or St George's, Windsor, at the present day), a School for boys, and an Almshouse for poor men. The foundation originally comprised a Provost and ten Fellows (all in holy orders), four Clerks, six Choristers, a Schoolmaster, twenty-five poor and needy scholars, and the same number of poor and infirm men. Owing to financial stringency, the Almshouse was actually suppressed during the Founder's lifetime, in 1468: the College of priests was finally abolished by the new statutes of 1872: with the result that to-day, of the three constituent elements in the foundation, only the boys' School remains, although, as at Winchester (founded by William of Wykeham in 1393, and originally combining a College of priests and a School for boys), the School has retained, or arrogated to itself, the name of College.

With the notable exception of the College of St Peter in Westminster (which is more popularly, if incorrectly, called "the Abbey"), no Collegiate Churches have been founded in Great Britain since the Reformation. In that single case, the traditional medieval pattern was still followed: for the College, as constituted by Queen Elizabeth I in the place of the Benedictine monastery, included (and to this day includes) not only the Dean and Chapter and the singing men (minor canons and lay clerks) together with the master of the choristers, but also the schoolmaster, the usher, and the forty grammar school boys (who are called the Queen's Scholars of Westminster). as well as twelve almsmen (now reduced to six, and known as the Queen's Bedesmen).

But even where the College of priests had been eliminated from the traditional structure or replaced by a solitary Chaplain, the other two elements remained. In 1557 a Derbyshire squire, Sir John Port of Etwall, provided in his will for "six of the porest of Etwalle paryshe" to "have wekelie and for ever twentie pence a peace, over and besides such lodginge as I or my Executours shall prouyde for theym in an almes howse, whiche God willing shall be buylded in or nere to the churche yarde of Etwall"; and "in licke manner" he charged his executors to find "a Preste well lerned and graduate and of honest and vertuous conversacyon freelye to kepe a Grammer Schoole in Etwalle or Repton from tyme to tyme for ever", and to say Mass or minister Divine Service at the altar thrice in every week. "And I will there be also an Ussher to assocyate to and with the said master to keepe the Scoole, and for theire travell in such behalf I will that the said Scoole master have yearelye twentie pondes and the Ussher tenne pondes": and "the Scollers of the said Scoole everye mornynge at their comynge to the saide Scoole, and also at the after nowne at and upon theire departinge from the Schole", were to pray for the soul of their Founder and for the souls of his parents, his wife, his children, his brothers and sisters, "and the soules of theym that I stande most bounde to pray for, as more playnlie shall appere in a Scedule, and all Christen soules. . . ". (One feels that all this must have taken some little time.) The school was in fact established not at Etwall (where the almshouses are) but in the neighbouring village of Repton, a few miles distant, in what remained of the buildings of a Priory of Austin Canons which had been dissolved in 1538: and it was there that I had my schooling under "a priest well learned and graduate and of an honest and virtuous conversation", who was a very great Head-master, and is now Archbishop of Canterbury and Primate of All England. In the middle of the nineteenth century, under the Reverend Steuart Adolphus Pears, D.D. (Headmaster, 1854-74), Repton was transformed from a small country gram-mar school into a great English public school: but it is to be noted that under the Charter (which was obtained in 1621) the Hospital at Etwall and the School at Repton were managed as one charity until 1874, when they were placed under separate control.

This is a somewhat conservative example, for Repton was founded during the Counter-Reformation under Queen Mary. But in the middle of the sixteenth century it was no longer possible to put back the clock completely to medieval time: and therefore, as Alec Macdonald wrote in his *Short History of Repton*, "the endowment of schools and almshouses made a convenient alternative to becoming the benefactor of a monas-tery for a rich man, who was nearing his end, and anxious for the good of his soul to devote his wealth to a pious object. The suppression (in 1545) of Chantries, or private chapels where masses were to be sung for the donor's soul, was an added incentive, for nothing was easier than for the founder of a school to insert a clause in his will, as Sir John Port and many others did, to the effect that the masters and scholars were to pray daily for his soul."

With the failure of the Marian Counter-Reformation and the restoration of the reformed religion, this latter incentive became less applicable. But the combination of school and almshouse, or of almshouse and school, continued to repeat itself. At Rugby, Warwickshire, in 1567, Lawrence Sheriff of London, grocer, founded a Free School and Almshouses, comprising a fair and convenient school-house, and four meet and distinct lodgings for four poor men, who attended prayers at the School, morning and evening, in their gowns: it was not until the middle of the nineteenth century that all direct connection of the almsmen with Rugby School was finally abolished. In 1595, Archbishop Whitgift founded The Hospital of the Holy Trinity, in Croydon, "for the abiding-place of such as were maimed, poor, needy, or impotent, for their sustentation and relief . . . together with a fair school-house for the increase of literature, and a large dwelling for the schoolmaster". In 1613, Edward Alleyn—actor-manager, Master of the King's Games of Bears, Bulls, and Mastiff dogs, Churchwarden of St Saviour's, Southwark, Lord of the Manor of Dulwich, and son-in-law of John Donne—began to build at Dulwich a Hospital, comprising a chapel, twelve almshouses, and a school-room; in 1616, a Chaplain was appointed (at a salary of £26 13s. 4d. a year), and six poor Brothers and six poor Sisters were admitted onto the foundation; and in the following year, a Schoolmaster was engaged (at a salary of £13 6s. 8d. and free meals), and twelve poor Scholars were admitted. (It is to be noted that the almspeople came first.) In 1619 the foundation was incorporated by letters patent as "The College of God's Gift", with the addition of a Master, a Warden, and four Fellows: and for the remainder of his life, Alleyn was happily engaged in compiling detailed and voluminous Statutes and Ordinances for his College, based upon information culled from many sources, including other recent educational foundations and a book on Hospitals for Orphans and Old Folks translated in 1611 from a History of Amsterdam, which tells of the founding in 1550 by a wealthy Dutch matron of a home for aged men and women and for the education of poor boys.[4]

In these and other instances which could be given, the priority seems normally to have been assigned to the almshouse rather than the school, though less perhaps in regard to ultimate values than to immediate necessity: for pauperism was recognized to be a social problem, as illiteracy was not. This is reflected in the Lady Dacre's foundation of "Emanuell Hospitall in Westminster" in 1594, where in fact, owing to the insufficiency of the endowment, the School did not come into existence until 1736. It is even questionable whether the Foundress herself contemplated anything definitely scholastic in the ordinary sense: the Charter of Incorporation which Queen Elizabeth granted to her executors on 17 December 1601 significantly speaks of a "Hospytall . . . of twenty poore aged people and twenty poore children", and the Statutes, drawn up in the same year, do no more than ordain

> that every of the said poor people shall have libertie to keep and bring up one poore Childe within the said Hospitall, so as the said Child bee brought up in some good and laudable art, or science, whereby hee or shee may the better in tyme to come lyve by their honest labour.

This was purely permissive, and no special accommodation was provided for the children: all that is implied is that any boys or girls who might be brought up in the Hospital should be given practical training by the other inmates in some trade or craft which would enable them to earn a livelihood when they came to riper years. Here, most conspicuously, the purpose of the foundation was charitable rather than educational (as indeed is indicated by the provision for girls as well as boys). It was also religious: the pensioners were required to attend prayers in the Chapel of the Hospital every morning and evening, on pain of a fine of 4d., and morning service at St Margaret's every Wednesday and Friday, and matins and evensong in the Abbey every Sunday, on pain of a fine of 2d. (Since their pensions were nominally £5 and actually £4 a year, these fines should have been an effective deterrent.) And when in 1736 an improvement in revenue finally permitted the opening of the School with a full complement of twenty children (10 boys and 10 girls), the Governors were careful to appoint as Master an "honest, sober and industrious Clergyman of the Church of England", subject to annual re-election, his wife acting as Matron or Mistress.[5]

The underlying problem in regard to all these various foundations (on their educational side) is the problem of motive. What did the pious founders of the ancient endowed schools of England imagine that they were providing? Or, to put the question in somewhat cruder language, what did they think that their money was going to buy?

In one single case, the answer is clear. William of Wykeham, Bishop of Winchester from 1366 until his death in 1404, founded his Colleges of St Mary at Winchester and Oxford, with a view to the numerical and intellectual replenishment of "the clerical militia", so lamentably depleted by "pestilence, wars, and other miseries of the world". The double foundation was conceived specifically as a clergy training school, or seminary: the grammar school at Winchester was to be "the quickening vineyard from which the buds are to be passed on" to St Mary College of Winchester in Oxford (known to us as New College) "to ripen into flowers and fruit" for the service of God and of his Church. The fundamental motive of Wykeham's foundation of Winchester College was, in fact,

the wish to have a learned clergy. The whole cast of the statutes is that of a collegiate church. Of forty-six chapters, or rubrics, as they are called, only six deal in any way with scholars and learning. The other forty might belong to any collegiate church. . . In dealing with the *personnel,* it is perhaps not significant that the Warden and scholars were to be clerks, clerics (*clerici*). All education was then a matter of clerical cognisance, and at Oxford even the bookbinders and parchment-sellers were clerks. It is significant that the Warden was to be a priest, and to wear in chapel an "amice" of grey such as canons of a cathedral wore. The ten Fellows were to wear "furred amices" like Vicars Choral, the elder scholars were to occupy stalls in chapel. All scholars were to have the first tonsure within a year of admission, if not before, except Founder's kin, who might put it off till the age of fifteen. None were to be admitted who had any bodily defect which "would render them unfit to take holy orders".

It is however necessary to qualify this impression by remembering in general that the clerical function in the Middle Ages was not so specialized as it is to-day, and in particular that, until the Reformation, the Civil Service was mainly recruited from the clergy, and financed by ecclesiastical endowments. Wykeham himself had risen in that service, and had accumulated numerous preferments while still in minor orders: not until 1362, when he was nearly 38 years old, did he become a priest: four years later he was nominated to the bishopric of Winchester, which was financially a higher prize than the archbishopric of Canterbury: and in the following year he succeeded Archbishop Simon Langham as Chancellor—the medieval equivalent of Prime Minister of England. It may therefore fairly be inferred that when Wykeham founded his Colleges for the recruitment and training of the clergy, he had more in view than that the parishes should be adequately staffed.[6]

But the essential point is that the purpose of his foundation was not so much educational as what would now be called vocational training: the two Colleges in which that training was to be provided, first at the scholastic and then at the academic level, were designed in the first instance to keep up the numbers and the quality of the clerical profession, rather than to develop the intellectual abilities of promising boys as an object desirable in itself. In other words, the human material was, in the last analysis, regarded more as a means than as an end.

The motives of the other "pious Founders" are more elusive. Did they—to use our modern jargon—"believe in education", or were they interested simply in philanthropy as such? Doubtless the faith of the Middle Ages that a religious and charitable endowment of any kind would prove in some way advantageous to the donor's soul after his death persisted only less precisely after the Reformation. In addition, the Renaissance had introduced the more secular idea of "fame", the ambition to create or to achieve something by which to be remembered in future generations upon the lips of men. It is a commonplace that the motives even of good and religious persons are seldom purely altruistic. Local pride, local patriotism, and a localized benevolence are also relevant as contributory factors; stimulated, no doubt, by the competitive instinct, the desire to emulate or to excel what had been done by others in the neighbourhood. This is perhaps as much as we can say, since we are unable to cross-examine the "Founders and Benefactors" of bygone times: and even if we were in a position to do so, it is highly doubtful whether they would be able to give us as clear and definite an answer as we might desire. How far did they think that they were in some way benefiting themselves, or in some way benefiting the community? What precisely did they suppose that the children to be educated in their charitable foundations were going to get out of the sort of education there provided for them? And what indeed did the children themselves suppose that they were getting out of it? We shall never know the answers to these questions: but they are, I submit, more serious and more suggestive than the conventional inquiries into the scholastic time-table and curriculum at any given period in the history of education.

They are, in any case, questions that may naturally suggest themselves to a Rector of St Margaret's, Westminster, if only because our choristers are exclusively recruited from Westminster City School. This large and admirable Church of

England secondary day school in Palace Street is one of a group known as the United Westminster Schools—two day schools and one boarding school for boys—which rest in the main upon six ancient Westminster foundations, historically connected with St Margaret's as the Parish Church of the City of Westminster, although reorganized and united by Act of Parliament in 1873 on the recommendation of the Endowed Schools Commissioners. These must be rapidly enumerated, because their foundation dates are not uninteresting. They were popularly known by the colour of the uniforms worn by their respective scholars. The oldest of these charities was Emanuel Hospital (or the *Brown Coat School*), founded, as has been already mentioned, by Lady Dacre, a maid of honour to Queen Elizabeth, in 1594, and incorporated by Royal Charter in 1601, although the School itself dates only from 1736. The *Green Coat Hospital*, founded by the Churchwardens of St Margaret's in 1624, was incorporated by Royal Charter in 1633 as St Margaret's Hospital, but, from the favour shown to it by Charles I and by Charles II (who endowed it with an annual sum of £50, in consideration of the crippling financial losses it had sustained from the Great Fire of London), was commonly known as the King's Hospital. Palmer's Hospital (or the *Black Coat School*) was founded by the Reverend James Palmer, B.D., in 1654; and *Emery Hill's Grammar School* was founded twenty years later, in 1674, by Mr Emery Hill, of the Worshipful Company of Brewers, a former Churchwarden of St Margaret's. A fifth old Westminster foundation, the *Blew Coat School,* founded by public subscription in 1688, was absorbed into the United Westminster Schools in 1910, although the original schoolhouse (attributed to Wren, and dated 1709), with a figure of a Blue Coat boy above the entrance, still happily survives. The *Grey Coat Hospital*, founded by eight parishioners of St Margaret's in 1698, eventually became a girls' school : it is fortunate in retaining the architecturally delightful building (on the site of a disused workhouse) into which it moved in 1701. The demolition, in the nineteenth century, of St Margaret's Hospital and of Emanuel Hospital is still a matter for regret. The site of the former is now occupied by the Army and Navy Stores, and of the latter by a block of residential flats.[7]

It is noteworthy that all these six Hospitals and Schools were founded almost within the span of a single century (1594, 1624, 1654, 1674, 1688, 1698). I now propose to isolate for our consideration two of the pious Founders, both of them commemorated in St Margaret's Church; the Reverend James Palmer by a fine alabaster monument, irreparably damaged by an oil-bomb in 1941; and Mr Emery Hill by a memorial tablet with a curious inscription and a heraldically questionable coat-of-arms.

A carpenter's son, and a native of St Margaret's parish where he was born in July 1595, James Palmer[8] was a graduate of Magdalene College, Cambridge. "The company of Carpenters in London gave him an exhibition towards his maintenance there", writes Thomas Fuller (in his *History of the Worthies of England*), "or lent it him rather; for since his own bounty hath repaid them the principal with plentiful consideration." He was ordained in 1605; proceeded to the degree of Bachelor of Divinity in 1613; and, three years later, was presented by the Dean and Chapter of Westminster to the vicarage of St Bride, Fleet Street. In this capacity it is probable that he officiated at the burial of Thomas Weelkes the musician, and at the christening of Samuel Pepys the diarist. It was a poor living: the stipend, which had not been augmented since the reign of Henry VIII, was only £16 a year, and there was no parsonage house. (The rights and emoluments of the rectory had been appropriated in 1505 to the Abbot and Convent of Westminster, "for the worship of God and Divine Service in the monastery that it might be better observed, hospitality increased, and the burdens of the monastery more easily borne", and they were to build a house for their vicar to live in: but nothing had been done about this.) Palmer, being a man of simple life and frugal habits, "used to lye in the steeple", or, in other words, lived in the tower of the church, in a little room above the porch. It is noteworthy that the Vestry offered his successor £140 a year, which was, to say the least, a very considerable augmentation of the stipend, and suggests a certain reflection on the Dean and Chapter.

James Palmer appears at one time to have had Puritan inclinations, for in 1637 information of divers irregularities was laid against him to the ecclesiastical authorities: he was reported to "omit the prayer for the bishops and the rest of the clergy, and to read divine Service in his gown, and sometimes without either surplice or gown, in his cloak". However, when he ceased to be Vicar of St Bride's in October 1645, *Mercurius Rusticus* leaped to the conclusion that he had been "sequestred for his Loyalty"; which, at that date, was a very natural conclusion, particularly in view of the fact that in March 1642 the House of Commons had ordered him to allow the free use of his pulpit twice a week to a Puritan lecturer, Simeon Ashe: and he is consequently included by Walker in his *Account of the Sufferings of the Clergy*. But the real reason was less heroic. There is indeed a hint of pressure brought upon him by the congregation to resign, but only because both they and he were conscious that, on grounds of health, he was no longer equal to his duties.

The true story can easily be traced in the Vestry Minute Books of St Bride's, Fleet Street. At a Vestry Meeting on 16 July 1645, it was agreed to send a deputation "to Mr James Pallmer, viccar, to treate with him about the resigninge upp his place in the parishe, hee haveing offred himself soe to doe, to some of the parishoners"; and they were "to returne his answere and resolucon in that perticuler the next vestrie [meeting]". On 23 September it was reported "that he had been spoken to concerninge the resigninge of his place . . . and that hee at first desired time to consider of it, and after mature deliberacon had for some dayes he gave a lovinge answer that he would leave it att Michaelmas next, which if hee did not, it was thought fitt and soe ordered, that Mr Thomas Webb soone after Michaelmas should repaire once more to the said Mr Pallmer to know his intentions therein, and why hee leaves it not according to his promise, and that they returne his answer to the vestrie the next meetinge."

It seems that a great many different individuals were involved in the delicate operation of persuading the vicar to resign, for Mr Thomas Webb had not been one of the original deputation (which consisted of "Mr Bressie, Mr Sedgwick, Mr Parrett, common councell men, Mr Lownes, churchwarden, Mr Wheatlye, Mr Hall, Mr ffydge and Captain Russell, or any five or six of them"); and at the Vestry Meeting on 9 October, it was Mr Thomas Gwatkyns who,

> on the behalf of himself and the rest chosen with him to take Mr Pallmers answere, did give an accompt thereof, as it was desired, when he declared that he had a great deale of discourse with him about the resigneinge of his place and that he found him very inclineable soe to doe. Amongst a many circumstances the substance was, that he desired the parish would be pleased to helpe him to 40 *li.* that was due to him from the Dean and chapter of Westminster for two yeares and a halfe sallary and then hee would goe along with such of the parishoners as should be appointed to the Committee for [Plundered] Ministers and that he might part lovingly and fairely he would relate to the Committee his infirmities, that he was ancient, his voice failed him, his hands shooke and he could not write and doe as he hath done, and much more to this purpose, and that if they thought fitt he would resigne his place to any such minister as the parish should thinke fit to make choice of and soe sitt downe, but if in case that were done he desired he might have the use of the roome over the church porch where his books and things are for this winter time until he can provide himself elsewhere, and that if the parish would proceed in the meantime to approve and make choice of an able minister, the said Mr Pallmer would be contented they should have the use of the pulpitt at wat time they please.

This offer was accepted with relief: and since there was no prospect of recovering any money from the Dean and Chapter of Westminster (who had been superseded and dispersed), the churchwarden, Mr Lownes, was desired forthwith to raise the said £40 "by way of loan and hee to engage himselfe for it, and what hee or any other person or persons shall advance for the same, the vestrie doeth undertake to see repaid . . . . as soone as they can gett the sallary allowed them from the committee of sequestracon who have sequestred the liveinge. . . ."

Alsoe this vestrie doeth nominate and appoint Mr Bressey and Mr Sedgwick, common councell men, Mr Lownes, churchwarden, Mr Turner, Mr Robinson, Mr Wheatley, Mr Gwatkyns and Mr Webb, Mr Shelton, Mr Hall, and Mr Cobb, Mr Peirson, Captain Russell and Mr Baker, upon Tewsday next ensuinge to goe alonge with Mr. Pallmer, viccar, to the Committee of Ministers [*sic*] att Westminster about the resigninge of his place or to attend them the next sittinge of the said Committee if they sitt not that day or as often as occasion shall require, and it is desired that Mr Thomas Gwatkyns doe repaire to the said Mr Pallmer to acquaint him hereof, and desire him to be in redines, and lett him know that the vestrie hath ordered to helpe him to his 40 *li.* for sallary upon resignacon of his place and that he shall enioy his roome this winter as he hath desired.

On the morning of 18 October there was another Vestry Meeting, at which "the peticon directed to the Committee for Plundered Ministers concerninge Mr Pallmer beinge drawn and penned by the consent of Mr Palmer was signed by all the vestrie men att this meetinge and appointed to be delivered this afternoone to the said Committee and the parties formerly nominated to treate with Mr Pallmer with what other parishoners vestrie men as pleased to attend." Finally, at a Vestry Meeting on 22 October, the following order made by the Committee for Plundered Ministers concerning Mr. Palmer was openly read and ordered to be entered in the Vestry Book:

Att the Committee for plundred Ministers
October 18° 1645.

Whereas Mr James Pallmer, viccar of the parishe church

of Brides London hath iointly with the parishoners of the said parishe proffered his peticon thereby setting forth that in regard of his old age and the palsey wherewith hee is visited and the grat decay of his voice he is disabled to discharge the duetie of pastor to soe great a congregacon, and hath therefore relinquished his interest therein to this committees disposall, it is therefore ordered by and with the consent of the said Mr Pallmer, that the said viccardige and the profitts thereof shall stand and be sequestred from the said Mr Pallmer to the use of some other godly and orthodox divine, and the parishoners of the said parishe are att liberty to present unto this committee with convenient speed some able and orthodox divine accordinge to their peticon to the end that hee may be settled in the said viccardidge in the steed of the said Mr Palmer.

Gilbert Millington.

There is ample pathos in this story, but no heroism. The Reverend James Palmer was not sequestered for his loyalty to Church and King: he "parted lovingly and fairly" with his parishioners at St Bride's, Fleet Street, and left the parish without a stain upon his orthodoxy or his godliness.

But what compels our admiration is his conduct after his voluntary, if not altogether spontaneous, retirement. "During his Abode at St *Bride's,* he had by an Honest Frugality gotten a pretty good Estate, which", as Walker tells us, "he Imployed to the Best Uses of Piety and Charity, in those continued Times of Misery, which so loudly called for the Exercise of these Duties: for he made it his Business to enquire out the Widows of Sequestred Ministers, whom he not only Relieved, but Doubled his Charity by the most Christian and Handsome Manner of Doing it; Using to drop the Money some where or other in the House, where it might come to their Hands. He was also very Charitable to other Poor, wherever he resided...." In 1652, he gave to the Worshipful Company of Carpenters in perpetuity the rents of three houses in the Great Almonry at Westminster for the relief of "the poor maimed carpenters of the said Company, or the poor widows of such carpenters deceased", in grateful memory of the fact that, fifty years before, when he was a lad, the Company had granted him an annual exhibition of 50s. to help to maintain him at the University. Two years later, in 1654, he built in Tothill Fields, in the parish of St Margaret, Westminster, "fayer Almes-Houses for 12 poore olde people with a Free School & a comodious habitation for the School-master & a convenient Chapell for prayers and preaching.... He indowed ye same with a competent yearly revinew of free hold estate comitted to ye trust & care of 20 considerable persons of ye place to be renewed as any dye. He cheerfully ended this life ye 5. of January 1659" [=1660 (N.S.)].

Palmer's Hospital (for the endowment of which he conveyed to his trustees six acres of land in Westminster and a farm in Berkshire of 120 acres) consisted of twelve almshouses, with gardens to every house, for six poor men and six poor women, with "a faire chappell" and a school-house to teach and educate free of charge twenty poor male children born within St Margaret's parish, and also a schoolmaster's house: the buildings were all of brick, and were enclosed within a brick wall. Here again we recognize the conventional pattern of Almshouse, Chapel, and School, with the school quite clearly an appendage to the almshouse. To act as chaplain to six poor old men and six poor old women was not in itself a whole-time job: therefore, over and above his duty to read prayers twice daily in the chapel, the chaplain's superfluous energies might profitably be directed to teaching twenty poor boys of the parish to read, write, and account. It is significant that the school was to be used not only "for educating the said poor children in learning," but also "for the catechising and instructing the said old men and women and children in religion and piety". For all this the schoolmaster-chaplain was to receive a salary of £12 a year and a house, with a chaldron of coals annually, and a new gown every other year. The boys were to wear black gowns and caps. During his own lifetime, the Founder himself acted as chaplain, reading prayers daily to the inmates of his Hospital, and constantly preaching to them a comfortable sermon once a week "He was", says Fuller, "a pious man and painfull Preacher."

The point has now come at which it is necessary for us to register the obvious distinction between elementary and higher education. The motive which inspired the Reverend James Palmer, B.D., to make provision for a Free School for twenty poor boys born in the parish of St Margaret, Westminster, was clearly different from the motive that had induced the Carpenters' Company in 1602 to award to the young James Palmer, a carpenter's son, an exhibition of 50s. a year to send him to the University of Cambridge; or— to cite a not dissimilar example —that moved the Churchwardens and Vestry of St Margaret's in 1628 to vote to Richard Busby, who was a former scholar of Westminster and the son of a parishioner, a grant of £5 to enable him to take his degree of Bachelor of Arts at Oxford, and an additional grant of £6 13s. 4d. three years later to enable him to proceed Master. I would suggest that what we find in the two latter instances was not so much (as it might be to-day) the desire to give the fullest educational opportunity to a poor boy who had shown intellectual promise, as rather an acknowledgment of a public duty to provide for the proper staffing of the learned professions—the Managerial Class of seventeenth-century society—and particularly, as with William of Wykeham two hundred and fifty years earlier, for the recruitment and training of the clergy. This policy was fully justified by results. It nurtured one of the most fruitful and creative stocks in the evolution of the English people—the clerical families of the seventeenth century, with an ancestry of yeoman farmers, turning into parsons and lawyers in the eighteenth century, and empire-builders in the nineteenth. What is more, its beneficiaries were grateful: James Palmer reimbursed the Carpenters' Company with compound interest; and the Churchwardens' Accounts of St Margaret's for the year 1649 acknowledge the receipt of £11 13s. 4d. "of Mr Richard Busby, it having formerly been disbursed for his use . . . .

86

which so soon as it was made known to him, he immediately repaid it". Nor did his gratitude stop there, for in 1685 he built at his own expense "two roomes the one above the other for the separate lodging of Twenty Boyes" at the King's Hospital (the Green Coat School), and procured a lease from the Dean and Chapter of a piece of ground in Tothill Fields "for the use and benefit" of the governor and boys of the said Hospital.

In 1649 Busby[9] had been Head Master of Westminster School for eleven years, and he was destined to hold his office for another forty-six, and also at the Restoration to be made a Prebendary of the Collegiate Church and to carry the *ampulla* at the Coronation of King Charles II. It is a remarkable testimony to his professional abilities, and also the magnanimity of the men in power who were prepared to recognize them, that throughout the period of the Interregnum he was undisturbed (although, of course, deprived of his ecclesiastical preferments), despite the fact that his Royalist sympathies were well known. (At the time of the signing of the Covenant he was reported "Sickly", and the authorities appear to have been content not to pursue the matter further.) He was in truth the most successful schoolmaster of his age, and under his prosperous if not humane direction Westminster may be said to have achieved the very purpose for which Wykeham had founded Winchester: for did not Dr Thomas Sprat (Minister of St Margaret's from 1679 to 1683) give thanks to God that though he had not been educated at Westminster, he yet became a Bishop?[10]

In one respect, however, Dr Busby left a more signal and decisive mark upon the educational structure of his country. Hitherto, while the sons of the upper middle and lower middle classes—of the gentry and clergy and farmers and tradesmen—had received a common education in the grammar schools, the sons of the nobility were very inadequately educated at home by private tutors. The results were so palpably unsatisfactory that academies for noblemen's sons, on the French model, were more than once projected. Had they been successfully established, the effect would have been to segregate even more rigidly the aristocracy from the middle classes, as a separate caste. To Dr Busby belongs the credit of a less dangerous solution of the problem. He was the first headmaster to effect the transformation, more widely reproduced in the nineteenth century, of a local grammar school into a "great Public School" of the modern type, by popularizing Westminster School with the titled families of Great Britain. He was in fact the originator of the English Public School as we know it to-day. It is true that the eighteenth century saw some reversion to the older system of private tutors for the sons of the nobility: but under George III, Eton, basking in the Royal favour, succeeded to—without monopolizing—the character that Westminster had previously attained. In the nineteenth century, a dividing line began to form between the upper and upper middle classes on the one hand and the lower middle classes on the other, and to distinguish public schools from grammar schools and from the inexpensive proprietary schools which for a period filled the gap between them. (Readers of Matthew Arnold's *Friendship's Garland* will remember that Lord Lumpington was educated at Eton and the Reverend Esau Hittall at Charterhouse, and both went up to Oxford, whereas Mr Bottles was brought up at the Lycurgus House Academy, Peckham, under Archimedes Silverpump, Ph.D., and went straight into business, where he made a fortune.) The gap was unintentionally widened by the well-meant but short-sighted eagerness of the doctrinaire Radical reformers to abolish the time-honoured abuses of our social system, among which they included close scholarships to the universities from obscure local grammar schools. Yet, largely thanks to Busby's work at Westminster, English secondary education has never been stratified by caste distinctions based on birth or wealth; and it is to some extent the consequence of this that our social structure has remained flexible, being composed of loosely defined classes, and not of castes. (As an American writer has acutely observed, we classify people first of all by ear: the basic social distinction in English life is between those who speak with a "public school accent" and those who do not: "the man who proves, by saying a few words, that his parents spent money on his education, can be sure he is firmly placed in the middle or upper classes"; and it is of course perfectly possible to acquire this cultivated way of speaking without having been educated at a public school. "For this reason alone it is not fair to call Britain a caste country. You can't change your caste in India, but in Britain it can be done through education, or even by means of an elocution teacher."[11]) The fundamental weakness of English society in the seventeenth century and after was that it made no systematic provision for the education of its helot class, the poor, and especially the urban poor. Thereby it created the two Nations of Disraeli's *Sybil*.

A national system of education could be provided only by the State. But when the State awoke to its responsibilities in the matter, the tragedy of the situation was that, as Sir James Graham wrote to Lord Brougham in 1841, "Religion, the keystone of education, is in this country the bar to its progress." Both Church and Dissent were politically formidable in the nineteenth century, and, as successive Reform Bills broadened the electorate, politicians were naturally frightened of losing votes. It is to the eternal credit of Mr Gladstone (himself suspect to his followers as a High Anglican) that he was prepared to grasp the nettle. What is perhaps less generally appreciated is that the Education Act of 1902 was as important as the Act of 1870. By it, Balfour pulled national education out of the rut of local sectarian quarrels by transferring power from the parochial School Boards to the County Councils, and also provided, for the first time, secondary education assisted by the State. Incidentally he gave the Nonconformists a much better deal than they realized or were ready to admit.

All this had to be accomplished by the State. The Church of England, and especially the clergy out of their own pockets, had done an almost incredible amount for popular education in the nineteenth century:[12] yet, because the Established Church not only had ceased to be, even in theory, coterminous and coextensive with the nation, but also, ever since the belligerent High Churchmen in the reign of Anne had thrown the apple of religious discord into the Charity School movement, was deadlocked with organized Dissent, it could not do enough.

Two centuries before Sir James Graham wrote to Lord Brougham the letter already quoted, the Reverend John Gauden, afterwards Bishop of Exeter, preaching before the House of Commons at their corporate Communion in St Margaret's on Sunday 29 November 1640, had urged his auditory to invite to England two distinguished educationists, Comenius from Poland and Dury from Denmark, and to give consideration to their designs. A footnote to the printed edition of the sermon pointed out that Members could easily get in touch with these "two *great* and *publique Spirits*" through Mr Samuel Hartlib, who had been in correspondence with them. On the strength of this sermon, Hartlib himself invited them to England. Comenius seems to have been under the misapprehension that this was an official invitation from the Parliament. The high expectations which Hartlib based upon their visit were doomed to disappointment: the House of Commons in 1641 had other things to think about, and Comenius returned home after six months. Yet the episode was not entirely fruitless, for the Long Parliament took a lively interest in education, and even in 1641 authorized the application of Church revenues "to the advancement of piety and learning": while thereafter until the end of the Protectorate the possibility of a system of national education for all classes continued to be ventilated in books and pamphlets. Hartlib himself in 1647, in his *Considerations tending to the Happy Accomplishment of Englands Reformation in Church and State*, called upon the Parliament to open and endow, throughout the country, schools of four kinds, namely, for the nobility and gentry, who were to fill important offices in the State; for scholars who were to teach the arts and sciences; for those who were called to be ministers of religion; and for "the Vulgar, whose life is to be Mechanicall". The Puritan outlook was not naturally democratic. Yet it is significant and memorable that Hartlib's scheme included the two classes whose education had been most neglected—the aristocracy and the labouring poor. It also envisaged State Inspectors of Education.[13]

But, for a loftier and more comprehensive view of national education—its structure, its method, and its purpose—we must look north of the Border, to the Book of Discipline of 1560 which John Knox "registered" in his *History of the Reformation in Scotland*, "to the end that the posterities to come may judge as well what the worldlings refused, as what Policy the godly Ministers required; that they (if God grant unto them occasion and liberty) may either establish a more perfect, or else imitate that which avariciousness would not suffer this corrupt generation to approve." The Policy of the godly Ministers was an organic whole, comprising Church government, education, poor relief: but its realization depended on the wealth of the old Church being liberated for the work of the new, and to implement this would have split the Reformation Party from top to bottom.

Even for "the posterities to come", the road to the establishment of a parochial system of schools in Scotland was beset with many obstructions, and was paved with a whole series of enactments, all more or less abortive, beginning with the Act of the Scottish Privy Council of James VI anent Plantation of Schools (1616), which was ratified by an Act of the Scottish Parliament in 1633. This was followed in 1646 by the Act for Founding of Schools in every Parish (rescinded in 1661, together with the other acts of the "pretended parliaments" of 1640-48). The Act for Settling of Schools (1696) is now regarded as "the Magna Carta of Scottish education", although even of this it has been said that "never was there a wiser law, and never was a law more studiously disregarded". What real progress was made in the establishment of schools during the eighteenth century in the Lowlands was due almost entirely to the Church of Scotland, and in the Highlands to the Society for Promoting Christian Knowledge. Yet when in 1776 Adam Smith compared the extent of the English Charity Schools with that of the

Scottish parish schools, it was a very notable compliment to the former, and was so intended.

The Policy of the godly Ministers was thus not entirely fruitless. They had been in advance of their age; and their ideal of a ministry chosen by and from an educated people was not to be fulfilled. But John Knox's blue-print for a national system of compulsory education is none the less heroic and remarkable.[14]

According to the Book of Discipline of 1560, every several church was to have a parish school with a schoolmaster competent to teach Grammar and the Latin tongue. Every notable town was to have "a College, in which the Arts, or at least Logic and Rhetoric, together with the Tongues, be read by sufficient Masters, for whom honest stipends must be appointed; as also provision for those that be poor, and be not able by themselves, nor by their friends, to be sustained at letters, especially such as come from landward" (i.e., from country districts). The ablest boys would then proceed to one of the three existing Universities (St Andrews, Glasgow, Aberdeen), with bursaries to finance them if required. All fathers, of whatever estate or condition,

> must be compelled to bring up their children in learning and virtue. The rich or potent may not be permitted to suffer their children to spend their youth in vain idleness, as heretofore they have done. But they must be exhorted, and by the censure of the Church compelled to dedicate their sons, by good exercise, to the profit of the Church and to the Commonwealth; and that they must do of their own expenses, because they are able. The children of the poor must be supported and sustained on the charge of the Church, till trial be taken whether the spirit of docility [= aptitude for learning] be found in them or not. If they be found apt to letters and learning, then may they not (we mean, neither the sons of the rich, nor yet the sons of the poor) be permitted to reject learning; but must be charged to continue their study, so that the Commonwealth may

have some comfort by them. And for this purpose must discreet, learned, and grave men be appointed to visit all Schools for the trial of their exercise, profit, and continuance; to wit, the Ministers and Elders, with the best learned in every town, shall every quarter take examination how the youth hath profited.

Two years "must be appointed to Reading, and to learning of the Catechism"; three or four years "to the Grammar, and the Latin tongue"; four years "to the Arts, to wit Logic and Rhetoric, and to the Greek tongue"; and the rest, till the age of 24 years, "to be spent in that study wherein the learner would profit the Church and Commonwealth, be it in the Laws, or Physic or Divinity".

Which time being expired, we mean in every course, the children must either proceed to further knowledge, or else they must be sent to some handicraft, or to some other profitable exercise; provided always, that first they have the form of knowledge of Christian religion, to wit, the knowledge of God's law and commandments, the use and office of the same, the chief articles of our belief, the right form to pray unto God, the number, use, and effect of the sacraments, the true knowledge of Christ Jesus, of his office and natures, and such other as without the knowledge thereof, neither deserveth man to be named a Christian, neither ought any to be admitted to the participation of the Lord's Table...

It was magnificent, even if it was not politics. We have only to compare, after the interval of more than a hundred years, the kindly, fumbling, amateur philanthropy of Mr Emery Hill,[15] that "great Example of Pietie and true Christianity" (as he is described upon his monument), who was Churchwarden of St Margaret's, Westminster, in 1651-3, and who in February 1642 had been one of the forty-two parishioners who signed the memorandum in our Churchwardens' Accounts recording the election of Stephen Marshall as Lecturer in place of Dr Wimberley.

Little else is known about him before August 1663, when, having passed through the usual gradations, he became Master of the Worshipful Company of Brewers. In December 1668 he was elected an Alderman of the City of London for the ward of Candlewick, and was sworn in on 12 January following, but simultaneously, at his own request, was discharged for insufficiency of estate, being "incompetent for the charge and duty of an Alderman". This was a very astonishing thing to happen, and it can only be supposed that he was in some temporary financial difficulty and felt unable to face the expense of an office requiring very substantial private means. However, his fortunes seem to have repaired themselves before very long, for in April 1672 we find him making the Brewers' Company a loan of £200 at 6 per cent; and a year or two later his standing was recognized by his appointment by the Secretary of State as one of the twenty-one commissioners for licensing hackney coaches. He seems to have made his money chiefly in real estate: it is significant that, at the end of his year of office as Master of the Brewers' Company, he was thanked "for the searching out of the title deeds of the lands in Ireland and the account thereof of which this Court heretofore hath been altogether ignorant": and, in his private capacity, he seems to have been adept at procuring leases of house property in Westminster from the Dean and Chapter at a negligible rent, and then subletting them at an enormous profit. Yet if he was capable of something very like sharp practice in his dealings with those reverend gentlemen, he was equally capable of devoting the entire proceeds to charitable purposes: for with shrewd business acumen he combined a strong philanthropic instinct.

In 1667, he is mentioned as Treasurer of Palmer's Hospital. In 1668, he assigned the rent from some of his own property "to be Imployed towards the teaching and instructing of poore orphans of this parish in Christian Literature and other charitable uses". Finally in 1674, three years before his death, he resolved to emulate the Reverend James Palmer, and made over to trustees certain premises, consisting of houses in the

ST MARGARET'S CHURCH, WESTMINSTER

MR. EMERY HILL

Strand, Buckingham Street, Duke Street, Villiers Street, and Office Alley, in order to the building of six almshouses for six poor old men (or six poor old men and their wives), and six almshouses for six poor old widows, and a "free school to teach 20 poor town-born children born in Westminster, and a chapel over the said school, and a territt at one end of the chapel to hang a bell in, to ring the poor people to prayers, and a house for the schoolmaster to live in, much after the manner of Mr James Palmer": and "20 poor male children, children of poor men, and born in the said parish (St Margaret)" were "to be taught free in the said school without charge to their parents, and to be taught both English and Latin, and to write and keep accounts, but especially to be well catechised and instructed in the principles of religion". The schoolmaster was to have a salary of £20 a year, with a house and certain allowances in coals and clothing; and the governors of the Charity were to have £10 every year, "to entertain them and their wives at two collations". Comparison of this with Palmer's Charity shows that Emery Hill had no originality, but wished at every point to go one better than his model: instead of six poor men and six poor women, there were to be six poor married couples and six poor widows; the schoolmaster was to be paid £20, instead of £12; and the children were to be taught Latin.

It is unfortunately typical that no attempt appears to have been made by Emery Hill's trustees to give effect to his intentions until 1708, when at long last the almshouses were built, and with them a school-room and a house for the schoolmaster. The governors cannot be entirely blamed: the funds of the institution were inadequate to the grandiose conceptions of the Founder, and there was not enough money even for the almspeople who, as usual, took precedence over the school. The fact remains that not until thirty years after the building of the school was the first schoolmaster appointed. Then, in 1738, it was ordered by the governors "that 20 poor boys, born in the parish of St Margaret or St John the Evangelist, Westminster" (which had recently been carved out of the mother-parish) ". . . be admitted into the school belonging to these almshouses . . . and that public notice be given of the same in the parish churches and chapels"; and at the same time the Reverend Wiseman Holt was admitted schoolmaster, at the stated salary of £20, "to teach the poor children, and to read prayers to the poor people of these almshouses". But, since apparently no children were in fact admitted at this time, his duties as schoolmaster must have been purely nominal, and in 1753, when the trustees were once again in financial difficulties, his salary was stopped, although, in recognition of his services in the almshouses (for which he received a gratuity until 1762, when this also had to be discontinued), he was suffered to retain his house together with the customary allowances of clothing and coals. On his death in 1767, the house was let for the benefit of the Charity. In December, 1773, it was agreed "that the Rev. Mr Ozanne be permitted to live in the schoolmaster's apartment belonging to the almshouses, during the pleasure of the trustees, he reading prayers to the poor people in the chapel, and visiting such of them as may be sick": he was also to receive a gratuity of 5 guineas for his services, and towards the charge of buying him a gown. But still no boys were being educated on the foundation.

However, from the First Report of the Commissioners on the Education of the Poor (1819), it appears that the Commissioners were satisfied that the governors had "never lost sight of this part of the founder's charity; though their first object has been to provide for the almspeople, for which purpose they gave up in 1775, half of the allowance appropriated by the founder for their own entertainment": in other words, they agreed to save £5 a year by having only one collation for themselves and their wives, instead of two. In 1791, they decided to reduce the allowances paid to the almspeople, in order to enable them to appoint a resident schoolmaster in accordance with the intentions of the Founder: and "the resolution respecting the appointment of a schoolmaster was inserted at the subsequent meeting of the governors; but the consideration thereof was always adjourned, until the 11th of

January 1805; since which period that resolution has not been entered." Finally in 1817, when Palmer's Hospital was rebuilt, and the financial position was also somewhat improved, Emery Hill's Grammar School came into existence a hundred and forty-three years after the date of its foundation, though not precisely in the form anticipated by the Founder. Twenty poor boys were admitted to be

> taught in a school-house belonging to Palmer's charity; and by the same schoolmaster. . . Most of the governors of Palmer's charity are also governors of this; and it was thought beneficial to both schools to unite the boys under one roof and one master; especially as Mr Emery Hill himself refers to Mr Palmer's charity, as the model by which he would wish to have his own conducted. They are taught the Latin grammar as well as English, according to the direction of the founder.

The boys were admitted between the ages of 7 and 10, and were discharged at 14. The schoolmaster (Mr James Thomas) was paid £20 a year by each charity: "the union of the two salaries was thought more likely to obtain a proper master for both schools".

The simple priest, the Reverend James Palmer, had shown more worldly wisdom than the hard-headed business man, Mr Emery Hill, in ensuring that his Hospital was established and his school opened during his own lifetime. Fuller comments: "O, it giveth the best light, when one carrieth his lanthorn before him! The surest way that one's will shall be performed, is to see it performed." Yet not even this is sufficient to command the future, for lanterns may go out. The Black Coat School was founded in 1654. The full quota of twenty scholars was not completed until September 1660, after which date the numbers fell off again until when Mr Doddington Clark the schoolmaster died in 1716, it was discovered that, by reason of his great age and inability, for several years past no children had been taught in the school. On 1 May 1717, the governors, being desirous that the charitable intentions of the Reverend

James Palmer should be rendered effectual, restarted the school. But in 1728 there were again no children being taught, and, owing to the gradual rise in the cost of living, the Charity was running into financial difficulties. "Whether any children were educated or not, subsequent to the year 1728, does not appear by the minutes or accounts; but as there are no memoranda concerning them, the probability is that the school was not kept up, notwithstanding the appointment of a schoolmaster in the year 1737." By 1746, the Charity was so heavily in debt, that the governors were obliged to discontinue the salary of the schoolmaster (the Reverend Rice Griffiths), and in the following year to let the house appropriated to his residence. The endowment had become insufficient even for the support of the twelve almspeople: the buildings had fallen into decay, so that it was absolutely necessary to rebuild them, and savings were suffered to accumulate for that purpose. In 1817 the Hospital was rebuilt, and the governors revived the school, twenty children being taught in the same room with twenty children belonging to Mr Emery Hill's Charity, "which for the purpose of saving expense to both foundations, has so far been united with this". At the time of the amalgamation of the United Westminster Schools in 1873, there was the requisite number of twenty boys on the Reverend James Palmer's foundation, although only twelve on that of Mr Emery Hill.

This melancholy story is important as showing how the intentions of the pious Founders were liable to be frustrated by economic circumstances against which they had been unable to provide: but it does not throw much light upon the question of their motives in founding charity schools. A little more illumination is, however, afforded by that quaint and garrulous document, the last will and testament of Mr Emery Hill, which was drawn up in 1677, three years after he had established his charitable trust. It contains, amid much miscellaneous matter (including an account of a conversation with Dr Busby on the subject of orphans, and sundry critical reflections on the morals and manners of the age), some further charitable and educational benefactions, the latter chiefly legacies to St Margaret's Hospital ("the Hospitall of Greene Coats in Tuttle ffieldes Westmr."), of which two are very typical of the testator and also of his testament: namely, a provision of 10s. a year for "some able Minister of the Parish to Examine the poore Hospitall Boys" on the day of the annual Audit, to ascertain "how the poore Children growes and thrives in theire Duties to God and man, and in their Learnings it will much encourage the Poore Children and also keepe a Check on theire Schoolmaster"; and furthermore

I will that there be five Chaldron of Sea Coales bee laid into the said Hospitall for the Poore Children every yeare yearly for ever, And that the Poore Children there have Rost meate and Plumporidge every Christmas day for ever to putt the poore Creatures in mind of that extraordinary food that God provided for theire Soules on that day, and that they may have greene Mittins every time they have new Cloathes, and that the Schoole Master may have a new Gowne every two yeares And that care bee taken to Supply the Poore Boys with Bookes fitt for theire Learning especially with Catikyses and Bibles And that every Boy that is putt forth may carry his Bible with him as his owne proper goods.

But more specific motives were now coming into play, and elementary education was about to become, not indeed less charitable, but more purposeful. These purposes were not, however, primarily educational. The menace of the Second Counter-Reformation necessitated measures of defence. When in 1685 King James II granted to the Jesuits permission to build a chapel in the Savoy, their Superior, Father Andrew Poulton, immediately opened a Charity School for the education of poor children, who numbered (it was alleged) over 400, more than half of whom were the children of Protestant parents. To counteract this method of proselytization, the Reverend Dr Simon Patrick, Rector of St Paul's, Covent Garden, and the Reverend Dr Tenison, Vicar of St Martin-in-the-Fields, opened a rival Charity School "in St Martin's Churchyard, adjoining to the library; which proved a flourishing school, under the care of an excellent master, Mr Postlethwait, now master of St Paul's School, in London. Thus it continued to the end of King James his reign, and some time after: but then we thought the money might be better employed, to the relief of poor Vicars. . .". Almost simultaneously, the Protestant Dissenters opened a Charity School in Southwark. In 1688, "divers well disposed persons Inhabitants of ye Parish of St Margaret Westr., and communicants of the new Church therein" (i.e., the Broadway Chapel), subscribed to found the Blew Coat School with the same object. These were the first-fruits of the Charity School Movement in the metropolis: and for some time after, Charity Schools were expressly recommended as "little garrisons against Popery".[16]

Another motive, equally powerful, and less evanescent, was also coming to the fore. "Item," wrote Mr Emery Hill in his last will and testament (1677),

> I give unto the Church Wardens and Vestrymen of St Margaretts Westmr for the time being my Colledge Lease of a Howse in the great Almory wherein Mr Aberry liveth held from the Deane & Chapter at Thirteene Shillings fower pence a yeare it is now lett at Seaven pounds a Yeare, it did go at Eight there is now Thirty yeares to come which said Howse I give for keepeing a Schoolmaster or a Schoolmistress to teach and educate the Poore fatherlese Children and Motherlese also that are kept at the Parish Charges, their Nurses not being able to keepe them at Schoole but *lett them Wander upp and downe the Streets a begging.* . . .

This theme, which was to become increasingly familiar, is developed in the records of the Grey Coat School[17] founded in 1698 by eight parishioners of St Margaret's, of whom five at least were local tradesmen, including a cheesemonger, a seller of soap and candles, a draper, a bookseller, and a vendor of brooms and leather goods. The first entry in the original Minute book of the foundation states that

Severall of the Inhabitants of the Parish of St Margaret, Westminster, having taken into their serious consideration the great misery that the Poor Children of the said Parish doe generally suffer, by reason of their Idle and Licentious Education; their nurses, or those that provide for them, generally suffering, if not encouraging, them to wander about and begg, by which means and the Evill customs and habits they contract thereby, they become (for the most part) the Curse and Trouble of all places where they live, and often by their wicked Actions are brought to shamefull and untimely death and Destruction: —

To prevent the like miseries for the future in the said Parish as much as in them lay, the persons hereafter named, in particular, did think it proper and convenient to Erect a Free School in the said Parish, where 40 of the Greatest Objects of Charity they could find, should from time to time be educated in sober and Vertuous Principles and instructed in the Christian Religion.

And for their Incouragement in their Learning, they did Propose that the said 40 Children should be cloathed as hereafter directed, and when fit to goe out Apprentices should be carefully placed out to Honest Masters, who should take care as well of their good Principles, as instruct them how to get an honest livelyhood by their labours and industry in the world.

In order thereto, they made choice of Thomas Ashenden to be master of the said school, to whom they agreed to allow a yearly sallary of twenty-six pounds, to be paid him out of such contributions as should be raised for maintaining the School. . . .

Then follow the names of the eight trustees: Robert Maddock, John Holmes, Thomas Wisdome, Richard ffyler, Charles Webbe, Symon Boult, John Wilkins, Samuel Michell.

The master was required to conduct prayers in school every morning and evening, and to catechize on Wednesdays and Fridays: he was also to take the boys to St Margaret's church for Morning and Evening Prayer on every Sunday and Holy Day, and for the Litany every Wednesday and Friday.[18] A Charity Sermon (endowed by an anonymous benefactor) was preached in St Margaret's on behalf of the School on the Feast of the Epiphany every year from 1689 to 1834.

All this was primarily an experiment, not in education, but in what we should describe as "rescue work". The school hours were purposely made long, in order to prevent the boys from being sent out to beg. This led to difficulties with their parents or nurses (with whom many of the boys were boarded out by the parochial Overseers of the Poor): and in 1701, in order to secure more regular attendance, and to keep the children from the contaminating influences of their homes, the day school for boys was transformed into a Hospital, to which girls also were admitted, and for the same purpose, namely, "for Setting on Work Poor Children of the Parish of St Margaret, Westminster". Long after, in 1874, the Grey Coat Hospital was reconstituted as a Church of England day school for girls. But, when we consider the original purpose of the foundation as stated by the eight Trustees, the significant phrase is this: *"they become (for the most part) the Curse and Trouble of all places where they live."*

The truth is that, without questioning the assumption that economic inequalities of wealth and poverty were part of the providential ordering of the world, the middle classes were becoming frightened of the poor: there were so many of them (since the breakdown of the Tudor Poor Law system so competently administered under the early Stuarts), and they were so brutal and degraded. As long ago as 1550, Bishop Latimer had warned the governing classes: "Thus much I say unto you, magistrates: if ye will not maintain schools and universities, ye shall have a brutality." Under the Commonwealth, the truth of this prediction was beginning to be realized. James Harrington, who (with John Skelton and Sir Walter Ralegh) lies buried in the chancel of St Margaret's, Westminster, wrote in his *Common-wealth of Oceana* (1656): "A Man is a Spirit rais'd by the Magic of Nature; if she does not stand safe, and so that she may set him to some good and useful work, he spits fire, and blows up Castles: for where there is life, there must be motion or work; and the work of idleness is mischief, but the work of industry is health. To set Men to this, the Commonwealth must begin betimes with them, or it will be too late: and the means whereby she sets them to it is EDUCATION, the plastic art of Government." Designed primarily, though not indeed exclusively, to condition the children of the poor for their appointed station and service to the community by making them "early accustomed to Awe and Punishment and Dutiful Subjection", the Charity Schools, a not ignoble product of the Benevolence of the eighteenth century, had something of the character of a social insurance policy. In 1786, the Reverend William Bickerstaffe, Curate of Ayleston, and fifty-eight of his parishioners, addressed a humble petition to the Duke of Rutland (then Lord Lieutenant of Ireland), in which they represented that "a charity-school at Ayleston, your Excellency's manor in Leicestershire, is an establishment highly necessary, to prevent barbarism", and solicited his patronage.[19] It remained for a mid-nineteenth-century Liberal politician, Robert Lowe,[20] to coin the well-worn maxim: "We must educate our masters." Latterly, however, the British have been losing faith in compulsory universal education as a talisman against juvenile delinquency, and have begun to pin their hopes on Youth Organizations, Playing Fields, Clubs, and even a possible Religious Revival, somewhat vaguely conceived. But the work of social reclamation accomplished by the expansion of public education between 1895 and 1935 is very remarkable, and should on no account be minimized or disregarded.

It is as striking as it is significant that up to this point education has been envisaged from the angle of supply, and not from the angle of demand. The scholastic scandals of the eighteenth century which were uncovered, three years after Waterloo, by the Commissioners appointed to inquire concerning Charities in England for the Education of the Poor, were largely due to inadequate endowments, though in part also to negligence and peculation. But the essence of the situation was not so much that the hungry sheep looked up and were not fed, as rather that the sheep looked fed-up and were not hungry. Because the Charity School Movement was not purely altruistic, it was regarded by the lower classes with distrust: Charles Dickens, himself brought up in the uncomfortable proximity of shabby-genteel poverty, embodied his detestation of it in the figure of Noah Claypole, the Charity Boy.

It was however one of the rare uncovenanted mercies of the Industrial Revolution that, by creating a popular demand for Scientific and Useful Knowledge (hitherto the private hobby of the well-to-do), it persuaded the abler and more ambitious of the proletariat that ignorance is a handicap in life. Peacock might poke fun at Brougham's "Steam-Intellect Society", but, because it was not sectarian nor avowedly redemptive, it had the advantage of not being suspect. From 1823 onwards, Mechanics' Institutes, the agencies of self-improvement, begun in Scotland by Dr Birkbeck, spread through industrial England: they were not paternalist but democratic, and the annual subscription was a guinea. This Adult Education movement is comparable with the growth of universities in the Middle Ages: and the new note was sounded by the young Disraeli when in October 1844 he dazzled the artisans and mechanics of the Manchester Athenæum with the vision of "Knowledge ... like the mystic ladder in the patriarch's dream". To-day the educational ladder, as a means of rising in the world, has become so commonplace an article of furniture in the Welfare State, that it is apt to be forgotten that ladders are intended to lead down, as well as up, and that one of the corner-stones of Dr Arnold's policy as Headmaster of Rugby was the conviction that "the first, second and third duties of a schoolmaster are to get rid of unpromising subjects". In the words of one of our leading educational authorities, Sir Will Spens, himself an Old Rugbeian, "What we need is not more ladders, but more snakes": and those who in their childhood were familiar with the game of Snakes and Ladders will require no further explanation of his meaning.

From this somewhat cursory and selective historical outline of the problem, it is now possible to draw some broad conclusions.

The first is that education must be given without ulterior motives. ("Take no thought for the harvest, but only for proper sowing.") It must not be administered as an antidote to Popery or Pauperism, or as a prophylactic against Revolution or Counter-Revolution. Yet it is not enough to say that the function of education must not be primarily negative. The converse is also true, that (in our modern jargon) it must not be propagandist. This rule applies in every field of study, not excluding the department known to an older generation as Divinity, but in the modern syllabus as "R.I." (Religious Instruction). The present Regius Professor of Divinity at Cambridge in his Inaugural Lecture (1953) quoted from the late Bishop Headlam's Inaugural Lecture as Regius Professor of Divinity at Oxford in 1918 the declaration that "the purpose of a Theological Faculty is to train ministers of religion", and retorted:

I cannot but regard this as a gravely mistaken judgment; and I hope that the Faculty of Divinity in this University will never consent to be treated as a seminary for ordinands. . . . It is for the Church in which a candidate for ordination is to serve, to decide what [the intellectual equipment of a clergyman] should be, and how far it can be covered by any course of theological study he may have pursued at the University. It is for the Divinity Faculty in the University to decide how its courses may best be fitted for the education of students and the advancement of knowledge in theology.[21]

Equally at the scholastic level there is a fundamental difference between a classroom and a conventicle: and the proper purpose of Religious Instruction is to teach Scripture (or Divinity), and not to inculcate religion. It is of course desirable, here as elsewhere, for the teacher to believe that what he teaches has the merit of being true, and also that it is sufficiently important to be one of the subjects with which every educated person ought to be familiar, at least in outline. But this is a part of what we mean when we say that the teacher should believe in his subject: and that applies to every subject in the educational curriculum, from algebra to anthropology. The good teacher believes in his subject as an intellectual discipline demanding intellectual integrity, and as a means of stimulating intellectual curiosity to ends that are neither frivolous nor futile. For the purpose of education is not the diffusion of knowledge, but the pursuit of truth: and this "stands not in the wisdom of men, but in the power of God". In this connection it is therefore profitable to remember Dr Hort's epitome of the doctrine of Maurice's *Lectures on Education* (1839), that all authority in matters of belief "is salutary only in so far as it is propædeutic, placing men in the best attitude for forming a judgment and helping them in the process, but never demanding to be listened to against judgment."[22]

Secondly, seeing that Christ has been made unto us wisdom as well as righteousness and sanctification and redemption (1 Cor. 1. 30), and since it is required of man that he shall serve God with all his mind, therefore the education even of those who are not intellectually gifted is too momentous a concern in its own right to be considered as a branch of charity. It is ultimately a debasement of the currency of culture if a School is founded as an appendage to an Almshouse. Education has indeed proved itself in countless ways to be a primary agent of social well-being, promoting public health and reducing crime: but these are, and must always be, uncovenanted mercies, the by-products that are added unto us when we are single-minded and educate with a view to educating. If the classroom is not a conventicle, it is equally true that a school is not a soup-kitchen, even when it is in fact desirable and expedient that it should supply soup. We have already established that education must be given without ulterior motives: and philanthropy constitutes an ulterior motive, even when it has no ulterior motive of its own.

It is a corollary of this that vocational and technical education, if it is to be admitted, needs to be very liberally conceived.

It must not be too specialized. If knowledge is merely utilitarian, it will not be truly useful. In the preface to his *Irish Essays*, Matthew Arnold, himself by profession a Government Inspector of Education, contemplated in 1882 "the actual civilization of England and America", and concluded that "it is a civilization with many virtues, but without lucidity of mind and without largeness of temper. And now we English, at any rate, have to acquire them, and to learn the necessity for us 'to live' (as Emerson says) 'from a greater depth of being'." That quality of depth of being is for the most part provided out of school: the bed-rock foundations of our culture, imparting to it solidity and coherence, have been the Authorized Version of the Bible and the Book of Common Prayer, the "set books" of our public worship. But from the standpoint of the community, education is not so much a device for communicating "depth of being", as a practical method of selecting and training an *élite*. It is however a matter of some consequence, from the same standpoint, that the supply should not be in excess of the available demand. If it is the business of the community to create or maintain the supply, it is not so much its business, nor indeed is it altogether within its power, to regulate the demand: the community cannot guarantee to those whom it has trained and educated for a particular calling that they will not become redundant, and consequently there is a real danger here of using men as means, and not as ends: it is not only in the lower strata of the social order that they are apt to be regarded as "hands", and not as souls. Moreover, as Lord Stowell said more than a century ago, "If you provide a larger amount of highly-cultivated talent than there is a demand for, the surplus is very likely to turn sour."[23] In that context, the word "demand" implies the epithet "economic". We may however question whether that is all that the Prayer Book Catechism means by the concluding phrase of "My duty towards my Neighbour": ". . . to learn and labour truly to get mine own living, and to do my duty in that state of life, unto which it shall please God to call me." It is not only the method of vocational training, but the whole conception of "vocation", that requires to be liberally, and indeed theologically, conceived.

Let us be realist. Education is, among other things, a means of rising in the world—and therefore also, for those who endow it or purvey it, a means of raising in the world; though this delectable fruit of education is normally more present to the consciousness of those who learn than of those who teach. The young will never be persuaded that it is too late to be ambitious: it is only in middle age that we discover that the structure of society is not a ladder, but a pyramid. The universities of to-day are mainly high-grade technical schools: the vast majority of those who attend them do so not from a disinterested love of learning for its own sake, but in the hope of qualifying to earn a higher income than would otherwise be open to them: the ceremonies of Commencement are a sort of distribution of trade union tickets of varying marketable value. We may perhaps be comforted to reflect that all this was equally true of the universities of the Middle Ages: it was only when they became the preserves of the upper classes that this ceased to be so conspicuously true, and even then the motive was seldom a disinterested love of learning. Although the Grammarian's Funeral has indeed been celebrated in every epoch of academic history, yet in every epoch of academic history it has been the exception rather than the rule.

But in the contemporary social and economic context, particularly in the Welfare State, what I think is dangerous is the tendency to regard higher education not as a privilege which confers a duty, but as a natural right. It was not altogether an unhealthy condition of affairs—certainly there was gain as well as loss—when parents had to pay to have their children educated. Many a father worked and saved (as mine did) to buy for his son a better education than he had himself enjoyed: and many a son has remembered with gratitude all his life the sacrifices that his parents were glad and proud to make in order to send him to the university. In a community in which the overwhelming majority of university students are subsidized by public money, it would be unreasonable to expect them to

feel a corresponding sense of gratitude to anything so impersonal as the Local Authority or the State. Moreover, in a
planned society, it is not unnatural for them to assume that
they have earned their place by attaining a certain standard
of proficiency in the qualifying examinations. Ideally, of
course, the purpose of an examination is to discover whether
a candidate has been educated, not whether he deserves to be.
But even when society begins to recognize—as ours has begun
to do—that "equality of educational opportunity" is a mirage
(and tends in practice to boil down to the less admirable principle that nobody shall have a better education than anybody
else), the mere fact that so crude a demagogic slogan should
have obtained so wide a currency reveals the extent to which
our measure of education has become quantitative, rather than
qualitative. So long ago as 1898, Bishop Creighton wrote: "We
are bringing up a generation on the supposition that all they
have to do is to sit like little pitchers under a pump, until the
proper amount of knowledge has been pumped into them."[24]

Our fundamental fallacy, however, is that we confuse the
subject with the object of education. With all their shortcom-
ings and their limitations, the pious Founders whose benefactions we have been considering did not make that particular
mistake. They may not have had much idea of what education
is for, but they had a very clear idea of what their schools were
for: whether to relieve poverty, or to provide prayers for the
dead, or to benefit the neighbourhood, or to mitigate human
misery, or to keep the lower orders contented in their station
in life, or to rescue them from a career of crime, or (with
William of Wykeham) to ensure the supply of what the English
Coronation Order describes as "a devout, learned and useful
Clergy", or (with John Knox) "that a seed may be reserved
and continued" for the profit of the Church and Commonwealth.

All these ends lie beyond the educative process, which sub-
serves them: and if not all of them are either adequate or
enlightened, they are at least less dangerous than the more
individualistic maxims of the twentieth century: "Knowledge

is wealth", "Knowledge is power", or—and this is at the root of much of the unrest in Africa today—"Knowledge is the white man's magic". Of all the various conceptions of the end of education, the noblest and the most ennobling is that set forth in the *First Book of Discipline* by the godly Ministers. Here is the fundamental Christian philosophy of education: and we find it elucidated in the prayer for Universities, Colleges, and Schools, in the Revised Prayer Book of 1928:

> that they who serve Thee therein, as teachers or learners, may set Thy holy will ever before them, and be led to the knowledge of Thy truth; that so both Church and Commonwealth may be bettered by their studies, and they themselves be made meet to be partakers of eternal life. . .

For in training men and women to serve God both as Churchmen and as citizens, education is directed to two ends which are complementary and mutually corrective, and of which neither is admitted to be ultimate. The emphasis on the Churchman's obligations to the Commonwealth is a necessary safeguard against the danger of his regarding the Church as an end in itself. What is perhaps more obvious, the emphasis on the citizen's obligations to the Church is a necessary safeguard against the danger of his regarding the Commonwealth as an end in itself, and also against the danger—of which the world has had sufficient experience in recent years—that the State may attempt to erect itself into what Dr Tillich has so aptly termed *eine in sich ruhende Endlichkeit*, a self-contained finality. It is possible to regard the system of public education as "a means of promoting a spirit of pride in the nation"; and the phrase might pass unchallenged until it is recognized as a quotation from *Mein Kampf*.[25] Yet it might be rash to assume that upon the lips of a liberal democratic politician it would be perfectly innocuous.

APPENDIX

EPITAPHS OF THE REVEREND JAMES PALMER, B.D., AND MR EMERY HILL IN ST MARGARET'S CHURCH, WESTMINSTER

THE PALMER monument was irreparably damaged by an oil bomb in 1941: but there is a photograph of it in *An Inventory of the Historical Monuments in London*, vol. ii, *West London*, published in 1925 by the Royal Commission on the Ancient and Historical Monuments in England, plate 151. The inscription was as follows:

> Heer under is interred ye body of James Palmer batchelor in divinity, borne in this parish of St Margts. in iuly 1585, a most pious & charitable man, exprest in severall places by many remarkeable actions & pticularly to this parish in building fayer Almes-Houses for 12 poore olde people wth a Free School & a comodious habitation for the School-mr & a convenient Chappell for prayers and preaching, where he constantly for divers yeares before his death once a week gave a comfortable sermon. He indowed ye same with a competent yearly revinew of free hold estate comitted to ye trust & care of 10 considerable persons of ye place to be renewed as any dye; he cheerfully ended this life ye 5. of Jany. 1659.
> Erected at ye Charge of Sr. Wm. Playter Knt. & Baronet

The memorial tablet to Emery Hill was restored in 1951 by the generosity of past and present members of Westminster City School. The inscription is as follows:

> ### SACRED
> ### TO THE MEMORY OF THAT GREAT
> ### EXAMPLE OF PIETIE AND TRUE CHRISTIANITY
> ### MR EMERY HILL
> Late Inhabitant of ye Parish & A worthy benefactor of ye same who departed ys Life upon ye 27 day of June Ao Dm

1677 in ye 68 yeare of his age & lyes here interred A person accomplished with all Chrian graces & vertues & most eminent for his charity besides wt. hee gaue in his Life time hee Left by his will at his death 1st the Revenue of severall howses in Westminster forever for ye use of the poor childrern of ye kings hospitall in tuttlefieldes of wch he was one of ye Governrs 2ly ye sume of 100li. for ye building of three Almes Houses in Petty france. 3ly 7li p an) in fee for ye teaching of ye poor Children of ye Parish 4ly 100li for A stock of Coales for ever for ye use of ye Poor of ys Parish 5ly 50li to ye Children of Christ church hospitall in London 6ly A bountifull Guift for ye setting upp of poor decayed tradesmen hee Left A plentifull Povision for ye building of twelve Almeshowses, A Chappell & schol for six poor men & their wifes six poor widdowes & teaching of 20 poor Childron wth sufficient maintenance for ye same for ever More 50li for the use of the poore of ye Company of Brewers Besides severall other charitable bequests which we haue not rowme to mention

NEW WINE AND OLD BOTTLES

UNDER the heading "Lecturers", the seventeenth-century jurist, John Selden, in his *Table Talk* passes some opprobrious remarks:

> Lecturers doe in a parish church what the ffryers did heretofore; gett away not only the affections, but the bounty that should be bestowed on the Minister.
>
> Lecturers gett a great deale of money, because they preach the people tame, (as a man watches a hawke) & then they doe what they list with them.[1]

The analogy between the Puritan lecturer and the medieval friar is interesting and unexpected: yet this, though from a different standpoint, was also the root of the objection most sharply present to the consciousness of the authorities, whether civil or ecclesiastical. For the lecturer was a kind of popular freelance, exempt from parochial cares and parochial ministrations, and less amenable in practice than in theory to episcopal supervision and control. He satisfied a genuine demand: but he was an anomaly in the ecclesiastical system. In the words of S. R. Gardiner: "The parish clergy could hardly avoid reading Morning or Evening Prayer in a more or less mutilated form: but a lecturer was under no such obligation. He was paid by a Corporation, or by individuals, to preach and to do nothing more. He might remain sitting in the vestry, if he chose, till the service was at an end, when he would come out to ascend the pulpit and to shine forth in the eyes of the congregation as one who was far superior to the man by whom the printed prayers had been recited. The lecturers were to be found chiefly in towns where there was a strong Puritan element in the population, and they were themselves Puritans almost to a man."[2] But preaching in the Church of England is primarily a function of the pastoral ministry, although it is not the primary function of that ministry. The Puritans objected that ministers not qualified to preach are not ministers.[3] The view taken by the ecclesiastical authorities was that preachers who do not minister are not qualified to preach. That is the intention—though not, perhaps, the sole intention—of Canon LVI of the Constitutions and Canons Ecclesiastical of 1604, which required that

> Every Minister being possessed of a Benefice that hath Cure and Charge of soules, although he chiefly attend to preaching, and hath a Curate vnder him to execute the other duties, which are to be performed for him in the Church, & likewise euery other stipendiarie Preacher that readeth any Lecture, or Catechizeth, or Preacheth in any Church or Chapell, shall twise at the least euery yeere reade himselfe the diuine Service, vpon two seuerall Sundayes, publikely and at the vsuall times, both in the Forenoone and After-noone in the Church which he so possesseth, or where he Readeth, Catechizeth, or Preacheth as is aforesaid, and shall likewise as often in euery yeere administer the Sacraments of Baptisme (if there be any to be baptized) & of the Lords Supper, in such maner & forme, and with the obseruation of all such Rites and Ceremonies as are prescribed by the booke of Common prayer in that behalfe. . . .

The position was complicated by the theoretical assumption, which we have already studied, that Church and State were coterminous. There is a petition in our Litany which couples "false doctrine, heresy, and schism" with "sedition, privy conspiracy, and rebellion": and the Ministers of the Crown were bound to keep a watchful eye upon the pulpits of the Established Church. Indeed, the student of English history in the first hundred years after the Reformation may be pardoned if he finds it difficult to recall whether at any given date the Government was engaged in endeavouring to make the clergy preach, or in endeavouring to make them desist from preaching —both very difficult operations, the clergy being what they are.

The nature of the problem is now perhaps becoming apparent. It is difficult for any institution which includes among its functions the control of opinion, to adjust itself to new ideas: although it is fatal for such an institution not to do so. An ideological conservatism, whether in politics or in divinity, is naturally intolerant of deviations from the established orthodoxy, and the disposition to preserve—especially when preservation is associated with self-preservation—is often more in evidence than the ability to improve. From the administrative standpoint, a steady, continuous, and effective propaganda is both necessary and desirable, but with the one proviso, that it must be the right kind of propaganda. In the sixteenth and seventeenth centuries, the principal organ for the dissemination of ópinion was the pulpit, and therefore both the civil and the ecclesiastical authorities, in the interest of public order and of doctrinal orthodoxy, were concerned to stimulate, to tune, or to restrain this vital instrument. But nobody has yet discovered how to apply a tourniquet without in any way interfering with a normal healthy circulation. If you wish people to agree with you, you must allow them liberty to differ; and you must reckon with the possibility that they may differ from you and from each other more violently than you can afford.

We should discount the allegation in Nalson's *Collections* that the Parliamentary Faction in September 1641 deliberately "set up a Spiritual Militia of these Lecturers, who were to Muster their Troops . . . neither Parsons, Vicars nor Curates, but like the Orders of Friers Predicants among the Papists, who run about tickleing the Peoples Ears with stories of Legends and Miracles, in the mean time picking their Pockets. . .".[4] For the origin of these lectureships was earlier in date, and it was spontaneous and not calculated. The morning lectures at St Antholin's, Watling Street, in the City of London, are supposed to have been established in 1559. They had been tinged with Calvinism from the outset. The original arrangement was that three lecturers should each preach twice a week at six o'clock in the morning, but the number of lectureships was subsequently increased to five, and finally to six. The next earliest lectureship known to me is mentioned in *The Orders and Dealings in the Church at Northampton* (1571). Richard Rogers became "Preacher of God's Word" at Wethersfield in Essex in 1574. The lectureship at Dedham (also in Essex) dated from 1577-8: the first lecturer was Edmund Chapman, who in 1582 organized a local presbyterian Classis, of which the Vicar of Dedham was an ardent member.[5] More familiar are the names of Walter Travers, Reader at the Temple, in the Inns of Court, from 1581 until his silencing by Archbishop Whitgift in 1586; and the silver-tonged Henry Smith, "an eloquent and a witty man" who in 1587 became "Reader or Lecturer at St Clement Danes without Temple-Bar, at the desire of many of the parishioners, and by the favour of the Lord Treasurer [Burghley], who dwelt in the said parish, and yielded contribution unto him."[6]

The best account of this development is to be found in Professor Haller's *The Rise of Puritanism*:

> Within the purlieus of the church, making use of Cambridge as its seminary, the reform party under the primacies of Bancroft, Abbot and Laud built up for itself what can fairly be called a kind of Puritan order of preaching brothers. The members sprang as a rule from the gentry or merchant class or had immediate connections with that class. . . . As a rule they accepted ordination, though as time went on they tended to avoid formal undertaking of the cure of souls, in other words regular appointment as parish priests. That too often involved responsibility for strict performance of observances which presented difficulties to their consciences. . . . Often they found support and the opportunity to preach as chaplains or tutors in great households, but the post which characteristically they found most congenial and, we may add, remunerative was that of lecturer or special preacher to a congregation for which the ordinary and prescribed services were performed by a regularly invested parson. . . . The lecturer . . . was selected to preach by the congregation, or by some member or group of members, or by some wealthy

adherent, any of whom might undertake the expense of his support. His ministrations might be sought out by people of many parishes round about. His duty was to lecture upon the Bible, that is to preach, on Sundays at times other than those of the usual services and in most instances upon week-days as well. He was supposed to be licensed by the bishop or other proper authority in the church, to whom he was accountable under pain of being silenced. . . .[7]

Taken by and large, the Puritans were neither saints nor hypocrites. There are times when one can do very comfortably in opposition: and it involves no reflection upon the sincerity of anybody's motives to point out that to be a Puritan in the 1580s, like being a Left Wing intellectual in the 1930s, was the obvious line for an able young man on the make. So the spiritual progeny of Chaderton and Sibbes and Perkins grew rapidly in numbers and in influence, until they came to command the most strategic pulpits in and about London, and to constitute a challenge to the established order in Church and State which could no longer be ignored. Yet they were not minded to destroy, but only to reform, the Church of England.[8] Their theology was Calvinist: but so, it could plausibly be argued, were the Thirty-nine Articles agreed upon by the Archbishops and Bishops of both Provinces, and the whole Clergy, in the Convocation holden at London in the year 1562, for the Avoiding of Diversities of Opinions, and for the Establishing of Consent touching True Religion: and there was indeed a touch of intellectual high-handedness about the Royal Declaration of 1628, still prefixed to the Articles in our Prayer Book, requiring that these shall be taken in "the literal and grammatical"—meaning, the Arminian—"sense". But the situation of the Puritans, though formidable, remained precarious. Minority opinions need to be sheltered by some measure of security of tenure until they can become majority opinions. In the year in which King Charles I succeeded his father on the throne, a circle of influential Puritans in London founded the first Party Patronage Trust in the Church of England with a view "to plant a powerfull Ministery in Cities and Market-Towns here and their in the Country for the greater propagation of the Gospell".

The committee of twelve residents in London—probably representing a much larger group of Puritans—who thus in 1625 associated themselves as feoffees or trustees to raise funds wherewith to purchase impropriations and land and appurtenances for the maintenance and relief of godly, faithful, and painful ministers of the Word of God, comprised four clergymen, four lawyers, and four merchants. Significantly they included six adventurers in the Massachusetts Bay Company, and one original member of the Providence Island Company. The clerical members of the association were Richard Stock, Rector of All Hallows, Bread Street; Richard Sibbes, Preacher of Gray's Inn and Master of St Catharine Hall, Cambridge; Charles Offspring, Rector of St Antholin's; and John Davenport, Vicar of St Stephen's, Coleman Street (afterwards pastor of New Haven, Connecticut, and finally of the First Church, Boston, Massachusetts). Stock died in April 1626, and was replaced by William Gouge, Rector of St Anne's, Blackfriars.

During an active existence of approximately seven years, the feoffees collected £6877 11s. 1d. (a total which compares favourably with the stocks raised by the Providence Island Co.), and disbursed an even larger sum—£8073 11s. 1d.—in the purchase of advowsons and in the maintenance or subvention of curates and lectures in widely scattered parishes throughout England and Wales, with a studied preference for towns which returned burgesses to Parliament. Their most important acquisition was the management of the St Antholin's lectureships, which they increased to six and planned to use as a kind of staff college from which, after a six years' apprenticeship, godly and fruitful preachers might be planted out in key-positions controlled by the Trust. But the Reverend Peter Heylyn, Fellow of Magdalen College, Oxford, happened upon their trail in Gloucestershire, and exposed their activities on Sunday 11 July 1630, in an University Sermon on the Parable of the Tares, which was in the nature of a sequel to Richard

Bancroft's Sermon at Paul's Cross on 9 February 1589. The sermon aroused considerable feeling; and Heylyn, for his own protection, sent a copy of it "to the Bishop of *London*, not long before made Chancellour of that University; and signified in a Letter therewith sent, that he was both able and ready to make good his charge, whensoever it should be required." Bishop Laud informed the King, who referred the matter to the attention of the Attorney-General. Legal proceedings were instituted in the Court of Exchequer, and in February 1633 the feoffees were dissolved, and all their properties were confiscated. This judgement undoubtedly stimulated Puritan emigration to New England.

It is impossible not to admire the ingenuity and the audacity of the conspiracy, which Laud regarded as "a cunning way, under a Glorious pretence, to overthrow the Church-Government, by getting into their power more dependency of the Clergy, than *the King*, and all *the Peers*, and all *the Bishops* in all the Kingdom had". Indeed, it was estimated that within fifty years the Trust would have acquired all the impropriations available for purchase. As Gardiner comments: "Of all modes of supporting a clergy yet invented, their maintenance by a body of capitalists living for the most part at a distance from the scene of their ministrations, is, in all probability, the worst. There are, however, times when the most irregular manifestations of life are welcome. . .".[12]

Be that as it may, there are certain palpable objections to the regularizing of irregular vitality by artificial means, and particularly by the power of the purse. It is one thing to find a way of getting new wine into old bottles: it is quite another thing to do so in such a fashion as to reserve those bottles in perpetuity for that specific vintage and no other. The Reverend Charles Simeon, at the beginning of the nineteenth century, when Cambridge was a seminary of the Evangelicals, was confronted by a similar problem, and adopted a similar solution. A congregation which had been edified by the ministrations of an Evangelical incumbent was liable, if his successor was a clergyman of a different stamp, to break up, and either to lapse or to hive off into Dissent: the only method of securing continuity of Churchmanship was to buy the advowson. The motive, therefore, of what Simeon called "my blessed work of purchasing Livings", was "love to immortal souls". "There is this difference", he wrote, "between myself and others: they purchase *incomes*—I purchase *spheres*, wherein the prosperity of the Established Church, and the Kingdom of our blessed Lord, may be advanced; and not for a season only, but if it please God, in perpetuity also", in all the principal provincial towns. "The object is of incalculable importance. The securing of a faithful Ministry in influential places would justify any outlay of money that could be expended on it." To this object, Charles Simeon devoted his private fortune: with this object, the Simeon Trust was constituted in 1817.[13] By the time of Mr Simeon's death in 1836 it controlled 21 advowsons: a century later, it controlled 152, although, as a result of the operation of various diocesan reorganization schemes since the War, the number for the time being stands at 142. The pious founder could not have foreseen the shifting of controversial interest from doctrine to ceremonial, nor the emulation of his policy by other and later Party Trusts more negative in purpose, more polemical in spirit, and less scrupulous in method.

It is, however, one of the little ironies of history that Simeon as Vicar of Holy Trinity, Cambridge, where Richard Sibbes had preached to crowded and enthusiastic auditories, should have suffered from the gainsaying of two successive lecturers, the titular successors of Sibbes and Preston and Goodwin, who were maintained by the dissident elements in his congregation, and whose opposition he was obliged to suffer for twelve uncomfortable years, until in 1794 he was himself elected to the lectureship.

For Laud had not succeeded in suppressing these Puritan foundations: and after his fall, the House of Commons, acting whether upon its own motion or at the request of the parishioners concerned, frequently recommended, or nominated, or sanctioned, a lecturer for a specific parish, in order to remedy "the great scarcity of preaching ministers throughout the whole Kingdom". Without as yet dispossessing the lawful incumbent—for it was only after the outbreak of hostilities that Parliament showed itself more ruthless in enforcing some degree of uniformity by depriving the disaffected clergy—the lecturer was ordered to have the use of the church and pulpit for (say) the afternoon of the Sabbath, and for one day in every week, preferably the market day, for the purpose of preaching a lecture. Thus on 18 February 1642, on the humble Petition of the Inhabitants of the Parish, the House of Commons recommended the celebrated Stephen Marshall, who had been Rogers' successor as lecturer at Wethersfield, to be made choice of as their Lecturer at St Margaret's, Westminster, "the House holding the said Mr *Marshall* a Person fit and able for the Discharge of that Place". The House had previously ordered, on 8 September 1641, that the parishioners of any parish in England and Wales might lawfully set up a lecture, and maintain an orthodox minister at their own charge, "to preach every Lord's Day where there is no preaching, and to preach one day in every week when there is no weekly lecture". But this, as Dr Bosher has observed, proved to be a game that two could play at: and groups of Anglican laity in London under the Commonwealth were quick to take advantage of the loophole so conveniently afforded them by their religious and political opponents. Thus on 23 June 1657, we find Parliament petitioning the Lord Protector to "be pleased to remove from Margaret's, Westminster . . . one Warmstree, who is employed as a Lecturer there, being a notorious delinquent . . .": and the future Dean of Worcester was expeditiously replaced by Mr Seth Wood, who was in turn ejected in 1660.[14]

It is a commonplace that institutions are tenacious, and exhibit a remarkable capacity for survival: and therefore it is not surprising to find lectureships persisting after the Restoration. There was, after all, no other provision made in the parochial system of the Church of England for popular preaching: and preaching was still popular, in an age which afforded few alternative facilities for entertainment or (we may add) for adult education. Bishops found some of the lecturers inclined to nonconformity, and even crypto-Dissenters: but the old association of lectureships with Puritanism was dying, and John Strype himself, the ecclesiastical historian, from 1689 to 1724 was lecturer of Hackney. At the beginning of the eighteenth century, most of the churches in London and its suburbs had lecturers attached to them who in the majority of cases were independent of the incumbent and were supported by voluntary contributions, "the amount of which put to shame the scanty stipends of the curates".[15] At St Margaret's, Westminster, on Sunday evenings there was a sermon endowed by a Friendly Society for the benefit of its members, which in the language of the times was called a Society Evening Lecture: and in connection with this Lectureship there occurred on Sunday 4 February 1739 an incident far-reaching in its consequences.

The regular Lecturer, the Reverend Mr Morgan, having to be out of Town that Sunday, had arranged for a substitute (the Reverend J. Majendie) to take his place. Meanwhile the officers of the Society, knowing that Mr Morgan would be absent, but not knowing that he had made other arrangements, had invited the celebrated revivalist, the Reverend George Whitefield, who had recently returned from Georgia, to preach the sermon. Such situations do occur, and they are always awkward: but what was particularly unfortunate in this case was that Whitefield's coach broke down on the way from Spitalfields to Westminster, with the result that he did not reach St Margaret's until half-way through the prayers. He made his way to the vestry, where he was informed that another minister intended to preach. Thereupon he repeatedly offered to go home: but his friends insisted that he must preach, or the congregation would walk out. "At my Request", he wrote in his *Journal*, "some went to the Trustees, Churchwarden, and Minister; and whilst I was waiting for an Answer, and the last Psalm singing, a Man came with a Wand in his Hand, whom I took for the proper Church-Officer, and told me I was to preach; I, not doubting but the Minister was satisfied, followed him to the Pulpit: and God enabled me to preach with greater Power than I had done all the Day before." This was in fact his third sermon that Sunday; and he was only 24.

Such an incident, involving so controversial a personality, could hardly escape calumny: and a highly garbled account of it was published in the *Weekly Miscellany* for 10 February, in a letter from the Reverend Richard Venn, who happened, by a curious irony, to be Rector of St Antholin's, and who had been the first clergyman in London to refuse his pulpit to Mr Whitefield.

On Sunday last, our new *Methodists* discovered a more violent temper than is consistent with their great pretensions to *meekness* and *sanctity*. The story is as follows, and it was related to me by the gentleman that read the prayers.

At St Margaret's, Westminster, there is a *Society* Evening Lecture; and when the Reader came, he found in the *church-yard*, at the *west door*, a number of people singing psalms. When he got into the *church*, he was affronted by some unknown persons as he passed through a great crowd to the vestry. As soon as the clergyman appointed to *preach* came, he was *solicited* (if an *overbearing importunity* may be so called) to resign the pulpit to Mr Whitefield, who (as is supposed by his not appearing at the *prayers*) was waiting at some neighbouring house to know the issue of the application. But the *preacher* continuing as determined to do his duty as Mr Whitefield was to do it for him, they at last effected that by *force* which they could not gain by *treaty*. So the *preacher* was safely confined in his *pew*, which was locked (the sexton being appointed by the *Society*, and in Mr Whitefield's interest), and guarded by several lusty fellows; while another party conveyed the *unlicensed intruder* triumphantly into the pulpit, and kept sentry on the stairs for fear he should be taken down in as forcible a manner as he got up.

There are many instances of these *unauthorised* teachers using *fraudulent* and *unfair* means of getting into pulpits against the inclination of the *proper minister* or *appointed preacher*. Sometimes they ask the pulpit for a *friend*, and then send Mr Whitefield or some other *Methodist*. Another method has been by slipping up into the pulpit as soon as the prayers are over, without asking any leave at all. And all these *disorders, irregularities,* and *artifices* are practised by persons who have no *warrant*, but *their pretended call from heaven*, to preach in *any* church in the diocese.

This travesty of the facts was categorically contradicted by one of the stewards of the Society in the *Weekly Miscellany* for 24 February: but it is difficult to catch up with a slander that has had a fortnight's start. Thenceforward Whitefield, although a priest of the Church of England, was to find almost all the churches in London and in the provinces closed against him, and was obliged to exercise his ministry of preaching either in the open air—it is extremely significant that it was on Saturday 17 February 1739 that he preached his first open-air sermon in this country to the Bristol colliers on Rose Green, Kingswood— or in unconsecrated buildings; and to the day of his death, which occurred in 1770 at Newburyport, Massachusetts, he was pursued by a virulent and implacable hostility to a degree to which John Wesley himself was never exposed. He still, however, had friends and sympathizers among the Evangelical clergy of the Established Church: and it is another of the little ironies of history that in the Countess of Huntingdon's Chapel at Bath his funeral sermon was preached by the Reverend Henry Venn, son of the former Rector of St Antholin's. None the less, viewed in its widest consequences, the unlucky contre-temps at St Margaret's, Westminster, on Sunday 4 February 1739 must be regarded as one of the most critical and decisive incidents in the history of the Evangelical Revival in the eighteenth century.[16]

From this somewhat cursory historical survey of a particular institution in the Church of England which here and there has still a titular and innocuous existence, we may now turn to consider the general nature of the problem to which it points.

It was superbly said of Archbishop Laud, who had been beheaded on Tower Hill before a jeering crowd on 10 January 1645, "He hath no memorial, save his University of *Oxford*, and this present Church of *England*": and the principle with which Laud identified himself, and which he bequeathed to the Anglican tradition, was the principle of allowing a generous liberty of theological speculation upon the basis and condition of a decent uniformity in the external worship of God, according to the doctrine and discipline of the Established Church.

At this point it may be necessary to explain that although the Thirty-nine Articles of Religion may properly be regarded as constituting a Protestant Confession, and were included as such in the *Harmony of Confessions* published at Geneva in 1581, yet, as Professor Dawley has observed, the Church of England is not a Confessional Church. At no time have the Articles been binding on the laity, who are in fact, and always have been, surprisingly unfamiliar with them; and since 1865, when the more stringent requirements of the Act of Uniformity of 1662 were relaxed by the Clerical Subscription Act, even the clergy have not been legally obliged to do more than register "assent". The Articles have never stood alone, and were never designed to stand alone, as a summary of the faith of the Church of England. They have always been received by English Churchmen together with the other Anglican standards, the Prayer Book and the Ordinal. Indeed, "the essential principles of Anglicanism stand out to view most conspicuously in the Book of Common Prayer. The Homilies and even, though in a less degree, the Articles have a temporary purpose, a transitory validity, a contingent worth. . . The Prayer-book, representing the purged and ordered current of traditional religion, exhibits the permanent effects of Reformation, and forms the true and abiding standard of Anglican orthodoxy. It embodies the Anglican version of the Catholic system."[17]

The declaration made by every clergyman of the Church of England at his ordination, and again whenever he is admitted to office, whether as a stipendiary curate or as an incumbent, reveals the extent to which the policy of Archbishop Laud has come to be accepted by the Church and State for which he died. It is as follows:

> I, *A.B.*, assent to the Thirty-nine Articles of Religion, and to the Book of Common Prayer, and of Ordering of Bishops, Priests and Deacons; I believe the doctrine of the Church of England, as therein set forth, to be agreeable to the Word of God: and in public prayer and administration of the Sacraments I will use the form in the said Book provided, and none other, except so far as shall be ordered by lawful authority.

The underlying assumptions are that the mind of the Church of England is made known supremely in the Book of Common Prayer, by which the clergy are to be controlled; and that, within that liturgical discipline, and because of it, there is room for a good deal of freedom of intellectual movement. But if the Laudian principle of ordered liberty is to secure the results which it is intended to achieve, then (if I may so express it) the game must be played according to the rules.

For example, there must be no specialization of function as between readers and preachers. The ministry of preaching is fundamentally a ministry of exhortation, based upon exposition of the Scriptures, and intended to the edifying of the flock in love. It is pastoral, rather than prophetic; and in normal circumstances the parish priest who "takes the service" will also preach the sermon. When "holy Mr Herbert" as an act of piety re-edified and furnished the church of Leighton Bromwold in Huntingdonshire (of which the prebend had been bestowed upon him by Bishop Williams of Lincoln in 1626), "by his order, the reading pew and pulpit were a little distance from each other, and both of equal height; for he would often say, 'They should neither have a predecency or priority of the other; but that prayer and preaching, being equally useful, might agree like brethren, and have an equal honour and estimation.' "[18] Above all, the ministry of the Word must never be sundered from the ministry of the Sacraments.

In the second place, although the Church can never be administered in accordance with the maxim which Lord Melbourne, as Prime Minister, is alleged to have proposed to a Cabinet in deadlock—"It doesn't much matter what we say, provided we all say the same thing"—yet neither can the cause of theological orthodoxy be promoted in the parishes by the method of the Lincoln-Douglas Debates, because the Church does not exist in order to be a debating society. The Church of England is admittedly indebted to the running controversy between Hooker as Master, and Travers as Reader, of the Temple, for that archetypal masterpiece of Anglican theology *Of the Laws of Ecclesiastical Polity*: yet it was more intellectually than pastorally edifying when "the pulpit spoke pure Canterbury in the morning, and Geneva in the afternoon, until Travers was silenced". Again, we may regard as more affecting than exemplary an anecdote of the Reverend John Rogers, Lecturer at Dedham from 1605 to 1636, which is narrated by Giles Firmin: "As for that description of Faith which that holy man, Mr *John Rogers*, hath given in his Book, the first that ever I heard opposed it in his own Pulpit, was his own Son, Mr *Nathaniel Rogers*, a man so able, and so judicious in Soul-work, that I would have betrusted my Soul with him, as soon as with any man in the Church of Christ: when his own Son thus in his Fathers own place opposed it, (as I have been informed) his reverend old Father, who dearly loved him, stood by and heard him with great attention; the people, they heard him with some amazement, and got him to preach over the Sermon again the next Sabbath." There is more pastoral wisdom and sagacity in Canon LIII (*No publike opposition betweene Preachers*):

If any Preacher shall in the Pulpit particularly, or namely of purpose, impugne or confute any doctrine deliuered by any other Preacher in the same Church, or in any church neere adioyning, before hee hath acquainted the Bishop of the Diocesse therewith, and recieued order from him what to do in that case, because vpon such publike dissenting and contradicting, there may grow much offence and disquietnesse vnto the people: the Churchwardens or party grieued shall forthwith signifie the same to the said Bishop, and not suffer the said Preacher any more to occupy that place which hee hath once abused, except hee faithfully promise to forbeare all such matter of contention in the Church, vntill the Bishop hath taken further order therein: who shall with all conuenient speed so proceed therein, that publike satisfaction may bee made in the Congregation where the offence was giuen. Prouided, that if either of the parties offending doe appeale, hee shall not be suffered to preach *pendente lite*.

In 1658, Jeremy Taylor, in a letter to John Evelyn, civilly declined an offer of a half-share in a pulpit with a divine of contrary opinions: "I like not the condition of being a lecturer under the dispose of another, nor to serve in my semicircle, where a Presbyterian and myself shall be like Castor and Pollux, the one up and the other down, which methinks is like worshipping the sun and making him the deity, that we may be religious half the year and every night serve another interest. . . ."[19]

But even more intolerable is the situation where the lecturer is regarded and indeed maintained by dissident elements in the congregation as a kind of Leader of the Opposition to the incumbent. The Evangelical Charles Simeon, as we have already noted, suffered from this at Cambridge for twelve years, until he completely won the confidence of his parishioners: while not long after, a "high and dry" divine of the old school, the Reverend Charles Fynes, D.C.L., Prebendary of Westminster, Minister of St Margaret's, and Rector of Cromwell, Nottinghamshire (where he normally resided), felt himself obliged to take drastic action in order to frustrate and set aside the popular election of an Evangelical as Lecturer of St Margaret's, in circumstances which were thus described in *The Times* newspaper of Monday 11 December 1820:

DISGRACEFUL OCCURRENCE. — Yesterday afternoon a disgraceful scene occurred in the Church of St Margaret, Westminster. To explain the matter, it is necessary to observe that the situation of Afternoon Lecturer had become vacant by the promotion of Mr Stevens (formerly Chaplain of the House of Commons) to the Deanery of Rochester. Six clergymen were candidates to succeed him, and at the election last week the Rev. Mr Sanders [sic], of St Ann's, Black-friars, was the successful candidate by a large majority. The Rev. Dr Fynes, Prebend of Westminster, and Rector [sic] of St Margaret's, has refused to him, with the concurrence of the churchwardens, the use of the pulpit, on the ground that Mr Sanders is one of that description of clergymen called methodistical. Yesterday afternoon the church was crowded to excess. Mr Sanders was refused the use of the vestry, and Mr Rodber, the morning preacher, approached the pulpit to preach. Instantly loud hisses, groans, and cries of "Shame, shame", proceeded from a great number of persons standing in the aisles of the church: a horrible confusion and alarm ensued: numbers sought their safety by getting over the rails, particularly women and children, and taking refuge literally at the altar. The beadles apprehended two of the rioters, after much contest. The prayer before the sermon, and the commencement of the sermon itself, were inter-rupted in a manner for which we know of no parallel, except the scenes at Covent-garden playhouse during what were called the O.P. rows. Any thing more disgraceful, and more revolting to pious minds, can scarcely be conceived than this dreadful transformation of the house of God into a theatre, exhibiting some of the worst features of a contested popular election.

It must, however, be admitted in extenuation that the atti-tude of the non-resident incumbent had been arbitrary, exas-perating, and provocative in the extreme. Six applications for the vacant Lectureship had been formally laid before the Vestry on Wednesday 20 October 1820, and the Vestry Clerk had been instructed to write to Dr Fynes informing him of the names of the candidates, and applying to him for the use of the pulpit for them to preach their probationary sermons. At the Vestry Meeting on Friday 3 November, a reply from Dr Fynes was read, in which he made the following observations: "Probationary Sermons are as I own very improper exhibitions in my opinion but as I believe Custom has made them usual upon such occasions, I cannot refuse the application of the Vestry... I could wish to make it a condition with the Lecturer that he should read the Afternoon Prayers on Sunday as well as preach the Lecture . . . and I would likewise suggest to the Vestry that since my Incumbency I have been materially injured in the receipt of Easter Dues by the Lecturer collecting his emolument before the Incumbent begins his Collection at Easter. Mr Stevens' Friends were very zealous in his behalf in this instance and I believe very successful." The next development was that the following Notice was served upon the Clerk of the Vestry.

Cromwell, Nov. 22d, 1820.

I hereby notify to all whom it may concern that I positively refuse Mr Isaac Saunders the liberty of preaching, or in any way officiating in the Parish Church of Saint Margaret, Westminster, and furthermore declare that I will prevent his appointment to the Lectureship of the said Parish so far as I am legally authorized.

CHARLES FYNES.

This Notice was laid before the Vestry Meeting on 30 November, when an explanatory letter from Dr Fynes was also read:

When I answer'd your letter which contained the List of Candidates for the vacant Lectureship I made no observation upon the name of Mr Saunders because at that time I was not aware of his being the person who officiates at the Broadway Chapel. . . . I could by no means consent to allow the use of Saint Margaret's Pulpit to Mr Saunders, and if notwithstanding this refusal, he should be elected Lecturer I would not give my sanction to such an Election. . . . After the sound and orthodox Doctrine delivered to the Parishioners of Saint Margaret so ably by the late Lecturer, I feel it my duty to guard them against being deluded and led away by the wild and visionary effusions of those who arrogate to themselves the character of Evangelical Preachers, and I trust that the good sense of the Vestry and the principal Inhabitants will induce them to co-operate . . . in our endeavours to avert such an evil, and to prevent, if possible, those disgraceful scenes which have sometimes been exhibited by Competitors upon similar occasions in other Parishes of the Metropolis. . . .

But, whatever Prebendary Fynes may have thought about it, the right of election of the Lecturer was "in the Inhabitants Men and Women rated to the Parochial Taxes": and they do not seem fully to have appreciated the solicitude for their orthodoxy so feelingly displayed by their official pastor, for they proceeded notwithstanding to elect the Reverend Isaac Saunders by 492 votes (out of a total poll of 992) and with a majority of 43 over his runner-up, the Reverend R. V. B. Sandilands. Dr Fynes immediately on hearing the news instructed the Vestry Clerk to inform the Churchwardens of his disapproval, and to remind them that no one could be authorized to perform the duty of Lecturer of St Margaret's Parish who was not sanctioned by the Incumbent and licensed by the Dean and Chapter. He had his way, in so far as the election of Mr Saunders was set aside, and a second ballot, taken on 28 December, resulted in the election of Mr Sandilands: although he was not able to prevail upon the Vestry to abolish the method of popular election altogether, since the Vestry took the view that so long as the Lecturers were remunerated by the parishioners, they should be elected by them, "and that the mode heretofore adopted of a Ballot is the most efficacious for determining the Choice of those Gentlemen who may offer themselves upon any Vacancy". But meanwhile Dr Fynes had had occasion to write again.

Cromwell, Dec. 16, 1820.

Sir,—. . . It is with the utmost concern I heard from Mr

Rodber, and read in the Newspapers the infamous behaviour of Mr Sanders' Partisans in Saint Margaret's Church on Sunday last. I trust the Ringleaders in this most disgraceful Riot will be brought to Justice and meet with the Punishment they justly deserve. It appears to me that the Vestry are call'd upon to express to the Public their unanimous detestation of the brutal Assault committed upon their Minister in the House of God, when engaged in the discharge of his sacred Duty; and that they ought to offer a reward for the Conviction of the Instigator and Promoter of such an atrocious unheard-of Outrage.

I beg you will communicate these sentiments to the Vestry, and am

Sir, your obedient Servant,
CHARLES FYNES.

In the event, it was left to Dr Fynes himself (who in the meantime had changed his name to Clinton by royal licence, being distantly related to the Duke of Newcastle) to bring an action in the Commissary Court of the Dean and Chapter of Westminster against Henry Hatchard, undertaker, who had been prominent in the disturbance at St Margaret's on that unhappy Sunday afternoon. Judgement, with costs, was given for the plaintiff, although, in consideration of the defendant's calling, the penalty of suspension *ab ingressu ecclesiæ* was limited to one month: and *Clinton* v. *Hatchard* (1822) became a leading case in English ecclesiastical law. Yet Dr Fynes Clinton's obituary notice in the *Gentleman's Magazine* (December 1827) made no reference whatsoever to the episode, and concluded simply with these words: ". . . The most useful characters in the sphere of ordinary life are not those which form the usual subjects of panegyric. The continued and gentle operation of a well-spent life is unobserved and unostentatious. Such was the tenour of the life of the departed. In it, however, the charity and good-will of that religion, of which he was a minister, were not to be mistaken. The poor of Westminster will remember the hand that liberally ministered to their wants;

and the love of peace and harmony, which guided his actions and threw their grace upon his demeanour, will not soon be forgotten."[20]

Our judgement on the character and conduct of Prebendary Fynes Clinton may be more critical than this, and it is possibly significant that the only one of his sons to be ordained became a narrow Evangelical fanatic. Yet it must be conceded that he was perfectly correct in his conviction that there must be no public opposition between preachers occupying the same parochial pulpit: which is the second rule on which the functioning of the Laudian principle of ordered liberty depends.

This is, however, qualified by the third rule, that, granted that no human teacher is infallible, and that no religious party can pretend to a monopoly of sacred truth, it follows that no school of theological opinion is entitled to deny or to forestall to any other the facilities that it demands for itself.

It may be noted that this principle is respected in the Reverend Charles Simeon's solemn Charge to his Trustees, which contains no partisan language about "men loyal to the principles of the Reformation", or the "distinctly Protestant and Evangelical principles" of the Church of England "as set forth in the Book of Common Prayer and Thirty-nine Articles of Religion"; although, as Hensley Henson pointed out, the omission, particularly in the second clause, of any reference to the Bishop of the diocese as having any pastoral responsibility, may perhaps be regarded as a blemish upon this otherwise admirable document,[21] which is as follows:

IN THE NAME AND IN THE PRESENCE OF ALMIGHTY GOD, I give the following Charge to all my Trustees, and to all who shall succeed them in the Trust to the remotest ages. I implore them for the Lord Jesus Christ's sake, and I charge them also before that adorable Saviour, who will call them into judgment for their execution of this Trust,

FIRST, that they be very careful, whenever they shall be

called upon to fill up a vacancy in this Trust, which they must invariably do within three months of a vacancy occurring, that they elect no one who is not a truly pious and devoted man, a man of God in deed and in truth, who, with his piety, combines a solid judgment and a perfectly independent mind. And I place this first, because a failure in this one particular would utterly defeat, and *that* in perpetuity too, all that I have sought to do for God and for immortal souls.

SECONDLY, That, when they shall be called upon to appoint to a Living, they consult nothing but the welfare of the people for whom they are to provide, and whose eternal interests have been confided to them [*sic*].

They must on no account be influenced by any solicitation of the great and powerful, or by any partiality towards a particular individual, or by compassion towards any one on account of the largeness of his family or the smallness of his income.

They must be particularly on their guard against petitions from the parishes to be provided for, whether on behalf of a Curate that has laboured among them, or any other individual.

They must examine carefully, and judge as before God, how far any person possesses the qualifications suited to the particular parish, and by that consideration *alone* must they be determined in their appointment of him.

Signed by me this 18th day of March in the year of our Lord, One thousand eight hundred and thirty-three.

CHARLES SIMEON

But a document so liberally conceived is liable to be narrowed by interpretation. Mr Simeon had included among his desiderata "a solid judgment and a perfectly independent mind". Until very recently (when a direct quotation from his Charge was substituted), it was stated in the *Official Year Book of the Church of England* that the Simeon Trust was founded in 1817 "for the purpose of holding Church Patronage which

is administered on Evangelical lines": and this is not necessarily the same thing. The Simeon Trust has in fact a particularly honourable record, and it deserves to be mentioned that
at the present time the eastward position at the Holy Communion is taken in almost half the parishes which it controls,
while in one parish the Eucharistic vestments are worn. Yet,
even when it is not the avowed object, it is the inevitable tendency of Party Patronage Trusts to set up in perpetuity little
enclaves of ecclesiastical partisanship, and to stereotype specific
phases of theological thought and religious habit by the
creation of vested interests in the cure of souls.

In the course of the past hundred years, the strife of parties
in the Church of England became exacerbated by developments in ceremonial and by varieties of use. Ceremonial is, of
course, only the outward livery of doctrine, and it is true not
merely that the basic controversial issues have always been
doctrinal, but also that the repercussions of the Gorham Judgment (1850) were more far-reaching and momentous than the
repercussions of the riots at St George's-in-the-East (1859-60),
which incidentally were precipitated by the election of an
ultra-Protestant Lecturer in opposition to a Ritualist incumbent.[22] Yet the fact remains that the majority of lay folk are,
not perhaps more influenced by, but more suspicious of what
they see than of what they hear.

That an exact and entire uniformity has never obtained in
the Church of England may readily be conceded: it does not
obtain even in the contemporary Church of Rome. Tudor or
Stuart despotism might issue an authorized Prayer Book, an
authorized version of the Bible, an authorized Catechism, and
even, for that matter, an authorized Latin Grammar, and
expect no other to be used.[23] But this was optimistic. The Act
of Uniformity enforcing the Revised Prayer Book of 1552
attributed the necessity for revision not to "any worthy cause",
but to "the curiosity of the minister and mistakers", which is
what we call sabotage. It was, incidentally, the kind of sabotage
at which clergymen, being men of strong convictions and high
principles, have always been rather good: for example, if you

are sufficiently determined, it is just as easy to be inaudible in English as it is to be inaudible in Latin. Again, after the Revised Prayer Book of 1559 had come into force, in 1564 Mr Secretary Cecil submitted to the Queen a memorandum on "Varieties in the Service of the Church". And again, after the Revised Prayer Book of 1662 had come into force, in 1682 an inquisitive Student in the Inns of Court desired "the satisfaction of an intire service performed exactly according to the Rubrick, without any exercise of the prudence of a private man, which does, methinks, but sully a Divine office of publick composure and authority. Which", as he complained to his friend the Dean of Durham, "is a felicity which I cannot yet discover in all London. . . . Wee have yet as many separate wayes of worshipp as wee have ministers, and every one that I could yet discover, offends in something that is clearly contrary to law."[24] And this, moreover, was long before the Anglican clergy had awoken to the occult potentialities latent in the phrase already quoted from their statutory declaration, namely, *"except so far as shall be ordered by lawful authority"*: for *"lawful authority"* can, by a little ingenuity, be interpreted to mean any authority to which any individual clergyman chooses, in conscience, to defer. It may however be admitted that the laity, being more simple and straightforward, have always been suspicious of, and genuinely puzzled by, this technique of conscientious interpretation of our ordination vow.

Nevertheless, although in every century absolute uniformity has been rather the ideal than a reality, yet, in regard to the externals of public worship, there was probably a more than merely relative uniformity in the Church of England as Catholic and Reformed, for the period from 1662 to 1850. Before that halcyon epoch, the authorities were obliged to cope with clergymen refusing to wear surplices,[25] and after it they had to cope with clergymen insisting on wearing chasubles. There is a story, possibly apocryphal, of Dean Stanley telling Dr Tait, Bishop of London (1856-69), that he had been to church at St Alban's, Holborn. The Bishop asked what he had seen. Stanley replied: "I saw three men in green, *and you will find it difficult to put them down.*"[26]

The Ritualists have not been put down: but neither have they succeeded in capturing the Church of England. It has been a hard-fought battle, and to anyone who does not understand the genius of *Ecclesia Anglicana*, it might appear to have ended in a draw. A slightly less superficial judgement might be that it has ended in a compromise. It is in fact ending in a synthesis. That is the Anglican way, the traditional English method of digestion.

One false solution has happily been averted simply by the anomalies of the system of patronage in the English Church. "Regional ceremonialism" is as unsatisfactory and as unedifying as "geographical morality": and, whatever individual bishops may try to do with the facilities at their disposal during their tenure of particular sees, the "monochrome diocese" is a phenomenon which we have not yet experienced in England. We are uneasily aware that in "heathen lands afar" competing missionary societies, supported respectively by Evangelicals and Anglo-Catholics, have established "zones of influence" recognized, and even strictly preserved, by our colonial administration: such as the C.M.S. and U.M.C.A. dioceses in Africa. Some of us have even heard travellers' tales from other continents of a Biretta Belt and a Bible Belt. (It is, however, a reassuring thought that at least one practice which in the Protestant Episcopal Church of the United States of America is the badge of the High Church party, is the badge of the Low Church party in the Church of England; and that at least one practice which in England is the badge of the High Church party, is the badge of the Low Church party in America.) But in England every townsman, and almost every countryman, can enjoy considerable varieties of liturgical experience within an easy radius of his home.

Yet, if the mind of the Church is not diocesan, still less is it parochial: and, upon mature reflection, the Church of England is becoming healthily impatient of individual incumbents seeking, on their own initiative and responsibility, to relieve "the present liturgical chaos" by an arbitrary and autocratic exercise, confined indeed to the territorial boundaries of their respective parishes (or, to speak more accurately, to the interiors of the particular parish churches in which they minister), of the *jus liturgicum* of the local parish priest. It is written large upon our history that it is not the business of a clergyman of the Church of England to take the world for his parish: but neither has he any business to take his parish for the world, and, when he does so, it is apt to be resented not only by the world, but even more by his own parish. Nor is this impatience confined to exhibitions of what Disraeli called "The Mass in masquerade": it applies almost equally to "mangled Mattins" and to the more woolly extra-liturgical devotions so dear to the Liberal Evangelical mentality.

There are two important factors in the contemporary situation. One is that the population is comparatively mobile: it is now rare for any man to live in the same parish all his life and never leave it, even for a holiday. The other is that, after a long and unhappy period of party bitterness and strife and litigation, the Church of England has, by the mercy of God, arrived at a condition of affairs in which, broadly speaking, the laity do not mind what garments the priest wears at the altar, so long as they can follow the service in the Prayer Book. By a sort of native wisdom, they have come, more readily than the clergy, to distinguish between what is not worth fighting for, and what they are entitled to expect.

Such is the pastoral opportunity which is now offered to the English clergy as ministers of Christ and stewards of the mysteries of God: and the main obstruction to it is still the presbyterian congregationalism which usurps the name of Catholic.

> *We are a Garden wall'd around,*
> *Chosen and made peculiar Ground;*
> *A little Spot, inclos'd by Grace,*
> *Out of the World's wide Wilderness.*[27]

Fundamentally it is not a liturgical but a pastoral problem.

Let me speak from my own experience as a parish priest. Here is a boy, from what could hardly be described as a religious home: he is prepared and presented for Confirmation; and it is our hope and prayer that he will grow up a devout and regular communicant. He comes back from his summer holidays, and reports that on the first Sunday he went to Holy Communion at the local parish church, but that he was so completely bewildered and humiliated by the unfamiliar order of service that he had not the nerve to go again. In that, and all its implications, you have the pastoral problem in a nutshell.

How far such an incident could be paralleled in other churches of the Anglican Communion, it is not for me to say. It is, however, not too optimistic to reflect that, because it is a pastoral problem, the Church of England, given time, is qualified to master it, because the genius of the Church of England is essentially pastoral. And we, the parochial clergy of the English Church, however some of us may be privately persuaded that the Book of Common Prayer is patient of "enrichment" from other sources or that the structure of our Communion Service is different from, and *ipso facto* liturgically inferior to, the structure of the Roman Mass, none the less know in every fibre of our being that our first duty is to care for the sheep of Christ and for his lambs "that they may be saved through Christ for ever", and not to put unnecessary stumbling-blocks in the way of those who have come to us from other pastures. It is necessary therefore that, before we choose to make our private fancies the rule of our public ministrations, we should, as we were bidden in the Ordinal, "consider the end of our Ministry toward the children of God".

Admittedly, this does not clear the problem of New Wine in Old Bottles: and, as Archbishop Cranmer said (though not precisely in these words), if sensible men had been listened to, we should still be eating acorns.[28] To accept the doctrine that the Holy Spirit is guiding the Church into all truth, is to recognize the necessity that the Church must change, although without losing or compromising its identity. That is the true Doctrine of Development. But it postulates continuity as well as change: and this continuity—which is more than a purely historic continuity—is supplied by assent to a Creed and by conformity to a Liturgy; the Creed oecumenical, and therefore primary; the Liturgy national, domestic, secondary, and not immutable. I would pause upon that word "domestic". Like the Father's House, the English Prayer Book contains many mansions of the human spirit: it is prophetic, it is priestly, it is pastoral: and, what is more, it admits of a wide range of devotional experience and of a generous latitude of theological interpretation. But there is a fundamental difference between those who regard it as a prison, and those who regard it as their home.

APPENDIX A

A Continuation of the Reverend Mr WHITEFIELD'S
Journal, *from his Arrival at LONDON, to his Departure
from thence on his Way to GEORGIA.* (London: printed
for James Hutton, at the *Bible and Sun, without
Temple-Bar.* 1739.) pp. 16-36.

LONDON.

Friday, February 2. Slept about two Hours, rose and went
and preached at *Islington*, and collected twenty-two Pounds
for my Orphan-house.

Had a great Number of Communicants, and was told my
preaching was attended with Uncommon Power. This is the
first time I have preached without Notes, (for when I preached
at *Deptford* and *Gravesend*, I only repeated a written Sermon)
but I find myself now, as it were, constrained to do it.

Expounded in the Evening, and collected three Pounds for
the Orphan-house, at Mr *Abbot's*; preached extempore, with
great Freedom at *Wapping-Chapel*; then expounded to another
Society, and returned Home without Fatigue or Weariness. . . .

Saturday, February 3. . . . Near nine Times has God enabled
me to preach this Week, and to expound 12 or 14 Times; near
forty Pounds, I believe, has been collected for the Orphan-
house.—*I find I gain greater Light and Knowledge, by preaching extempore.—So that I fear I should quench the Spirit, did
I not go on to speak as he gives me Utterance.*

Sunday, February 4. Had a comfortable Night's Rest; was
warmed much by talking to an almost Christian, that came to
ask me certain Questions.—Preached in the Morning at St
George's in the East, collected eighteen Pounds for the Orphan-
house, and had, I believe, 600 Communicants, which highly

offended the officiating Curate. *Poor Man, I pitied, and prayed for him sincerely.*

Preached again at *Christ-Church, Spittlefields*, gave thanks, and sung Psalms at a private House: Went thence to St *Margaret's, Westminster*; but something breaking belonging to the Coach, could not get thither 'till the middle of Prayers.— Went through the People to the Minister's Pew, but finding it locked, I returned to the Vestry till the *Sexton* could be found. Being there informed that another Minister intended to preach, I desired several Times that I might go Home: My Friends would by no means consent, telling me I was appointed by the Trustees to preach, and that if I did not, the People go out of the Church; at my Request, some went to the Trustees, Churchwardens, and Minister; and whilst I was waiting for an Answer, and the last Psalm singing, a Man came with a Wand in his Hand, whom I took for the proper Church-Officer, and told me I was to preach; I, not doubting but the Minister was satisfied, followed him to the Pulpit: And God enabled me to preach with greater Power than I had done all the Day before.

After this, prayed with, and gave a Word or two of Exhortation to a Company that waited for me, then took a little bodily Refreshment, and then went to a Love-Feast in *Fetter-Lane*, where I spent the whole Night in watching unto Prayer, and discussing several important Points with many truly Christian Friends. About Four in the Morning we went all together and broke bread at a poor sick Sister's Room, and so we parted, I hope, in a Spirit not unlike that of the primitive Christians.

This has been a Sabbath indeed! How has God owned me before near Twelve thousand People this Day.—How he has strengthened my Body! How has he filled and satisfied my Soul. Now know I, that I did receive the Holy Ghost at Imposition of Hands.—For, I feel it as much as Elisha did, when Elijah dropped his Mantle. Nay, others see it also; and my opposers, would they but speak, cannot but confess that God is with me of a Truth. Wherefore do they fight against God?

Monday, February 5. Went about gathering for my poor

Flock, had a little Time to write my Journal, was somewhat weak part of the Day, but grew strong by expounding to four Companies at Night. *I always get Strength by working. What great things has God done for my Soul! Oh that I could praise him with my whole Heart!*

Tuesday, February 6. Was refreshed much this Morning, and found that the Sleep of a labouring Man was sweet.— Waited on the Bishop of *Gloucester* with Brother *John Wesley*, and received his Lordship's liberal Benefaction for *Georgia.* . . . .

·   ·   ·   ·   ·   ·

BASINGSTOKE

Sunday, Feb. 11. . . . A most beneficial and comfortable Meeting have I had with my dear Christian Friends, and many, I hope, will have Reason to bless God for what they have seen and heard.—A Vestry, I find, was called to stop my Proceedings, and I hear I am to be presented to the Diocesan.—Several Lies have been told in the News about my Preaching at St *Margaret's* last Sunday.—*Blessed be God that I can rejoyce in these lower marks of my Discipleship.—Wherever I go, God causeth me to triumph, knits the Hearts of his People most closely to me, and makes me more than Conqueror through his Love.— The Comforts I enjoy within are inexpressible, they have a great Effect upon my outward Man, and makes me of a chearful Countenance; which recommends my Master's Service much.— Oh Free Grace in* Christ Jesus!

·   ·   ·   ·   ·   ·

BATH and BRISTOL

Wednesday, February 14. After Family-Prayer, and giving a Word of Exhortation, I set out for *Bath*, and was greatly comforted there with some Christian Brethren.—I then waited on Doctor *C—y*, desiring I might have the Use of the Abbey Church to preach for the Orphan-house, the Trustees having obtained Leave of the Bishop before I went to *Georgia*. But he was pleased to give me an absolute Refusal to preach either on that, or any other Occasion, without a positive Order from the

King or Bishop. I asked him his Reasons. He said, *he was not obliged to give me any.* Upon which, I took my leave, and retired with my Friends, and prayed for him most fervently.— *The Time will come,* says our Lord, *when they shall thrust you out of their Synagogues.*

After Dinner, other Circumstances concurring, we thought God called us to *Bristol.* And with Cheerfulness of Heart, we reached that Place about Seven in the Evening.—But who can express the Joy with which I was received? To add to my Comfort, many Letters came to my Hands from *London* Friends, which rejoyced me exceedingly. And what was the chiefest Pleasure, somebody or other thought me considerable enough to write a Letter in the *Weekly Miscellany* against me, and with several Untruths, about my preaching at St *Margarets Westminster.*—*Thou shalt answer for me, my Lord and my God. Yet a little while and we shall appear at the Judgment-seat of Christ. Then shall my Innocence be made clear as the Light, and my just Dealings as the Noon-day.*

BRISTOL

Thursday, February 15. . . . After having breakfasted and prayed with some religious Friends, I went with Mr *Seward* to publick Worship; from thence to the Reverend Mr *G — s,* Minister of St *Mary, Ratcliff* [= *Redcliffe*], who, as I was informed, had promised to lend me his Church to preach in for the Orphan-house. But he, in effect, gave me a Refusal, telling me, *that he could not lend his Church without a special Order from the Chancellor.*—Upon this, I immediately waited upon the Chancellor, to whom I had sent the Night before. But he told me frankly, that he would not give me any positive Leave, neither would he prohibit any one that should lend me a Church: but he would advise me to withdraw to some other Place till he had heard from the Bishop, and not preach on that or any other Occasion. I asked him his Reasons. He answered, "Why will you press so hard upon me? The Thing has given a general Dislike."—I replied, "Not the Design of the Orphan-house,—even those that disagree with me in other

Particulars, approve of that. And as for the Gospel, when was it preached without Dislike?" Soon after this, I took my leave, and waited upon the Reverend the Dean, who received me with great Civility. When I had shewn him my *Georgia* Accounts, and answered him a Question or two about the Colony, I asked him, "Whether there could be any just Objection against my preaching in Churches for the Orphan-house?"—After a Pause for a considerable Time, he answered, "He could not tell." But somebody knocking at the Door, he replied, "Mr *Whitefield*, I will give you an Answer some other Time; now I expect Company." "Will you be pleased to fix any, Sir?" said I. "I will send to you," says the Dean. *O Christian Simplicity, whither art thou fled? Why do not the Clergy speak the Truth, that it is not against the Orphan-house, but against me and my Doctrine, that their Enmity is levelled. Had another come in his own Name, him they would have received.—But do thou, O Lord, behold their Enmity, and grant unto me, and all thy despised Servants, that with all Boldness we may speak thy Word.*

About three in the Afternoon, God having given me great Favour in the Jaylor's Eyes, I preached a Sermon on the *Penitent Thief* to the poor Prisoners in *Newgate....*

At seven I expounded for an Hour with very great Power to a young Society, which God has caused to be established since I was in *Bristol* last: And many, I heard afterwards, were pricked to the Heart, which was manifest enough by the Tears that were shed by almost all that heard me. . . . The Lessons were very remarkable, and the People made an Application for me.—The first was the Opposition made against *Aaron's* Priesthood, and God's determining who was in the right, by causing his Rod to blossom when the other Rods produced nothing. *So let it happen, O Lord, to me thy unworthy Servant.* —The second was the Eleventh Chapter of St *Paul's* 2d Epistle to the *Corinthians,* where the Apostle recounted his sufferings for *Christ,* against the Insinuations of the false Apostles. *Blessed be God, in most of the Things there recorded, I have, in some small Degree, had Fellowship with the Apostle, and before I die, I doubt not but I shall sympathize with him in most other*

Articles.—While I was reading it, I could not forbear blushing much. The People were intent upon me, their Eyes bespoke the Language of their Hearts: Each seemed to say, *Thou art the Man. Suffering is the best Preferment.*

Friday, Feb. 16. Begun this morning to settle a daily Exposition, and reading Prayers to the Prisoners in *Newgate....*

Saturday, Feb. 17. Read Prayers and expounded the Parable of the Prodigal Son at *Newgate* to a great Number of People; and afterwards was much refreshed by the coming of a dear *London* Friend and the Receipt of several Letters; for the Writers of which, I with many others immediately kneeled down and gave Thanks. One Thing affected me much in these Letters, *viz.* Their News of a great Opposer's being given over by the Physicians.—*Alas poor Man! We all prayed most heartily for him, Knowing how shortly he must give an Account of what he had most unjustly said and wrote against me and many true Servants of* Jesus Christ. *Father lay not this Sin to his Charge.*

About One in the Afternoon I went with my Brother *Seward,* and another Friend, to *Kingswood,* and was most delightfully entertained by an old Disciple of the Lord.—My Bowels have long since yearned toward the poor Colliers, who, as far as I can find, are very numerous, and yet are as Sheep, having no Shepherd.—After Dinner therefore, I went upon a Mount and spake to as many People as came unto me. They were upwards of two hundred.—*Blessed be God that I have now broken the Ice; I believe I never was more acceptable to my Master than when I was standing to teach those Hearers in the open Fields. —Some may censure me.—But if I thus pleased Men, I should not be the Servant of* Christ.

About five, we returned full of Joy; and I wrote to the Bishop of *Bristol* (as I had done before to the Bishop of *Bath* and *Wells*) for Leave to preach in his Lordship's Churches, for the Benefit of the Orphan-house. *May God incline him to send me an Answer of Peace!*

At seven, I went to expound to a Society of young Men for near two Hours. . .

Sunday, Feb. 18. Arose this Morning about six . . . read Prayers, and preached at *Newgate*. . . At ten, I preached at St *Werburgh*'s with great Freedom, and to a large Audience.—Blessed be God, I thought yesterday I should not have the use of any Pulpit; but God, who has the hearts of all Men in his Hands, disposed the Reverend Mr *Penrose* to lend me his, who thanked me for my Sermon; and the Reverend Mr *Gibbs* sent to me, and offered me the Use both of St *Thomas* and St *Mary Ratcliff*.—The latter of these I accepted of, and preached to such a Congregation as my Eyes never yet saw, with great Liberty and Demonstration of the Spirit.—Many went away for want of room; and Mr *Gibbs* and his Lady were exceeding civil both to me and Mr *Seward*. . . .

Monday, Feb. 19. Read Prayers and expounded as usual at *Newgate*, and preached in the Afternoon to a great Multitude at the Parish-Church of St *Philip* and *Jacob* [*sic*], and collected Eighteen Pounds for the Orphan-house.—Thousands went away, because there was no room for them within. . . .

. . . Amongst the Letters I received from religious Correspondents, one writes to me thus,—"Mr——, who wrote that Letter in the *Miscellany*, died Yesterday."—*He is now gone to give an Account of the many hard Speeches contained therein. —And is convinced that Orthodoxy in Notions is not the whole of Religion.*—. . .

Tuesday, Feb. 20. This Day my Master honoured me more than ever he did yet.—About Ten in the Morning, in Compliance with a Summons received from the *Apparitor* Yesterday, I waited upon the Reverend Mr *R——l*, the Chancellor of *Bristol*, who now plainly told me, he intended to stop my Proceedings. . . . "I am resolved, Sir, if you preach or expound any where in this Diocese, till you have a License, I will first suspend, and then excommunicate you."—I then took my

Leave.—He waited upon me very civilly to the Door, and told me, "What he did was in the Name of the Clergy and Laity of the City of *Bristol*;"—And so we parted.

... At four there was a general Expectation of my preaching at St *Nicholas*; thousands went to hear me.—But the Lecturer sent Word, that Orders were given by Mr *B—r*, that I should not preach in his Church; which rejoyced me greatly. *Lord why dost thou thus honour me? ...*

Wednesday, February 21. .... At three in the Afternoon, according to my appointment, I went to *Kingswood* amongst the Colliers. God highly favoured us in sending a fine Day, and near two thousand People were assembled on that occasion. I preached on *John* ch. iii. ver. 3. and enlarged for near an Hour, I hope, to the Comfort and Edification of those that heard me. ....

APPENDIX B

Reports of Cases argued and determined in the Ecclesiastical Courts at Doctors' Commons, and in the High Court of Delegates. By J. ADDAMS, LL.D. An Advocate in Doctors' Commons. . . Vol. 1: containing cases for the Hilary Term 1822, to Trinity Term 1823, inclusive. In continuation of The Ecclesiastical Reports of Dr Phillimore. (London: 1823.) pp. 96-104.

1822 *Hilary Term.*
In the Commissary Court of the Dean and Chapter of Westminster.

The Office of the Judge, promoted by CLINTON *v.* HATCHARD

This was a proceeding by articles against Henry Hatchard, of the parish of St Margaret, Westminster, at the promotion of the Rev. Dr Charles Fynes Clinton, prebendary of the collegiate church of St Peter, Westminster, and incumbent curate of the said parish. The articles, after pleading, first the *general* law touching the orderly demeanour of persons who repair to their parish churches; and secondly, that part of 5 & 6 Edw.6. c.4, which respects *quarrelling, chiding,* or *brawling,* in any church, went on to charge, *that* the said Henry Hatchard did, in the afternoon of Sunday the 10th of December 1820, whilst at the church of St Margaret, Westminster, and during the celebration of divine service therein, behave in an irreverant [*sic*] and disorderly manner, and annoy and interrupt the Rev. William Johnson Rodber, assistant curate of the said parish, whilst he was passing from the vestry-room to the pulpit, and endeavour to prevent him from preaching a sermon therein—*that* he, the said Henry Hatchard, in order to effect his said purpose, had caused, or induced a number of persons to collect about the vestry door, by shouting, in a loud tone,

"We want some friends about the vestry-room door;" so that the said Rev. William Johnson Rodber could with difficulty effect a passage from the said vestry-room to the pulpit—*that*, during the said Rev. William Johnson Rodber's passage from the said vestry-room towards the pulpit, the said Henry Hatchard took hold of his gown, and, addressing himself to him, said, "Here is Mr Saunders, ready to do his duty; why won't you let him preach?"—*that* upon the said Rev. William Johnson Rodber disengaging his gown, and still proceeding towards the pulpit, he, the said Henry Hatchard, followed him, repeating the word "Shame"; and adding, in an angry, chiding, and reproachful manner, "For shame, Mr Rodber; Mr. Saunders was regularly elected—why not let him preach? For shame"—and *that*, by such irreverent and improper conduct, he, the said Henry Hatchard, greatly annoyed and disturbed, as well the said Rev. William Johnson Rodber in the performance of his duty, as the congregation then assembled in the said church, for the purpose of divine worship.

A responsive allegation was given, and admitted, on the part of the said Henry Hatchard, which pleaded, in substance, *that*, in the autumn of the year 1820, the afternoon parochial and unendowed lectureship of the parish of St Margaret, Westminster, having become vacant, the Rev. Isaac Saunders, Rector of St Ann's, Blackfriars, was chosen lecturer, against several competitors, by a majority of parishioners, at a poll taken by the churchwardens on the 6th, 7th, and 8th of December in that year—*that* it being *doubted*, during the said election, whether Dr Clinton, the incumbent, would grant Mr Saunders the use of the pulpit, if elected, much curiosity was excited among the parishioners to know the result, which led to the assemblage of an unusual number of persons at the afternoon service, at St Margaret's, on the ensuing Sunday, being the 10th of December—*that*, among others, the said Henry Hatchard went, and arrived there towards the conclusion of prayers; and having learnt, upon his arrival, that the said Mr Saunders was in the vestry, he went thither to enquire whether he was, or was not, allowed to preach—*that* being answered by that gentleman in the negative, he withdrew from the vestry into one of the aisles of the church, where, having learnt, soon afterwards, from one of the beadles, that the said Mr Saunders had retired into the churchyard, upon the vestry being *cleared*, he also went there, and found him in conversation with a friend, who suggested that it would be proper to give *formal notice* to Mr Rodber, the officiating curate, that Mr Saunders was in attendance, as a matter of curtesy [*sic*]; and that the said Henry Hatchard, as a supporter of the said Mr Saunders, was a proper person to communicate such notice to Mr Rodber—*that* the said Henry Hatchard thereupon proceeded towards the *vestry*, for the purpose so suggested; but that, encountering Mr Rodber in his way from the said vestry, which he had just left, to the pulpit steps, he said to him, in a very low tone of voice, and in a mild and respectful manner, "Mr Rodber, Sir, the Rev. Isaac Saunders is here to perform the duty to which he has been elected"—*that* the said Rev. William Johnson Rodber taking no notice thereof, the said Henry Hatchard immediately turned away, and left the said church, which he did not re-enter during that afternoon—*that*, on the said Henry Hatchard so turning away, several persons cried out "Shame, Shame", and "For shame, Mr Rodber," or to that effect; and there was a noise, a hissing, and a considerable tumult, in the said church; but *that* the said Henry Hatchard took no part in the same— *that* he had not *previously* shouted or said, in a loud tone of voice, or otherwise, "We want some friends at the vestry-room door;" and that he did not, *subsequently*, accompany the said William Johnson Rodber towards the pulpit steps, exclaiming, "For shame, Mr Rodber," or to that effect; or address him in any other words than those before pleaded.

No evidence was adduced in support of this allegation; but three witnesses were produced and examined upon the articles.

Frederick Price, one of the *bearers* of the parish, deposed (in substance)—that he was at the parish church of St Margaret, Westminster, on the afternoon in question, and that, just after the evening prayers were finished, he observed Mr Hatchard (whom he had never seen at the church before but at a funeral, he being an undertaker) standing very near the vestry door, *by* the *deponent*, whose office it was to attend the officiating clergyman from the vestry to the pulpit—*that* he distinctly heard him say to a person who stood close to him, "we want a few friends near the vestry-room door"—*that*, as Mr Rodber was passing from the vestry towards the pulpit, he was closely followed by Mr Hatchard, who said to him, in the deponent's hearing, plainly and distinctly, "Shame, Mr Rodber, Mr Saunders is regularly elected—why not let him preach?—for shame of you"—*that* immediately upon Mr Rodber's ascending the pulpit, a number of persons began to hiss and shout, and call out "Shame"—whereby so great a tumult was excited, that a very few of the congregation could possibly distinguish Mr Rodber's sermon, although preached in his loudest tone,—and *that* after the service was over, the crowd, which was greater than ever the deponent had seen there, either before or since, would not quit the church till a magistrate was sent for, and arrived, from the Queen Square Police Office, accompanied by several constables—and that it was between five and six o'clock before the church was cleared. The witness further deposed, that "although there was some talking, and a kind of murmuring noise, *before* Mr Hatchard addressed Mr Rodber, as above —yet there was nothing violent or outrageous until *after* he had so addressed him."

The Rev. William Johnson Rodber (in substance) deposed, that on Sunday, the 10th of December, 1820, he attended the parish church of St Margaret, Westminster, as assistant curate of the parish—*that* as soon as the clergyman who read the prayers, had finished, he left his pew, and retired to the vestry —*that*, on leaving the vestry for the pulpit, where the deponent was about to preach, his progress was impeded by a great number of people about the vestry-door, among whom was Henry Hatchard, the party proceeded against, so that the deponent had great difficulty in effecting a passage towards the pulpit— *that* he had proceeded but a short way from the vestry, when he felt the left sleeve of his gown pulled, and heard his own name called out; whereupon he turned round, and saw the said Henry Hatchard, who immediately said, "Mr Rodber, here is Mr Saunders, ready to do his duty, will you choose to let him preach?" [The deponent says, that he had observed the Rev. Mr Saunders in the said church during the afternoon prayers, and knew him to have been elected afternoon preacher, by the parishioners, although he had been denied the use of the pulpit, even for a probationary sermon, and had been told that it would still be denied him, in the event of his being elected]—*that* the deponent did not make any reply to the said Henry Hatchard, but passed on—*that* the said Henry Hatchard kept close to the deponent, and, as he was passing near the rail of the altar, again addressed him, saying, angrily, "Mr Rodber, why won't you let Mr Saunders preach—he has been regularly elected?—for shame"—*that* the deponent still not answering, but forcing his way through the crowd, a most violent outcry and noise immediately took place—*that* in his passage through the crowd, to the pulpit steps, which the deponent, with difficulty, effected, by aid of two of the church beadles, he was kicked till both his legs were black and blue, and hissed at, and spit upon—whilst there were many persons crying out "Mr Rodber, come back, don't disgrace yourself"—*that* the deponent delivered his sermon in the midst of an uproar, which continued during the whole service, and was loud enough, at times, to drown the sound of the organ, and the voices of the congregation and the charity children—*that* this uproar was such as the deponent had never, upon any occasion, before witnessed, and *that* after the service, the crowd was obliged to be dispersed by constables—*that* it was evidently the intention of the persons who hustled the deponent in his way to the pulpit, to prevent him from reaching it—and *that* the said Henry Hatchard was principally instrumental in this attempt, and in exciting the tumult and disorder which otherwise existed in the said church.

The evidence of John Woodward, also one of the bearers of the parish, was precisely corroborative of that of Price, the first witness, and that of Mr Rodber.

JUDGMENT

Dr SWABEY. [after stating the charge, and recapitulating the evidence.]

Upon this view of the case I conceive it impossible to deny that the offence imputed to this defendant, and which, as appears, may be one of grave *consequence*, is brought home to him by the clearest and most indisputable evidence. In particular, no language can be a "chiding and brawling" within the state of Edw. 6, in a *truer* sense of the words, than the defendant's expostulations, or remonstrances, with Mr Rodber, as spoken to by the several witnesses, upon the occasion in question. The attempted justification set up (*in plea*) can be regarded in no other light than of a mere pretence. Not only was a "formal notice" to Mr Rodber that Mr Saunders was in attendance purely superfluous, but its delivery can scarcely, I think, under the circumstances, be ascribed, by any stretch of charity, to a laudable motive. But be that as it may, it is certain, that the scene of tumult and disorder which ensued was the actual, if it was not the designed, consequence of the delivery of this "notice" *by* the defendant; who therefore has been selected, in my judgment, with great propriety, as the person against whom these proceedings have been instituted. A very little inquiry, which it was his duty to have made, if inclined to meddle in this matter at all, would have instructed him, that in the case of every, at least *unendowed*, lectureship, no choice, by the parish, of a lecturer is effective, without the consent or approval of the rector (*a*); whose undoubted right it is, in every such case, to grant to, or withhold from, the lecturer so chosen the use of his pulpit. At all events, however, he could not be ignorant that if Mr Saunders had a legal right to the pulpit in the instance in question, there must be a legal mode of enforcing it—that any other mode of attempting to enforce it *was* as unjustifiable, as it must *eventually prove* unavailing; and that an appeal to private judgment, or rather to popular feeling upon such a subject (which this defendant's conduct amounted to, in my apprehension of it), was illegal, as well as, in the highest degree, indecorous.

It remains only to pronounce the sentence of the law, which assigns to this species of offence, the offender being a layman, the penalty of suspension *ab ingressu ecclesiæ*, for a discretionary period. I am induced to limit that period to one month only (to be computed from Wednesday next) in the present instance, from the circumstance of this defendant being an undertaker. I trust that he will be sensible of the lenity of the Court in this respect—and that, in future, he will be led to his parish church by better motives, and conduct himself in it with greater caution and propriety.

I accompany this sentence of suspension with a decree for *costs* against Mr Hatchard, as a matter of course.

(*a*) No person can be a lecturer, endowed or unendowed, without the rector's consent, unless there be an immemorial custom to elect without his consent—where there is such a custom, it is binding on the rector, as it supposes a consideration to him. The *endowment* only seems material, in this respect, as it does (or may) furnish an argument in support of the custom, and to shew that it had a legal commencement. See 2 Str. 1192. 1 Wils. ii.   Rex *v.* Bishop of London, 1 T.R. 331; and Rex *v.* Field and others, 4 T.R. 125.

Even after the rector's consent is obtained, the bishop's license is also necessary—if not as forming part of the title of the lecturer, still, at least, to exempt him from the penalties of 13 & 14 Car. 2. * c.4.   Vide 1 T.R. 331.

* Vide *s.* 19 and Canons of 1603. Canon xxxvi.

THE CHURCH AND LIBERALISM

SOME forty years ago in Westminster, at a Sunday evening supper party at St Margaret's Rectory (which was then No. 17, Dean's Yard), when the company included Bishop Welldon, Professor Kirsopp Lake, and Mr Bertram Christian, the publisher, to whom I am indebted for this anecdote, the Rector, Canon Hensley Henson, standing with his back to the fire and spreading his coat-tails, narrated with sardonic amusement the receipt of a letter which he described as "conceived in the following terms":

Very Reverend and dear Sir,

Some weeks ago I called your attention to the wide departure in your pulpit utterances from the teaching of the Bible and the true principles of religion, and begged that you might be enabled to see the error of your ways.

Since, however, as I have been pained to observe, you have rejected the opportunity of making any amendment in the opinions you express, I regret to have to inform you, with great respect, that I have no alternative but to pray to Almighty God to strike you dead. I am,

Very Reverend and dear Sir,
Your obedient servant, ...

For better or for worse, we belong to a generation that is both more sophisticated and less self-confident; with the result that the fires of orthodox zeal no longer burn at so high a controversial temperature.

The theological convulsions of the nineteenth century have often been described as "The conflict between Science and Religion", and the lamentable clash between Bishop Wilberforce and Professor Huxley at the meeting of the British Association at Oxford in 1860 is commonly regarded as the central incident in that conflict. But the agony of traditional orthodoxy in the Victorian era did not centre round *The Origin of Species* (1859), of which in fact the argument had already been foreshadowed in the anonymous *Vestiges of the Natural History of Creation* (1844) by Robert Chambers, so flippantly epitomised in one of the novels of Disraeli.[1] As Dr Raven has observed, "The development of a mechanistic philosophy, involving the restriction of the field of science to the categories of weight and measurement and the extension of it to include the organic and the human, was obviously the most serious challenge to religion":[2] and we may add that it reached its logical climax in the Behaviourist psychology of only yesterday, which virtually reduced all human conduct to a matter of conditioned reflexes. Yet this fundamental challenge, strangely enough, was perceived more clearly by the Romantic poets than by the orthodox divines. It is worth remembering that the alienation between Religion and Science in the first three-quarters of the nineteenth century was less profound than that between Poetry and Science, about which less has been written only because it is irrelevant to the religious polemics which (as in the late sixteenth and early seventeenth century) were the leading intellectual interest of the age. Intuitively, Cowper, Keats, and Wordsworth revolted against the contention of eighteenth-century Rationalism that "Man's customs and habits depend on his nature, his nature is conditioned by his body, his body is composed of matter, and the laws of matter are known." That philosophy had been adumbrated by Montesquieu, displayed in Godwin's *Political Justice*, and developed into a pseudo-scientific dogmatism by the Encyclopaedists: and the French Revolution was its sanguinary outcome.[3] Evangelicalism, whether within the Establishment or outside it, was Tory in grain; and, like the Oxford Movement, it matured in the new universe of discourse created by Romanticism, which was a counter-revolution against the tyranny of the Age of Reason. But for Churchmen the central and all-embracing controversial issue was the authority of the Bible: and the conflict between Religion and Science, which broke out in the departments of geology and biology (in that order), and of which the outbreak was recognized in 1829 by the endowment and inauguration of the Bridgewater Treatises, was only a corner of the battlefield on which the authority of the Bible was being challenged and defended all along the line.

Most of the tumult and the shouting came from the clerical rank and file, the spiritual descendants of the men who had rallied so exuberantly to the slogan of "The Church in Danger" in the days of Dr Sacheverell.[4] When that gifted entomologist, the Reverend Octavius Pickard-Cambridge, as a young deacon attempted to defend the views of Darwin at meetings of local clergy who denounced without having read them, his efforts were not well received: and it was the Archbishop of Canterbury and the Bishops of London and Llandaff who braved clerical opinion in 1831 by appointing Charles Lyell to the Professorship of Geology at King's College, London.[5] Perhaps in no period has the Church of England owed more to the beneficent influence of the State connection than in the ensuing hundred years: the system under which high ecclesiastical appointments are made by the Crown on the recommendation of the Prime Minister may be open to theoretical objections, but if the alternative of election by the clergy, or by the clergy and laity, had been in force, we should never have had Frederick Temple as Bishop of Exeter (and finally Primate of All England), nor Hensley Henson as Bishop of Hereford (and subsequently of Durham), nor Charles Gore as Bishop of Worcester (and subsequently of Birmingham and of Oxford); and it is inconceivable that Buckland would ever have become Dean of Westminster, or Milman Dean of St Paul's.

But all this in the nineteenth century was a new kind of problem, and one for which the Church was wholly unprepared. For Fundamentalism, no less than Modernism, involves an intellectual judgement as to the value of the Bible as an authority, in the ordinary secular meaning of that phrase: and it was a very long time before it occurred to anyone to think of the Bible in that way, or to perceive that such a judgement was demanded. The Deist, Anthony Collins, sarcastically observed

ARCHDEACON FARRAR
from *Vanity Fair*, 1891

CANON HENSLEY HENSON
from *Vanity Fair*, 1912

that nobody thought of doubting the existence of God until the Boyle Lecturers had undertaken to prove it: [6] I believe it to be far more true to say that nobody really believed in the verbal inspiration of the Holy Scriptures until the geologists began to question it. Hitherto, broadly speaking, people believed everything they read in the Bible, in the same way that some people believe everything that they read in the newspapers. This applied to the opponents as well as to the adherents of orthodox Christianity: a typical piece of anti-Christian polemic was *The Man after God's own Heart*, an attack upon the moral character of David, unhampered by any esoteric knowledge about J and E. Theologians might find themselves obliged to attempt to harmonize ostensibly contradictory texts, but the attitude to Scripture as such was uncritical: the documents contained within the Sacred Volume were accepted at their face value, and used as data from which inferences could be deduced. Thus for example the Reverend John Lightfoot, D.D., Master of Catharine Hall and, in 1654, Vice-Chancellor of the University of Cambridge, in a sermon preached upon Exodus 20. 11. and entitled *The Sabbath Hallowed*,[7] ingeniously works out, upon the basis of the opening chapters of the Book Genesis, the actual season of the year at which the Creation must have taken place:

That the world was made at *Æquinox*, all grant, but differ at which, whether about the eleventh of *March*, or twelfth of *September*; to me in *September* without all doubt. All things were created in their ripeness and maturity; Appels ripe, and ready to eat, as is too sadly plain in *Adam* and *Eves* eating the forbidden Fruit. . . .

The implicit assumption, "that *Adam* fell on the very day he was created", will be found to rest upon a profoundly moving but typically medieval parallel between the Fall and the Redemption, in which the chronology of our Saviour's Passion is projected back onto the narrative in Genesis.

. . . *Redemption* was wrought on the sixth day, as the *Fall* had been on the sixth day. And when Christ had wrought that great work, he rested the seventh day in his grave, as

God rested on the seventh day, when he had wrought the great work of Creation. . . . About the *third* hour, the hour of sacrifice and prayer, it is very probable *Adam* was created. And *Mark* tells you, *Chap.* XV. 25. *And it was the third hour, when they crucified him*; that is, when they delivered him up to *Pilate* to be crucified. About the *sixth* hour, or high noon, *Adam* most probably fell, as that being the time of eating. And *John* tells you, *Chap.* XIX. 14. that about the sixth hour he was condemned, and led away to be crucified. And about the *ninth* hour, or three a clock afternoon Christ was promised, which *Moses* calls the cool of the day: and about the ninth hour Christ *cried out with a loud voice, and gave up the Ghost.* Such Harmony may be found between the day and hours of the one and of the other: the latter helping to prove and clear, that *Adam* fell on the *sixth* day, the day on which he was created, and *continued not in honour all night.*

And Dr Lightfoot then proceeds to demonstrate that the first sabbath, observed by Adam upon the seventh day, was both of moral and of evangelical institution, for "the institution of the Sabbath is mentioned, *Gen.* II, before the fall of Adam is mentioned, *Gen.* III". All this admittedly presupposes a theory of verbal inspiration: but not in the sense in which we understand it, for the modern theory of verbal inspiration derives its character and its form from the historic circumstance that it was intended to answer and refute the critical attack upon the integrity of Scripture.

Equally remote from us, in this respect, as Dr Lightfoot, is William Cowper, the poet of Evangelicalism, as he regards with a kindly but quizzical superiority the activities of the geologists, who fondly suppose that they are able to reopen a question authoritatively settled in the opening pages of the Bible:

> *Some drill and bore*
> *The solid earth, and from the strata there*
> *Extract a register, by which we learn*
> *That he who made it, and reveal'd its date*
> *To Moses, was mistaken in its age.*[8]

This kind of attitude (apart from the apparent conflation of Moses with Archbishop Ussher, which is a minor detail) was all very well so long as its premisses remained unchallenged. But when in 1782 Priestley applied to the development of Christianity what he named the "historical method", and five years later Eichhorn inaugurated "the higher criticism", the mood of serene and uncritical assurance began to give way to a panic-stricken defensive fundamentalism. "Some 50 years ago", wrote Dr Pusey in 1860 in his introduction to the Prophet Zechariah, "there was a tradition at Göttingen, where Heyne had lived, that he attributed the non-reception of the theories as to Homer in England to the English Bishops, who 'apprehended that the same principle would be applied to Holy Scripture'."[9]

This was a new phenomenon. The Church has never defined inspiration. Medieval exegesis, while assuming that all Scripture was authoritative and inspired, allowed that it might have four different senses. The Reformers never fully realized what their conception of the Bible as the Word of God implied for exact Biblical study: Luther, at once reactionary and radical in his attitude to the sacred writings, was gloriously inconsistent: Calvin laid down as axiomatic the inerrancy of Scripture, but was forced to admit that it contained erroneous statements. Legalism, rather than literalism, characterized the Puritan attitude to the Bible: it was their authority for impugning the propriety of surplices and caps and tippets, or for unbishoping Timothy and Titus.

But at the beginning of the nineteenth century, the precision of the critical attacks in all the quarters from which they emanated, imposed upon the orthodox for the first time the necessity of defining precisely what they meant by inspiration.[10] Not all, indeed, accepted this necessity. Bagehot wrote: "One of the most remarkable of Father Newman's Oxford sermons explains how science teaches that the earth goes round the sun, and how Scripture teaches that the sun goes round the earth; and it ends by advising the discreet believer to accept *both*. Both, it is suggested, may be accommodations to our limited intellect—aspects of some higher and less discordant unity."[11]

But this was felt to be over-subtle. The normal reaction was simpler and more crude: the foundations were being cast down, and the Church was in danger.

It was not the first time. When Jerome published his Vulgate, St Augustine enlarged upon the perils to be apprehended from it: "If any error should be admitted to have crept into the Holy Scriptures, what authority would be left to them?" Martin Dorpius repeated these words when Erasmus published his New Testament. Dr John Owen, Dean of Christ Church, Oxford, under the Commonwealth, could see no excuse for the publication of Bryan Walton's *Biblia Polyglotta*, although the work had been undertaken with the patronage of Cromwell himself: for "to print the original and defame it: gathering up translations of all sorts and setting them up in competition with it" is "to take away all certainty about sacred truth", and to leave men "no choice but to turn Atheists or Papists".[12] And the same blind and obstinate conservatism became articulate and indeed vociferous as the citadel of orthodoxy was bombarded and undermined from every side. When Milman's *History of the Jews* was published in 1829 in Murray's Family Library, "it was received with suspicion and indignation, so as, in fact, to put a stop to the series": and it argued considerable moral courage on the part of Sir Robert Peel when, six years later, he offered the author a prebendal stall at Westminster with the living of St Margaret's. In 1840, when for the first time —apart from a brief interlude in the sixteenth century when the Abbey was dissolved—St Margaret's was constituted a wholly independent and unappropriated parish within the diocese of London, Milman thus became our first Rector. In 1849 he was nominated by Lord John Russell to the Deanery of St Paul's.

That Anglicanism weathered the storm of the scientific and historical renaissance of the nineteenth century is not a little owing to the steadfast and scholarly determination with which Henry Hart Milman consciously endeavoured to avert "a breach between the thought and the religion of England". But to John Henry Newman, who in his *Apologia* characteristically praises Hugh James Rose for most of the wrong reasons, Milman seemed one of the epigoni of that theological liberalism which so mistakenly claimed "to determine on intrinsic grounds the truth and value of propositions which rest for their reception simply on the external authority of the Divine Word".[13] Newman's suspicions of the Rector of St Margaret's, Westminster, were not indeed without foundation. Henry Crabb Robinson in his diary records under the year 1838 a conversation with Milman at the Athenæum. Dr Pye Smith, a Congregationalist minister, had published an article denying the spiritual character of the Song of Solomon, and had in consequence been threatened at a meeting of Congregationalist trustees that he should have no further share in distributing charity money, because he had assailed the integrity of the Holy Scriptures. Crabb Robinson asked Prebendary Milman whether Dr Pye Smith's interpretation was a novelty to him, and received this reply: "In the first place, I must caution you against putting such questions to us clergymen. It is generally thought we are pledged to maintain the plenary inspiration of the Scriptures. It is not true, by-the-by. However, as you have put the question, I will say that I never knew a man with a grain of common sense who was of a different opinion."

John Henry Newman was a man of transcendent intellectual genius, but how far he was endowed with what Hensley Henson once described as "that rare quality so strangely called common sense" remains an open question. On 25 February 1840 he wrote to his sister:

> Everything is miserable. I expect a great attack upon the Bible—indeed, I have long expected it. At the present moment indications of what is coming gather. Those wretched Socialists on the one hand, then Carlyle on the other. . . . Then, again, you have Arnold's school, such as it is (I do hope he will be frightened back), giving up the inspiration of the Old Testament, or of all Scripture (I do not say Arnold himself does). Then you have Milman, clenching his "History of the Jews" by a "History of Christianity" which

they say is worse; and just in the same line. . . . And then your geologists, giving up parts of the Old Testament. All these and many more spirits seem uniting and forming into something shocking.

. . . I begin to have serious apprehensions lest any religious body is strong enough to withstand the league of evil but the Roman Church. . . .

We may be painfully reminded of a passage from the essay on "The Miscellaneous Works of Conyers Middleton" in Sir James Fitzjames Stephen's *Horæ Sabbaticæ* (2nd series, 1892), in which he speaks of those who "instead of hovering between Atheism and Popery, fly for refuge to Popery from Atheism, and hug its chains, not because they really believe it to be true, but because they think that a desperate determination to do so is their best chance of not being compelled to believe Atheism". And again: "If experience had not put the fact beyond all possibility of doubt, it might have seemed surprising that mankind should yet have to learn that the truth, the whole truth, and nothing but the truth, is the one thing needful to be believed; and that, of all pestilent inventions, none is more deadly and soul-destroying than a contrivance for enabling men to believe a thing whether it is true or not. Few errors are so injurious that it would not be better to hold them in good faith, and because they were honestly believed to be true, than to hold even the most important truths upon any other terms. It is sad to think how much theology in our days, whether Protestant or Popish, holds out to its disciples this great inducement: Come to me, all ye that are weary of doubt, and I will give you this security that, if your creed is false, you shall be the last to discover it." [15]

The fundamental trouble with John Henry Newman—if I may borrow one of those expressive idioms for which the Old World is so much indebted to the New—is that he didn't have what it takes to be an Anglican. This indeed is evident, not only from Milman's magisterial review, so highly praised by Mr G. M. Young, of Newman's *Essay on the Development of*

Christian Doctrine, but also from Newman's review in the *British Critic* (January 1841), so highly praised by Fr Philip Hughes, of Milman's *History of Christianity, from the Birth of Christ to the Abolition of Paganism in the Roman Empire*.[16] Newman's fundamental criticism of Milman, constantly reiterated, is that "he will write *rather as an historian than as a religious instructor*", which Newman regarded as conduct highly unbefitting in a clergyman, who should observe and depict the Christian history as "an outward visible sign of an inward spiritual grace", and not "as an external political fact". Harking back to Milman's earlier *History of the Jews*, his Oxford critic observed with pained surprise that "he evidently considers that it is an advance in knowledge to disguise Scripture facts and persons under secular names. He thinks that it is much gain if he can call Abraham an Emir or a Sheik." And, more disgraceful still, he actually "compliments ... the sceptical and infidel writers of Germany ... on 'their profound research and *philosophical* tone of thought' "! So, more in sorrow than in anger, Newman embarks upon his peroration:

It is indeed most painful, independently of all personal feelings which a scholar and a poet so early distinguished as Mr Milman must excite in the minds of his bretheren that a work so elaborate and so interesting should be composed upon principles which are calculated to turn all kindly feeling into mere antipathy and disgust. Indeed, there is so much to shock people that there is comparatively little to injure. To one set of persons only is he likely to do mischief, those who just at this moment are so ready to use the principle of Mr Milman for the demolition of Catholic views, without seeing that it applies to the New Testament's history and teaching just as well ....

And that, of course, was something too horrible to contemplate, a prospect from which Mr Newman instinctively recoiled.

"Newman's fatal defect", says Mr G. M. Young, "was want of historic learning ... The *Essay on Development* is, as its title declares, nothing if not historical: and of historical evidence, as of the methods of historical inquiry, it may be safely affirmed Newman knew nothing. . . ." I think it may be said with more precision that Newman's fatal defect was a complete lack of any sense of the continuity of history. His method of historical interpretation was purely typological: it consisted in recognizing something in the past as the image of something entirely different in the present. "I saw my face in that mirror, and I was a Monophysite . . . Rome was what she now is: and the Protestants were the Eutychians." That was in August 1839: but in the middle of September he was distracted by Wiseman's article in the *Dublin Review*, which suggested an alternative hypothesis, that the Anglicans were really Donatists; whereas Newman had always assumed that Donatism was an antetype of the Non-Juring Schism. And then, in the summer of 1841, at Littlemore, when he was working on the history of Arianism, "the ghost" came "a second time", and "in a far bolder shape", and he perceived with startling clarity that "the pure Arians were the Protestants, the semi-Arians were the Anglicans, and that Rome now was what it was then."[17] It must have been very unsettling: if the Anglicans were not Monophysites, they were Donatists, and if they were not Donatists, they were semi-Arians; and the Protestants were Arians if they were not Eutychians: indeed the only constant factor in the problem seemed to be Rome, which curiously enough, was always what she is, and is always what she was.

A refreshing contrast to these exercises in typology is afforded by the robust and panoramic scholarship and massive intellectual integrity of H. H. Milman. He had his limitations: he was unsympathetic to "sacerdotal power" and "monkish superstition": he was in some ways a survivor from the eighteenth century. I once ventured to describe him as "a kind of Christian Gibbon, without the indecency and without the fun"; but Mr. Duncan Forbes[18] has drawn attention to a passage in the *History of the Jews* which seems to qualify that verdict: "The cloud still led the way; but their prudent leader likewise secured the assistance of Hotah . . . who had been accustomed to traverse the desert." Grote in the *Westminster Review* described this epoch-making work as "written in a perfectly religious spirit, but exhibiting some disposition to economise the supernatural energy": [19] and what caused the sharpest shocks to religious opinion were no doubt the details rather than the spirit of the narrative—the representation of Abraham as "an independent Sheik or Emir", and the suggestion that natural causes, albeit instrumental to Divine Providence, might in part account for the destruction of the Cities of the Plain, or for the provision of quails and manna in the desert. "Manna is now clearly ascertained by Seetzen and Burckhardt to be a natural production; it distils from the thorns of the tamarisk, in the month of June. It is still collected by the Arabs. . . . The preternatural part therefore of the Mosaic narrative consists in the immense and continual supply, and the circumstances under which it was gathered, particularly in its being preserved firm and sweet only for the Sabbath-day." But Milman's primary and positive achievement was that he introduced his contemporaries to the truth that the Chosen People had a secular as well as a religious history, and that the latter was "accommodated" to, or (as we should say) conditioned by, the former.

By missing the fact of development in Old Testament history, and by choosing to embrace "the notion that the Mosaic narrative is uniformly exemplary, not history", the pious involuntarily gave a handle to the adversaries of revealed religion who scoffed at the morals of the patriarchs and their descendants. Milman, in whose three great masterpieces (*History of the Jews*, 3 vols., 1829; *History of Christianity*, 3 vols., 1840; *History of Latin Christianity*, 6 vols., 1854) the Liberal Anglican philosophy of history finds its most complete expression, did not compromise, but on the contrary vindicated the authenticity of revelation and the truth of God. And this he was able to effect precisely because, in his own words, "The object of this work is strictly historical, not theological": or, as the scandalized John Henry Newman put it, "he will write *rather as an historian than as a religious instructor*". There were those who could not abide the novelty of so objective an approach to sacred history, for it was as much a novelty to the unbelieving as to the believing world: but no man did more in the long run to persuade his generation that Christianity has nothing to fear from truth. In the memorable words of Professor Hort: "Criticism is not dangerous except when, as in so much Christian criticism, it is merely the tool for reaching a result not itself believed on that ground but on the ground of speculative postulates; while such postulates though they may be suggested by a multitude of facts (*sc.* the irrelevant facts) yet draw their strength rather from the temporary feeling of an age, in other words from a masked authority or tradition, or because an individual mind feels them needed for its own inner repose, and will not be disturbed by new facts."[20] It was also characteristic of Dean Milman that, almost alone among Anglican dignitaries, he subscribed to the Bishop Colenso Defence and Testimonial Fund, not because he agreed with the conclusions of that prototype of Modernistic prelates, but because he considered that Colenso had not had fair play.

The notorious Bishop of Natal had once been a mathematical master at Harrow: and on one of his visits to England, Farrar, who was then a housemaster there, "indignant at the utterly shameful treatment which he was receiving at all hands, and glad to show my humble sympathy with a noble-hearted man, conspicuous for the ardent and fearless sincerity of his love of truth",[21] invited him down for a week-end. On Sunday in the School Chapel the Bishop naturally gave the blessing; and an avalanche of letters from parents, indignant that their offspring should be blessed by an heresiarch, descended upon the unfortunate Headmaster.

The Liberalism of Frederic William Farrar, Rector of St Margaret's and Canon of Westminster from 1876 to 1895, was of a different order from that of Milman. Broadly speaking, the Liberalism of Milman was scholarly, impartial, and objective: the Liberalism of Farrar was emotional, subjective, and impassioned. We must, however, qualify this by recalling that

Milman hated intolerance and injustice, and that Farrar, who, among his other accomplishments, did more than any other single individual to introduce the teaching of Science into the English public school curriculum,[22] had an astonishing range of erudition in a variety of fields. One of his studies in philology, *An Essay on the Origin of Language* (1860), attracted the notice of Charles Darwin, who on the strength of it proposed him for election as a Fellow of the Royal Society. His Bampton Lectures on the *History of Interpretation* (1885) are still useful, while the thirteen-page "Bibliography of Exegesis" so modestly appended to the volume—"It is possible that some readers may be glad to be referred to the works mentioned in the following list. . ."—has barely ceased to be intimidating. A more popular work, his *Life of Christ*, written while he was Headmaster of Marlborough, ran through twelve editions in as many months, and was translated into almost every European language. He was indeed sufficiently regarded as a scholar to be invited to contribute to Smith's *Dictionary of the Bible*. It was unfortunate, in view of the conditions prevailing at the time, that the subject allotted to him was the Deluge: and, on discovering that in his article he maintained that the Deluge was not universal, the editor and the publisher decided that it would be prudent to postpone its publication, and in vol. i inserted "DELUGE: see FLOOD". But when the second volume was ready for the press, they were still irresolute, and inserted: "FLOOD: see NOAH". The article on Noah, however, had already been assigned to Dr Perowne, afterwards Bishop of Worcester (who in fact came, though more guardedly, to much the same conclusion): and thus Farrar's contribution was sacrificed to the exigencies of the contemporary predicament in Old Testament studies.

Yet Farrar, though something of a polymath, was not a scholar in the real sense. His industry was inexhaustible: his reading was encyclopaedic: his memory, if inaccurate, was prodigious. But he was essentially a popularizer: moreover, as Hensley Henson wrote of him after his death, "It would perhaps be true to say that his wide learning and genuine intellectual power were obscured, rather than commended, by the Asiatic richness of his literary style, and the purple rhetoric of his preaching." He was unquestionably one of the leading popular preachers of his day, and had a considerable following on both sides of the Atlantic: a pew in St Margaret's was specially reserved at Morning Prayer for visitors from the United States. It has been estimated that Farrar preached about 120 sermons every year. His multifarious activities seldom allowed him to devote more than three or four hours to the preparation of a pulpit discourse; and "the ink upon the paper was often damp as the chimes for service marked time for eager multitudes." When, in accordance with his almost invariable custom, the Rector preached in his own church on Sunday mornings, he attracted enormous and influential congregations: every inch of standing room was occupied : on the Sunday on which a census was taken of church attendance, St Margaret's had a larger congregation than either the Abbey or St Paul's. Conversely, whenever the Canon occupied the Abbey pulpit on Sunday evenings, the notice "ABBEY FULL" sent an overflow congregation to St Margaret's. Fastidious critics thought his style too florid, and deprecated his love of ornament and quotation: the writer of his obituary notice in *The Times* regretted that he had not paid more attention to the maxim, "No flowers by request". Yet so austere a critic as Bishop Lightfoot once declared that a Temperance Sermon preached by Farrar before the University of Cambridge, on Jonadab the son of Rechab, was the finest he had ever heard.

When Farrar came to Westminster in 1876, of the five other Canons only one could be regarded as a preacher above the ordinary, while three were aged and decrepit. A sensational course of sermons from the Abbey pulpit in November-December 1877 entitled *"Eternal Hope"* defined his ecclesiastical position and determined his ecclesiastical career. When Dean Stanley died, and Farrar was hoping to succeed him, Queen Victoria wrote to her friend and confidant, the Dean of Windsor: "The Queen admires Canon Farrar, and likes him personally, but thinks he is too vehement and violent in his expressions. . . . The Queen *owns* she would *not* like to see him in our dear friend's place. . .".[23]

The Liberalism of Farrar was emotional. He assailed the popular conception of Eternal Torment because he felt it to be intolerable, and because he knew the anguish that it caused to timid souls. It is true that his attack upon the crude old-fashioned doctrine did not go beyond the position at which educated theological opinion had already arrived: in the words of a supercilious agnostic, Leslie Stephen, "Canon Farrar does not himself deny the existence of hell; he only thinks that fewer people will go there, and perhaps find it much less disagreeable than is commonly supposed."[24] It was not so much Farrar's views that were startling, as rather the crusading fervour with which he gave expression to them.

Thank God, my own hopes of seeing God's face for ever hereafter do not rest on ten times refuted attempts to read false meanings into the Greek lexicon, in order to support a system far darker than St Augustine's, from whose mistaken literalism it took its disastrous origin. But here I declare, and call God to witness, that if the popular doctrine of Hell were true I should be ready to resign all hope, not only of a *shortened*, but of *any* immortality, if thereby I could save, not *millions*, but *one single human soul* from what fear, and superstition, and ignorance, and inveterate hate, and slavish letter-worship have dreamed and taught of Hell. I call God to witness that so far from regretting the possible loss of some billions of æons of bliss by attaching to the word αἰώνιος a sense in which scores of times it is undeniably found, I would here, and now, and kneeling on my knees, ask Him that I might die as the beasts that perish, and for ever cease to be, rather than that my worst enemy should, for one single year, endure the hell described by Tertullian, or Minucius Felix, or Jonathan Edwards, or Dr Pusey, or Mr Furniss,[25] or Mr Moody, or Mr Spurgeon. Unless my whole nature were utterly changed, I can imagine no immortality which would not be abhorrent to me if it were accompanied with the knowledge that millions and millions and millions of poor suffering wretches—some of whom on earth I had known and loved—were writhing in an agony without end and without hope.

That was not indeed uttered from the pulpit: it will be found in an Excursus on the word αἰώνιος in the printed edition of *Eternal Hope*: but it is no wonder either that these sermons, in Farrar's words, "awakened an echo throughout the world", or that Dr Pusey was moved to reply to Farrar's challenge in *What is of Faith as to Everlasting Punishment?*, dispassionately supporting his argument by citations from no less than eighty-four Patristic documents. Pusey was not himself an obscurantist: it was he who first pointed out to the young William Ewart Gladstone in the 1820s "that there were *some* errors of fact in the Gospels": [26] but he was conservative in regard to doctrine. However, an exchange of letters, published in the preface to the thirtieth thousand of *Eternal Hope*, left Dr Farrar satisfied —more satisfied, indeed, than Dr Pusey—that the differences between them were less than might at first appear.

Farrar believed that it was these sermons on *Eternal Hope* that blocked him for preferment: and there was a sense in which that was true, although it was less the sermons than the preacher that constituted the obstruction. Not until 1895, when he was old and tired at 64, was he given the Deanery of Canterbury: nor did he disguise the fact that he regarded this promotion as both tardy and inadequate. This was in truth the flaw in the bright metal of his character. [27] For a priest there is only one thing more demoralizing than to think that he ought to be made a bishop, and that is to think that he ought to have been made a bishop: and if he is unable to prevent that thought from preying on his mind, no further evidence is required to prove that he is mistaken. Farrar was far more than a popular preacher: but to be a popular preacher is always a highly dangerous occupation. None the less, it is to his credit that *Eternal Hope*, together with its sequel, *Mercy and Judgment*, ventilated the question of Everlasting Punishment at a popular level, and thereby constituted a landmark in the progress of Liberal Theology in the Victorian age.

A third Liberal type is represented by the most eminent of his successors, Herbert Hensley Henson, Rector of St Margaret's and Canon of Westminster from 1900 to 1912; afterwards Dean of Durham, then Bishop of Hereford, then Bishop of Durham, and, for a brief period after his retirement, Canon of Westminster for a second time. Not long before his death, which occurred on 27 September 1948, he wrote in "An Open Letter to a Young Padre":

> In the course of my long life, I have heard comparatively few sermons, mainly because I have myself preached so many. My place has normally been in the pulpit, rarely in the pew; but in the impressionable years of boyhood and adolescence, before I had bent my neck to the yoke of Ordination, and become bound to the obligation of frequent preaching, I was fond of hearing sermons, and I was not unaffected by those I heard. Particularly there stands out in my memory the sermon preached to undergraduates in St Mary's [Oxford], which, being myself at the time an undergraduate, I heard, sitting in the crowded gallery. The church was thronged, for the preacher was Canon Farrar of St Margaret's, Westminster, whose fame as doctrinally suspect was widespread, and whose reputation as an eloquent preacher was at its height. His text was Hebrews xii. 1, 2: *"Therefore let us also, seeing we are compassed about with so great a cloud of witnesses, lay aside every weight, and the sin which doth so easily beset us, and run the race which is set before us, looking unto Jesus, the author and perfecter of our faith."* ...

He adds that the preacher, in language of passionate fervour, presented Christianity as a personal allegiance to a Crucified Master. "That was the view which gained my acceptance, and which has ever since retained its hold on me."[28]

But Henson's personality was more complex than that of Farrar, as Farrar himself had a more complex personality than

Milman. Whether we like it or not, a man's theological position is always to some extent conditioned by his temperament. To read Henson's autobiography—so characteristically entitled, *Retrospect of an Unimportant Life*—is to be reminded of a phrase from Henry Nettleship's review of the *Memoirs* of Mark Pattison, the formidable nineteenth-century Rector of Lincoln College, Oxford: "It is the picture of a beautiful soul, marred by self-inflicted wounds, but constant and undaunted in its struggle towards the light."[29]

Hensley Henson came of middle-class Nonconformist stock: his parents could not afford to give him a proper education, and it was only his native intellectual genius that enabled him to enter the University of Oxford (as a non-Collegiate student) and to win the glittering distinctions of a First in History and a Fellowship at All Souls before he was 21. All his life he laboured under a queer sense of social inferiority: he was never able to forget the miserable conditions of his education and the privations and difficulties of his early days. Even after his election to All Souls, he had still to pass through a long period of repeated disappointment and frustration, of penury and ill-health.

Ordained deacon on Trinity Sunday 1887, he was immediately appointed Head of Oxford House, the recently established University Settlement in the slums of Bethnal Green. It was a post for which, by contrast with his successor (Winnington-Ingram), he was obviously unsuited, and he had already determined to resign when in the autumn of 1888 he was offered the College living of Barking, a large industrial parish in Essex. He had been in priest's orders for less than six months, he had had no previous parochial experience, and he was only 25. He threw himself "with almost fierce energy" into his new duties: but after seven arduous years his health began to fail under "the too-heavy burden" of work and worry, and his Bishop procured him a remove to the Chaplaincy of the little ancient Hospital of St Mary and St Thomas of Canterbury at Ilford, where his obligations were limited to the Sunday services and the oversight of a small body of alms-folk. One of the Bishop's motives in placing him there arose from the awkward and distressing circumstance that the previous Chaplain, after introducing "divers ceremonial eccentricities which had aroused public notice", had seceded to the Church of Rome. Henson was intended to restore the balance. But his situation had no prospects, and no apparent issue: his stipend gave him a bare subsistence: his reputation as a controversialist of the type that writes letters to the newspapers stood in the way of his return to Oxford either as Vicar of St Mary's or as a College Tutor: and time was passing. Then, at the end of October 1900, when he was already 37, and it was beginning to appear that his course had come to a dead end, there arrived, "like a bolt from the blue", a letter from the Prime Minister (Lord Salisbury) offering him a Westminster Canonry which carried with it the Rectorship of the church with which his name will always be associated. He was installed on 24 November.

"Dean Stanley in the Abbey, and Canon Farrar in St Margaret's, had linked the churches in the public mind with religious tolerance and theological liberty. With this tradition I heartily accorded. I resolved that I too would stand for a national Christianity which was religiously inclusive and theologically liberal."[30] With that determination he came to Westminster, and to this conception of the Church of England he remained constant through all the variegated phases of his ecclesiastical career. His training was that of an historian: his mind was legal: he had a passion for intellectual integrity. (It was not for nothing that, when he was Rector of St Margaret's, his little Aberdeen terrier, immortalized with his master in a *Vanity Fair* cartoon, bore the name of "Logic".) He also tended to regard his triumphs over difficulties less as an uncovenanted mercy than a refutation of his critics. In his second turn of official residence at the Abbey, he alarmed the Dean by announcing "a course of Sermons designed to facilitate Intercommunion with non-Episcopal Churches": the sermons were attended by very large congregations, and were subsequently published in a volume entitled *Godly Union and Concord*. As Dr Alington has said of him: "the ambiguities and uncertainties of the Anglican position were a constant trouble to his restlessly honest mind, and his amazing facility in writing, coupled to his command of incisive language, led him to utterances which caused the public to believe that he loved controversy for its own sake." It might be more accurate to say that he loved truth, while he enjoyed controversy; although it was his weakness, like that of many other brilliant controversialists, that he showed himself more eager to outspar than to persuade. His nature was fundamentally generous, "but he held his own opinions with so firm a conviction that he was quite unable to do justice to the doubts or convictions of others", and his dangerous facility for the caustic phrase "emphasised his disagreement and often roused their anger".[31] He was indeed the Rupert of ecclesiastical debate. The forensic taunts with which, as Bishop of Durham, he enlivened the discussions of the Revised Prayer Book in 1927 and 1928—"the Protestant underworld", "an army of illiterates generalled by octogenarians"—have lodged in the public memory, but they swayed no votes. He was one of the last controversialists, as he was also one of the last pulpit orators, of the classical tradition.

He was naturally combative. When in 1909 Bishop Gore, who had been his colleague on the Westminster Chapter, and by whom he felt at once so strangely fascinated and repelled, inhibited him from preaching in a Congregational Church Institute at Birmingham, Henson defiantly framed the inhibition and hung it on the wall of his study as a trophy. He was instinctively distrustful of finding himself in a majority: he regarded with ineradicable suspicion every movement temporarily dominant, whether in Church or State: and he displayed a chivalrous and even reckless sympathy with the under-dog, partly because he always regarded himself as an under-dog. When in 1911 the Reverend J. M. Thompson, Fellow and Dean of Divinity of Magdalen College, Oxford, scandalized the orthodox by the radicalism of his *Miracles in the New Testament,* and Gore, now translated to the see of Oxford, refused him permission to officiate in the diocese,

Henson not only invited Thompson to deliver the St Margaret's Lectures for the ensuing Lent,[32] but added a special preface to his own new book, *The Creed in the Pulpit*, in which, after a provocatively apposite quotation from the preface to *Lux Mundi* (which Gore had edited in 1889), he declared roundly: "One thing is unquestionable. In setting a ring-fence around the narratives of Christ's birth and resurrection, and exempting them from the operation of critical methods allowed to control the rest of the New Testament, Mr Thompson's opponents have taken up a position which it is really impossible to justify on any other principles than those which direct the policy of the Vatican."

It is perhaps not altogether surprising that when this "enigmatic Ishmaelite" (as he once described himself) was consecrated in the Abbey Church of Westminster on 2 February 1918 as Bishop of Hereford, it was "in singular circumstances of public obloquy" which left a permanent scar upon his mind.

Yet Henson never went the whole way with the Modernists. Of all the published volumes of his sermons, *The Value of the Bible* (1904), though prefaced by an "Open Letter to the Bishop of London", is, in my judgement, the most valuable and the most constructive. It is true that in the "Open Letter" Henson is a little insistent upon "the legal limits of theological liberty" which neither he nor his episcopal critic has the right either to enlarge or to restrict; but, a few pages further on, he writes, with reference to a quotation from Professor Sanday: "results of critical investigation have not the same character, or the same claim on our acceptance, or the same power over us, as the results of religious conviction; and any confusion between the two, any attempt to clothe critical conclusions with the authority of Divine credenda, and to read into the necessarily provisional results of historical inquiry the vital and immutable character of Divine Truth, will surely draw in its train consequences hurtful to honest criticism, and not less hurtful to honest belief." So also, even in the preface to *The Creed in the Pulpit*, we find him writing: "I doubt if many 'liberal' theologians remember sufficiently that revision or 're-statement' implies the preservation of the truth which has to be revised and re-stated": and then he goes on to quote the text which was always in his heart and often on his lips: "Jesus Christ is the same yesterday, and to-day, yea and for ever." ("Everything else fails us: He alone remains. One is untrue to oneself: He is true to us always."[33]) Finally in 1922, as Dean Inge recorded in his *Diary*, he said a thing that the Modern Churchmen's Union never forgot or forgave. He said: "I have come to think that no Liberal Churchman can be a good parish priest."[34]

That is, of course, the fundamental point at issue. We need not, indeed, assume that Henson's verdict is of universal application: but it cannot be too much emphasized that, for the Christian, Truth is not an abstract personification, but a real Person; and that, although a priest is required to "be ready, with all faithful diligence, to banish and drive away all erroneous and strange doctrines contrary to God's Word", yet the end of his ministry is pastoral: "to teach, and to premonish, to feed and provide for the Lord's family; to seek for Christ's sheep that are dispersed abroad, and for his children who are in the midst of this naughty world, that they may be saved through Christ for ever." It is highly improbable that for most of them "all other things which a Christian ought to know and believe to his soul's health" will include what it was once fashionable to describe as "the assured results of modern criticism". The first duty of a pastoral ministry is the edifying of the Body of Christ in love: and it is perfectly possible for a preacher to be intellectually honest without laying stumbling-blocks before simple believers in the shape of sermons which are ostensibly negative and destructive.[35]

Pastoral fidelity: that is indeed the heart of the matter. When in 1863 the Bishop of Manchester (Dr Prince Lee) attributed to the Bishop of Natal a "savage glee and exultation, which would rather become a *successful fiend* ... than a minister of a Christian congregation",[36] he was at least applying a true criterion, although his application of it might be somewhat bizarre and hyperbolical. It could be said of Colenso *On the Pentateuch*, as it has been said of Dr Barnes' *The Rise of*

Christianity, that the Bishop "adopts an aggressive and destructive tone throughout, and almost gives the impression that he is attacking historical Christianity instead of expounding it" : [37] and indeed there is, if not ridicule, at least material for ridicule in the arithmetical calculations that, if the statements in the Pentateuch are to be accepted at their face value, the number of boys in every Hebrew family must have averaged 42; that on the occasion of the second Passover the priests sacrificed 50,000 lambs at the rate of 400 lambs per minute; and that every priest was required to consume at least 88 pigeons daily. But in fact Colenso was a missionary-hearted bishop, and the origin of his curious researches was a perfectly sincere desire to allay the doubts of "a simple-minded but intelligent" Zulu, who, with the realism of a child, had asked him certain awkward questions about the Flood which had not previously occurred to him. [38]

So also, if we regard the work of the three representatives of the Liberal tradition whom we have been considering—Milman, Farrar, Henson—we shall observe that they had one thing in common: they were all pastorally-minded men. When Milman was Rector of St Margaret's, the modern conception of a parish priest had scarcely been invented. But he was faithful to his lights, which were those of the eighteenth century, the Age of Benevolence, to which he naturally belonged, translated into the idiom of the nineteenth century. At a time when the most densely populated portion of the parish, where Victoria Street now runs, was, in his own description, "one reeking and irreclaimable centre of filth and misery", he was qualified to describe it from first-hand acquaintance, "from my intercourse with the poor"; and, throwing himself heart and soul into the schemes of the Westminster Improvement Commissioners, he was a pioneer in the work of slum clearance by which the face of London has been steadily transformed. Although more actively involved in the establishment of the London Library, he did not disdain in the same summer of 1840 to lay the foundation stone of the Westminster Literary, Scientific and Mechanics' Institution, when he delivered himself of the weighty observation that "to advance the intellectual is one very great subsidiary towards promoting the moral elevation of human beings". He was also an assiduous and an invaluable member of the Board of Governors of Westminster Hospital, the first modern Voluntary Hospital in the metropolis, founded in 1716. And, from a passing reference in Chadwick's Supplementary Report on Urban Burial Grounds, we know that at St Margaret's the funerals of paupers were not, as in some other London parishes, conducted with maimed rites.[39] ("There is nothing", said Lord Shaftesbury, "which the poor feel so keenly as dishonour to their dead."[40]) Although the evidence is scantier than we could wish, and although he might have been embarrassed and repelled by such modern clerical clichés as "a love for souls", there is good reason to suppose that Milman, amid his herculean labours as a scholar—and it does not always come easily to a scholar in the parochial ministry to "draw all his cares and studies this way"—was recognizably a diligent and conscientious pastor according to the standards of his time.

Farrar belonged to an entirely different generation. Assisted by a team of able curates, he organized the work of the still overpopulated and poverty-stricken parish as it had never been organized before. In the words of one of his old curates: "He completely changed the conception of parochial work that prevailed in the parish of St Margaret's, and made a church, that probably had been saved from demolition chiefly on account of its historical associations, the centre of an active and vigorous religious life." He built a Mission Hall, he taught in the Church Schools, he founded clubs and societies, and gave popular lectures on Dante, Milton, and other literary subjects: he gathered a large band of voluntary workers, with all of whom he kept in constant touch: and his Sunday Schools, with their sixty teachers, were one of the show-pieces of the Diocese of London. Despite his other preoccupations, he "made it a regular part of his work to familiarise himself with everything that was going on. He required his colleagues to report all cases of sickness or distress, and presided regularly at the meetings of district visitors, where the circumstances of the infirm or indigent were fully discussed with a view to their relief. . . . Systematic house-to-house visitation had, of course, to be left to the curates; but when the Rector's presence could afford any comfort, he was always ready to go." Farrar was a typical Late Victorian in his capacity for moral indignation, but his crusading fervour was invariably detonated by something in his personal experience: it was, for example, what he had seen with his own eyes, in the back streets and alleys of his parish, of the ravages of drink and crime and prostitution, that made him a fanatical advocate of total abstinence, and an unflinching champion of General Booth and the Salvation Army: for, ambitious as he knew himself to be, he never shrank from identifying himself with unpopular causes at whatever detriment to his worldly prospects. In the words of another of his curates: "Dr Farrar worked for his people, thought of them, and prayed for and with them. . . . I have seen letters from many young men and young women in business addressed to him, thankfully acknowledging the blessings they had derived from his influence and teaching; and this, after all, is the true test of ministerial success."[41]

There remains the "enigmatic Ishmaelite". Only men of first-class intellect fail to perceive that there is always something intimidating about a first-class intellect: but it is a delusion that a tongue as quick and as sharp as a rapier is incompatible with a warm and generous heart. A brother priest once said to Hensley Henson: "If only you could remember that you are not the most intellectual clergyman in the Church of England, but that you are the most affectionate!" Those who regarded him only as a stormy petrel little knew the pastoral tenderness of which he was capable, and which comes out in the pages of his autobiography—as for example in the phrase, "There is something wonderfully humbling about the loyalty of the young. It is so tenacious and so trusting"—and in the very remarkable pastoral epistle which, when he was Bishop of Durham, he wrote to his chauffeur (whom he had converted, baptized, and confirmed) on the young man's twenty-first birthday.[42] In 1916, when he had left St Margaret's and was Dean of Durham, the Reverend the Honourable James Adderley (better known as Father Adderley), who stood for most of the things that Henson instinctively detested, but who had known him at Oxford House in his East London days, wrote of him with remarkable perspicacity and insight: "He has more heart than he gives himself credit for possessing, and he wilfully (I think) hides it. It is a thousand pities that he has not been kept at parish work much longer. His monthly service for communicants at Barking was one of the most inspiring services I ever attended, and I am not at all sure that he will not make an excellent Bishop one day, just because he will then once more come in contact with the souls of sinners and weak Christians who want comfort rather than dialectics and diatribes."[43]

That prophecy (with certain reservations as to dialectics) was indeed remarkably fulfilled. We may allow that, as a preacher, Henson was at his prime during his twelve years as Rector of St Margaret's, Westminster: his sermons—sincere, thoughtful, and expository—are admirable specimens of his scholarship and of his fastidious lapidary prose. But, as Bishop of Durham, he gave to the Church of England two volumes of Ordination Charges—*Church and Parson in England* (1927) and *Ad Clerum* (1937)—which, because they are directly pastoral, and therefore intellectually uninhibited, will continue to be treasured long after his published sermons are forgotten. I go back to them time and time again, and find them very searching and very humbling. Here is a typical passage from *Ad Clerum*: [44]

Nearly fifty years have passed since I was ordained in Cuddesdon Parish Church on a lovely summer morning in June 1887. How well I remember the tumult of conflicting thoughts which raged in my mind, and perhaps hindered me from entering as fully as I would have entered into the solemn yet exalting service! How little I guessed what lay before me! The immense failures which would overtake my too-ardent beginnings; the disappointments which would shadow my later course; the growing sense of inadequacy which would become a settled resident in my mind. The happiest years of my ministry were those in which, as the vicar of a great industrial parish, I was nearest to the people. Faces look out at me from the past—toil-worn faces radiant with love and confidence. Nothing of what men call success is worth comparison with the experiences which those faces recall. This exceeding great reward of ministry is within your reach, and it is the best thing you can have—far better than prominence, and great office, and the applause of crowds and senates. I suppose that, after all these years, I may speak to you, not only with the authority of my Apostolic office, but also with the added authority of long and varied experience. I say to you then—love God and love your people. Count nothing excessive which you can do for them. Serve them in your office for the love of Christ, and they will surely give you back more than you can give them. "Give, and it shall be given unto you: good measure, pressed down, shaken together, running over, shall they give into your bosom. For with what measure ye mete, it shall be measured to you again."

I think now, looking back over the years, that, though all the conditions of religious ministry have become more difficult and perplexing, and though the clergyman's office no more commands the kind of deference from society which it did when first I became a clergyman, yet a sincere man, loving Christ and his brethren, can do more good as a clergyman than in any other position. But all depends on the spirit with which that office is regarded, and the ends to which it is made serviceable. . . .

For all priests, whether liberal or orthodox, the pastoral calling must be paramount. There is a place for scholars in the ministry: but, unless they are prepared, like their less intellectually gifted brethren, to say their prayers and love their people, their orthodoxy or their liberalism will be sterile as regards the purpose for which they have been ordained.

6

THE PRODIGALITY
AND CAREFULNESS OF GOD

"THE INIQUITY of oblivion blindly scattereth her poppy,
and deals with the memory of men without distinction to merit
of perpetuity."[1] That this should be so in the temporal fortunes of mankind is a commonplace of moralists and of poets.
Humanity is for ever kicking down the ladders by which it has
climbed. Yet it is disquieting to a Christian that it should
seemingly be true also in the concerns of that eternal City
which hath foundations, whose Builder and Maker is God.
"The wicked are always punished," said Flaubert: "so are the
virtuous." So far as the lives of individuals are concerned, our
religion provides us with an answer. It is not quite so easy,
however, to know the answer in regard to the fate of institutions
and of churches that have in their time been clearly blessed of
God, and a source of blessing to many. How much was lost
when, in the seventh century of our era, the Arabs overran
North Africa, the cradle of Latin Christianity; or when, at
long last, in 1453 Constantinople fell to the Turks, and the
Byzantine Empire, which for eight centuries had heroically
held the pass against the armies of the infidel, crumbled into
ruin! It is not easy to reconcile disasters so mysterious and so
far-reaching with the pious and orthodox hypothesis of a
Providential ordering of history. How shall we argue that the
Judge of all the earth did right when, in July 1187, the fate of
Jerusalem and the Holy Places was sealed by the capitulation
of the Crusading army in the tragic battle of the Horns of
Hattin; or when, in August 1526, the flower of the Hungarian
chivalry was destroyed on Mohacz field, and the victorious
armies of the Crescent thrust on into the heart of Europe?
Have we not seen, even in my own life-time, the Russian Ortho-
dox Church with its millions of adherents reduced to a shadow

of its former self as a consequence of the Ten Days that Shook the World; and the army of Kemal Ataturk in 1922 obliterating the Eastern Orthodox Church in Asia Minor, the cradle of Greek Christianity?

History has witnessed the removal of many candlesticks, and not necessarily the worst. Nor will the cheap explanation suffice, though heartless ignorance still repeats it, that the Church was overthrown in North Africa, in the Middle East, in Holy Russia, because it had forsaken its first love, because it no longer had a genuine experience of God, because it was sunk in sloth and superstition and self-complacency, or politically compromised by its association with a doomed regime. "It would not be difficult indeed to show that the Christian societies of the East stamped out by Mohammedanism had many grievous faults; it would only be difficult to show that we in the West who escaped had fewer and less grievous faults. Nor had we need of historical research to teach us this, if we had remembered our Saviour's words about the Galileans whose blood Pilate had mingled with their sacrifices."[2] This is a great mystery. It has always been so. When the Son of Man cometh, shall he find faith upon the earth?

On a diminutive scale, the same tremendous problem is constantly reflected in the annals of parochial history. The present church of St Margaret, Westminster—the third to stand upon its site—was consecrated on 9 April 1523. The rebuilding had been initiated by the widow of a Chief Justice of England, Lady Mary Billing, whose liberality paid for the south aisle: she died in 1499. The chancel was built by Abbot Islip († 1532), the last of the great business executives (if I may so describe them) who ruled the Benedictine Monastery of Westminster, which from the beginning had been Rector of the parish church: in the east wall may be seen two stones bearing his rebus, in the form of the letters I S from which projects a slip of a tree. The architect of the church was Robert Stowell, Master Mason of the Abbey, who died in 1505, the year after the completion of the nave. The work continued under his successors, first Thomas Redeman, and then his son Henry. This Henry Redeman (†1528), who designed and built the steeple, was so devoted to the church that, although he regularly drew his weekly wage of 3s. 4d., he as regularly returned it to the Churchwardens as his personal contribution to the Building Fund.[3] Smaller gifts came from the workmen themselves—the stone-masons, the chalk man, the smith, the plumber, and the carter. In 1500 a donation of 6s. 8d. was received from "my lord Edmund the King's third son to the behoof of the church work".

The parishioners were evidently very proud of their new church, and expended money freely in making it beautiful. There is evidence of constant expenditure up to the very year 1540 when the Reformation may be said to have reached Westminster. The Abbey was surrendered into the hands of the King on 16 January. Its Dissolution is not noticed in our parochial records, except for a marginal note in the burial register under the thirty-second week of the same year: "This is the first week that the churchyard came into the churchwardens' hands", and they collected the burial fees.

The appearance of St Margaret's in 1540 must have been striking and brilliant. There were perhaps as many as eleven altars in the church. A Tabernacle was set up in honour of St Catharine, and in 1531 there were sixty-nine subscribers towards the gilding of the Tabernacle of St Margaret. There were nine religious fraternities connected with the church: the Guilds of St Margaret, St John, St George, St Christopher, St Cornelius, St Erasmus, St Anne, the Assumption of our Blessed Lady (also known as Our Great Lady Brotherhood), and Our Lady of Rounceyvall: the records of these two latter have fortunately been preserved. "As you entered St Margaret's by the porch under the new steeple, the most conspicuous feature which met your gaze was the great Rood standing above its 'loft', flanked by figures of St Mary and St John, all richly painted. St George's Chapel also possessed its 'loft', and everywhere the church was full of statues of the saints, resplendent with paint and gilding. Some, if not all, the windows were filled with stained glass. The floor of the church was for the most part covered with pews appropriated for money down to the parishioners, and held apparently for life."[4] Our earliest record in 1460 contains a list of pew-holders with their payments varying from 1s. 8d. to 3d. On St Margaret's Day (20 July), being the Patronal Festival, the virgins of Westminster went in procession through the streets headed by a minstrel (whom the Churchwardens provided), and collected money from the townsfolk for the adorning of the parish church. On these and other festal occasions the four men and six children who normally sang the Mass were reinforced or replaced by the "singers of the Abbey" or the "singers of the King's Chapel", and the Brotherhoods carried their banners in procession to the church, which was hung with embroidered cloth of arras borrowed from the Palace, or from the Abbey, or from some neighbouring parish.

What followed in the ensuing years is tersely recorded in the Churchwardens' Accounts (1546-48):

Payd for a honest dysshe of mete & for wyne for the Kyngs Visitours   xij*s.* viij*d.*

Also payd for the takyng downe of the Tabernacle in the Trinitie Chapell   viij*d.*

Also payd to Patryke Kelley playsterer for lyme & other Stuff for the whyttynge of the Churche   viij*s.* x*d.*

Also payd for lyme & Workmanship for the wasshyng of both the sydes of the hie Alter   ij*s.* j*d.*

Also payd to Thomas Stokedale for xxxv ells of clothe for the fronte of the Rode loft where the X commaundements be wrytten, pryce of the ell viij*d.*   xxiij*s.* iiij*d.*

Item payd to hym that dyd wryght the said X commaundements and for the drynkyng   lxvj*s.* ix*d.*

Also payd for ij waynscott bords for the hye Alter   xij*d.*

Also payd for the wryghtyng of the Scriptures upon the same bords   v*s.*

Receyved for Images & for iiij Curtens   lxvj*s.* viij*d.*

(1550) Also payde for a new table for the Blessed communion.   x*s.*

Then Edward VI died in 1553, and Mary came to the throne, and the Churchwardens were busy "Repeyrynge of the Churche" and undoing the work of the past few years. They paid four labourers 4d. "to helpe up the high Alter stone", and an additional 2d. for the same service to "our Lady alter stone". They purchased "iij great Antiphoners, ij Grayles and a Masse Booke" at a cost of 49s. They also purchased "a blew Chesable of Sattyn, a holly Water stock, an owlde Legente, a processionall, an owlde Antiphoner, a pix of copper all gylte, a Canapy for the Sacramente, a censer of copper, iij payre of Candellstickes, ij Albes, Corporas Clothes, a ship for ffranken-sens and a Lenten Crosse". The Rood was set up again, and in 1554 a painter was paid 1s. "for wasshyng owte of the Scripture of the highe Alter table". "The clothe that hung before the Rodeloft wrytten wt the commaundementes" was taken down: "the Lawndresse" (whose "hole yeres wagis" were only 7s.) received 2s. "for whityng of the same clothe & wasshyng owt the staynyng", and it was then cut up and made into "iij Serplys" (surplices) at a further cost of 2s. One of the more expensive items of expenditure was "the Bysshoppes Dynner at the Reconcyliacon of the Churche" (after the sacrilege committed by William Flower), for which the Church-wardens provided 3 capons, half a veal, 4 green geese, a dozen of rabbits, a dozen pigeons, a sirloin of beef, and 2 gallons of wine (costing altogether 28s. 11d.): they also paid 3s. 2d. for "breade beere and Ale in the Vestry" for the hangers-on. Finally, Cooper the mason and three labourers received 1s. 6d. between them "for takyng down an Image" which Nycholas Clarke was paid 40s. for converting (with the aid of "a patterne" supplied by "Caro the Carver" of London) into "an Image of Saynct Margaret", to replace the statue that had been destroyed by the iconoclasts of the preceding reign.

Like the Queen's re-establishment of the Benedictine Monastery of Westminster under Abbot Feckenham, it was all rather makeshift but none the less a gallant effort. Then in 1558 Mary died, and Elizabeth came to the throne. At first it seemed uncertain whether she would maintain or uproot the work of the Counter-Reformation. But this uncertainty was soon resolved. The monks were once again evicted: the Abbey was reconstituted as a Collegiate Church under a Dean and twelve Prebendaries: and the accounts of the Churchwardens of St Margaret's for 1559-60 tell their own story:

Fyrst, payde for a Bybill and a Paraphrawse   xvjs.

Item for a chayn and ij stapilles for the paraphrawse   xd.

Item for a Communion Booke bound in Parchemyne . vjs.

Item payd to John Riall for his iij dayse work to take down the Roode Mary & John   ijs. viijd.

Item to John Riall for takynge down the Tabill on the highe alter and takyng down the Hollywater stock   xijd.

Item, for clevyng and sawyng of the Roode Mary & John   xijd.

Item payd for a Communion Tabill   xijs. viijd.

Item [received] of Andrew Holborne for the beame the Rode stoode on for boords and other tymber parcell of the Roode loft   xlijs.

Item payd for Ropis pully & other necessaries to take downe the saide beame   iijs. iiijd.

Item for a paper wt the X commandements   xvjd.

Thus St Margaret's, Westminster, settled down again under the Reformed Religion, and nothing remained to show for the work of the Marian Counter-Reformation except Nicholas Clarke's converted statue of our patron saint—now decapitated, but still showing traces of its original colour[5]—and an Inventory, made by the Churchwardens in 1560, of the vestments, copes, altar cloths, and ornaments belonging to the church, concluding with this detail: "Item a Ship and iij holly water stocks all brokyn." So we may take leave of our Churchwardens' Accounts: except that I cannot forbear to mention in passing, because it is the sort of thing that never finds its way into the history-books and yet throws a flood of light upon the worship of our forefathers, an item from the Accounts for 1610-11: "Payd to goodwyfe Wells for salte to destroye the fleas in the

Churchwardens pewe, and for makinge cleane of the same pewe ... vj*d*."

Time marches on, and we must move forward with it to the historic scene in St Margaret's, Westminster, the Parish Church of the House of Commons, on Monday 25 September 1643, when the Honourable House (or what remained of it), together with the Commissioners from Scotland, and the Reverend Assembly of Divines, with great solemnity subscribed the Covenant. There was a touch of real eloquence in the Exhortation made to them by Mr Philip Nye before he read the Covenant aloud: [6]

A great and solemn work (Honourable and Reverend) this day is put into our hands, let us stir up and awaken our hearts unto it. . . .

That which the Apostles and Primitive times did so much and so long pray for, though never long with much quietnesse enioyed; that which our Fathers in these latter times have fasted, prayed and mourned after, yet attained not; even the cause which many deare Saints now with God, have furthered by extreamest sufferings, poverty, imprisonment, banishment, death, even ever since the first dawning of Reformation: That and the very same is the very cause and work that we are come now, through the mercy of Jesus Christ, not only to pray for, but to sweare to. And surely it can be no other, but the result and answer of such prayers and teares, of such sincerity and sufferings, that three Kingdoms should be thus born, or rather new born in a day; that these Kingdoms should be wrought about to so great an engagement, than which nothing is higher, for to this end Kings raign, Kingdomes stand, and States are upheld.

It is a speciall grace and favour of God unto you Brethren, Reverend and Honourable, to vouchsafe you the opportunity, and to put into your hearts (as this day) to engage your lives and estates in matters so much concerning him and his glory. And if you should doe no more but lay a foundation stone in this great work, and by so doing engage posteritie after you to finish it, it were honour enough: But there may yet further use be made of you, who are now to take this Oath, you are designed as chiefe master Builders and choyce Instruments for effecting of this settled Peace and Reformation; which if the Lord shall please to finish it in your hands, a greater happinesse on earth, nor a greater means to augment your glory and crown in heaven, you are not capable of. And this let me further adde for your encouragement; of what extensive good and fruit in the successe of it, this very Oath may prove to be, wee know not. God hath *set his Covenant like the Heavens*, not onely for duration, but like also for extension: The Heavens move and roule about, and so communicate their light, and heat, and vertue, to all places and parts of the earth; so doth the *Covenant* of God; so may this gift be given to other Covenants that are framed to that pattern. How much this solemn League and Oath may provoke other Reformed Churches to a further Reformation of themselves; what light and heat it may communicate abroad to other parts of the world, it is only in Him to define to whom is given the *utmost ends of the earth for his inheritance*, and worketh by his exceeding great power great things out of as small beginnings.

There was indeed, however, another passage in the same sermon which the Scottish Commissioners cannot have relished, for it gave notice of the inevitable rift between the Independents and the Presbyterians after the Civil War was won. It was as follows:

... What doe we covenant? What doe we vow? Is it not the preservation of Religion, where it is reformed, and the Reformation of Religion, where it needs? Is it not the Reformation of three Kingdomes, and a Reformation Universall, Doctrine, Discipline, and Worship, in whatsoever the Word shall discover unto us? To practise, is a fruit of love; to reform, a fruit of zeale; but so to reforme, will be a token of great prudence and circumspection in each of these Churches. And all this to be done according to Gods Word, the best Rule; and according to the best reformed Churches, the best interpreters of this Rule. If *England* hath obtained to any greater perfection in so handling the word of righteousnesse, and truths that are according to godlinesse, as to make men more godly, more righteous: And if in the Churches of *Scotland* any more light and beauty in matters of Order and Discipline, by which their Assemblies are more orderly : Or if to any other Church or person it hath beene given better to have learned Christ in any of his wayes than any of us; we shall humbly bow, and kisse their lips that can speak right words unto us in this matter, and help us unto the nearest uniformity with the word and minde of Christ in this great work of Reformation.

Mr Alexander Henderson, who responded for the Kirk of Scotland, made no reference to these very liberal sentiments in his reply. Henderson was certainly more open-minded than many of his compatriots, who had no mind "for keeping a door open in England to Independency", and frankly stated that "the chief aim of the Covenant was for the propagation of our Church discipline in England and Ireland". But not even Henderson was disposed humbly to bow and kiss the lips of the ragged regiment of "gifted brethren" who claimed to be inspired by God: and in 1644 we find him writing home about "such sects and monsters of opinions as are daily set on foot and multiplied in this kingdom through the want of that Church government by Assemblies which hath preserved us, and we hope, through the blessing of God, shall cure them." The difference between the Scottish Presbyterians and the English Puritans was, broadly speaking, the divergence between the standpoint of a Government and that of an Opposition: the English Puritans had consistently contended for the liberty of prophesying, and in so doing were thinking in terms of their own liberty to prophesy without at all clearly envisaging the wider implications of such a liberty when once established : whereas the Scots had a very shrewd idea of the advantage that would immediately be taken of it by unauthorized persons, the extremely and undesirably articulate lunatic fringe of orthodox English nonconformity. To them it was readily apparent that for the English a great deal more "light and beauty in matters of Order and Discipline" was to be desiderated: as Dr Robert Baillie, the Principal of Glasgow University, grimly remarked, "No people had so much need of a Presbytery."[7]

The rift widened into an open breach: and, after the defeat of Charles II and the Scottish Presbyterian army in the Battle of Worcester, from the very pulpit of St Margaret's, Westminster, from which, only eight years before, Nye and Henderson had encouraged the Honourable House and Reverend Divines on the occasion of the taking of the Covenant, Oliver Cromwell's favourite chaplain preached before the House of Commons on 5 November 1651 a thanksgiving sermon with the inflammatory title: *"England's Deliverance from the Northern Presbytery compared with its Deliverance from the Roman Papacy.* By Peter Sterry, once Fellow of Emmanuell Colledge in Cambridge, now Preacher to the Right Honourable Councell of State, sitting at White-Hall." We may presume that it was Cromwell himself who caused a Scottish edition of this sermon to be published at Leith, ostensibly for the benefit of the English army of occupation.[8]

But in any case nobody reads these sermons now. As Thomas Carlyle wrote in his introduction to *The Letters and Speeches of Oliver Cromwell* (1845):

All past Centuries have rotted down, and gone confusedly dumb and quiet, even as that Seventeenth is now threatening to do. . . . The Fast-day Sermons of St Margaret's Church Westminster, in spite of protests, are all grown dumb! In long rows of little dumpy quartos, gathered from the bookstalls, they indeed stand here bodily before us: by human volition they can be read, but not by any human memory remembered. . . . They are dead and gone, they and what they shadowed: the human soul, got into other latitudes, cannot now give harbour to them. Alas, and did not the honourable Houses of Parliament listen to them with rapt earnestness, as to an indisputable message from Heaven itself? Learned and painful Dr Owen, learned and painful Dr Burgess; Stephen Marshall, Mr Spurstow, Adoniram Byfield, Hugh Peters, Philip Nye: the Printer has done for them what he could, and Mr Speaker gave them the thanks of the House: —and no most astonishing Review-Article, or tenth-edition Pamphlet, of our day, can have half such "brilliancy", such "spirit", "eloquence",—such *virtue to produce belief*, which is the highest and in reality the only literary success,—as these poor little dumpy quartos once had. And behold, they are become inarticulate quartos; spectral; and instead of speaking, do but screech and gibber! All Puritanism has grown inarticulate; its fervent preachings, prayings, pamphleteerings are sunk into one indiscriminate moaning hum, mournful as the voice of subterranean winds. So much falls silent: human Speech, unless by rare chance it touch on the "Eternal Melodies", and harmonise with them; human Action, Interest, if divorced from the Eternal Melodies, sinks all silent. The fashion of this world passeth away.[9]

Yet this devaluation was of course too sweeping. In point of fact, Puritanism was still very far from inarticulate at the time when Carlyle was writing: and it has left an abiding mark upon the English character. As Dr Kitson Clark has observed: "What is of permanent living importance is not what it did, but what it was. . . . It gave strength, it enhanced personality. . . . It produced human beings who were capable of working out their own freedom, however meagre the inheritance with which society had endowed them. . . . In addition to this, Puritanism also produced a tradition which denied the right of the State to interfere with matters connected with religion. . . ."[10]

That is the long-term legacy of English Puritanism. The immediate reaction against it was, however, drastic. The bodies of the Cromwellian magnates—including not only John Pym, William Stroud, Dr Dorislaus, and Stephen Marshall, but also

Oliver Cromwell's mother, and even Colonel Robert Blake, Admiral at sea—were ignominiously exhumed from Westminster Abbey and flung into a common pit in St Margaret's churchyard, in what (as it happened) had once been the garden of the prebendal house of Mr Prebendary Laud.[11] Not only were the Churchwardens instructed by the Vestry (3 October 1660) to "prepare the Kings Majesties Armes to be richly Carved made and gilded after the best manner that can bee invented and with as much grace as may bee to bee sett up in the parish Church of St. Margaretts Westminster and to bee as faire and beautifull in everie respect as the Kings Armes are sett up in any Church in and about the Cittie of London. And . . . to use their best endeavours speedily to putt the worke in hande soe soone as money can be raised for that purpose": [12] but also in 1674 it was decided to erect an organ at a cost of £200. This was built by the celebrated "Father" Smith (Bernard Schmidt), who was himself appointed (1676) Organist of St Margaret's: he received a salary of £5 a quarter, and the parish paid an additional 10s. to the Blower.[13] We may recall the surprise and gratification with which Mr Samuel Pepys, on 4 November 1660, listened to organ music in the Abbey church, "the first time that ever I heard organs in a Cathedral". Pepys was a frequent attendant—perhaps that is a better word than worshipper—at St Margaret's. On 26 May (Lord's Day) 1667, he pursued Mrs Martin thither, and, being offered by Mr Howlett a pew in the gallery, "did entertain myself with my perspective glass up and down the church, by which I had the pleasure of seeing and gazing at a great many very fine women; and what with that, and sleeping, I passed away the time till sermon was done, and then to Mrs Martin. . . ." But Pepys ordinarily listened to sermons, of which indeed he was something of a connoisseur. (It was in St Margaret's on 13 May (Lord's Day) 1666, that he "heard a young man play the foole upon the doctrine of purgatory".) Here we may recognize another legacy of Puritanism, in the average Englishman's inveterate reluctance to go to church unless there is going to be a sermon, and his almost equally inveterate habit of criticizing the sermon when he comes out of church. It is, I think, profoundly symbolic that the one contribution of Puritanism to ecclesiastical furnishings was the velvet cushion in the pulpit, upon which rested the Bible from which the minister expounded the Word of God.

Under Charles II and James II, the morals of the Restoration and the menace of the Second Counter-Reformation brought their own reaction, and the eighteenth century opened for the Church of England under very favourable auspices. In 1698 the parishioners of St Margaret's, or some of them, subscribed to have prayers read in the parish church every evening of the week at 6 o'clock, and so late as 1759 this arrangement was still in operation. But, with few exceptions, my predecessors, the ministers of St Margaret's from 1683 to 1827, were unedifying specimens of the clerical profession. They were all Prebendaries of the Abbey: one of the recommendations in a confidential memorandum on ecclesiastical patronage compiled for King William III in 1691 was that the minister of St Margaret's should be, as always, one of the Prebendaries of Westminster, "because the House of Commons go to that church, and therefore it is fit there should be encouragement for a good preacher."[14] But the implicit assumption, that the minister of the Parish Church of the House of Commons would normally reside upon his cure and perform the duties of his office, was neither constantly nor conspicuously fulfilled: and, instead of the prebends of the Abbey being used for the encouragement of the minister of St Margaret's, the benefice of St Margaret's tended to be used for the quite superfluous encouragement of the Prebendaries of the Abbey. It was not a prize of any great financial value, but, for what it was worth, it was in the patronage of the Dean and Chapter, who naturally kept it as a perquisite among themselves in an age when preferment was awarded on the principle that "unto him that hath shall be given", and—except in regard to offices of high executive responsibility (what George Grenville called "bishoprics of business", as distinct from "bishoprics of ease")—there was "no damned nonsense about merit".

The twelve prebends of Westminster, each worth £300 a year, were in the patronage of the Crown, and Prime Ministers regarded them as particularly useful for purposes of barter in the trade of Hanoverian politics. Thus Prebendary John Taylor, LL.D., the friend and former schoolfellow of Dr Johnson, owed his preferment to the influence of the powerful Cavendish family, who could not but requite his services to the Whig interest in Derbyshire. Dr Taylor was minister of St Margaret's from 1784 to 1788, having previously held other small pieces of patronage in the gift of the Dean and Chapter, in addition to the Rectory of Market Bosworth in Leicestershire. He resided for the greater part of the year at his home in Ashbourne, Derbyshire, where he bred prize cattle: as Johnson said, "His talk is of Bullocks." Boswell, who visited him there in Johnson's company, admired him in the character of a country squire and magistrate, and noted in his *Journal*: "If Taylor were not a Clergyman, he would be truly creditable." He did not, however, totally neglect his ministerial duties at St Margaret's, which is indebted to him for the singular distinction of being the only church in which a sermon by Dr Johnson is known to have been preached in the actual presence of its author.[15]

Taylor's predecessor, Prebendary Thomas Wilson, D.D., son of the saintly Bishop of Sodor and Man, was minister of St Margaret's from 1753 to 1784. He was at the same time Rector of St Stephen's, Walbrook, a valuable City living. He resided at Bath. A radical in politics, he was the lifelong friend of the notorious John Wilkes, M.P. (whom he actually made Churchwarden of St Margaret's in 1759), and the admirer—until her second marriage—of the republican blue-stocking, Mrs Catharine Macaulay, to whom, in her lifetime, he erected in 1777 within the altar-rails of St Stephen's, Walbrook, a statue which the outraged Vestry obliged him to remove. It was, however, partly thanks to him that St Margaret's was enabled to acquire and to retain its crowning glory, the great east window of Flemish glass, which had once formed part of the dowry of Catharine of Aragon.[16]

197

To explore this chapter of our history in larger detail would be superfluous, though we may note that it significantly opens with the son of a tavern keeper, and closes with a distant relative of a Duke. The minister of St Margaret's from 1683 to 1720 was Dr Nicholas Onely, Prebendary of Westminster, Chaplain of the Savoy, and Rector of Cottesmore in Rutland, who exploited with unspeakable meanness a luckless Huguenot refugee, the Reverend Gabriel D'Emilliane, whom he employed as his assistant curate.[17] The minister of St Margaret's from 1798 to 1827 was Prebendary Charles Fynes, D.C.L. (who changed his name to Fynes Clinton in 1820 by royal licence). He already held the Rectory of Cromwell, Nottinghamshire, to which he had been presented in 1789 by his kinsman, the Duke of Newcastle, the head of the Clinton family, whose influence had secured him a prebend of Westminster in the preceding year. Being accustomed to spend at least half of every year at his country rectory, "the best parsonage house in the Midlands", he actually did not discover for two years that the chimes of St Margaret's, which in 1748 had been set to the new loyal and patriotic tune of "God Save the King", had, for reasons of economy, been taken down and sold by order of the Churchwardens.[18] His solicitude for the eternal wellbeing of the souls committed to his care was illustrated principally by his firm and resolute conduct in vetoing the election of an Evangelical clergyman to the Sunday afternoon Lectureship at St Margaret's, Westminster. He was no worse than many other contemporary pluralists. "Whenever you meet a clergyman of my age", said Canon Sydney Smith of St Paul's to the young Mr Gladstone in 1835, "you may be quite sure he is a bad clergyman."[19]

Here is the reverse aspect of our problem: for it is as mysterious that the Hanoverian Church of England was not allowed to suffer the retribution it invited by its lethargy and by its avarice, as that the zeal of earlier generations, whether Catholic or Puritan, should seemingly have availed for nothing to avert the obliteration of their work. It is true indeed that the eighteenth century was the age of Parson Woodforde and Parson Adams and the Vicar of Wakefield, as well as of Prebendary Wilson and Prebendary Taylor, and that the character with which it has been branded wholesale by nineteenth-century Evangelicals and Anglo-Catholics is not universally deserved. Yet when Dr Thomas Arnold, the Headmaster of Rugby, wrote to a member of the Society for Promoting Christian Knowledge on 10 June 1832, "The Church, as it now stands, no human power can save", he uttered a true saying, albeit a saying that is true in every generation of the Church's life: for at all times and in all places the Church stands not in the wisdom, the zeal, the piety of men, but in the power of God, whose judgements are unsearchable, and his ways past finding out. Incidentally, it is not everyone who knows how Dr Arnold finished that sentence, which is seldom quoted in its entirety: ". . . my fear is that, if we do not mind, we shall come to the American fashion, and have no provision made for the teaching Christianity at all. . . ."[20]

But the energy which was perhaps the most conspicuous attribute of our Victorian forebears expressed itself in all departments of the national life, and not least in the National Church. The besetting sin of the Hanoverian Establishment had been a quiet worldliness: but now the standard of clerical duty was transformed. An old gentleman, Mr Thomas Grenville, who died at the age of 91 in 1846, remarked that no change which had taken place in his lifetime was so great as the change in the clergy of the Church of England.[21]

The transformation was probably less obvious to those outside the Anglican Communion. On 20 November 1850, *The Times* newspaper published with unconcealed disgust a letter, occupying six and a half columns of small close type, from Dr Nicholas Wiseman, recently Vicar Apostolic of the London District, and now proclaimed Cardinal-Archbishop of Westminster. The Dean and Chapter of Westminster had been among the first to protest against the new archiepiscopal title, and therefore the Cardinal-Archbishop, pulling out the *vox humana* stop, dramatically disowned any intention of disturbing them in their enjoyment of "the stately Abbey, with its adjacent palaces and its royal parks", the portions of His Eminence's diocese to which "the duties and occupation of the Dean and Chapter are mainly confined", and with which he ventured to contrast "the concealed labyrinths of lanes and courts, and alleys and slums" which pullulated beneath the shadow of the Collegiate Church:

> nests of ignorance, vice, depravity and crime, as well as of squalor, wretchedness, and disease; whose atmosphere is typhus, whose ventilation is cholera, in which swarms a huge and almost countless population, in great measure, nominally at least, Catholic; haunts of filth, which no sewage committee can reach—dark corners, which no lighting board can brighten. This is the part of Westminster which alone I covet, and which I shall be glad to claim and to visit, as a blessed pasture in which sheep of Holy Church are to be tended, in which a bishop's godly work has to be done, of consoling, converting and preserving. . . .

The Cardinal-Archbishop did not, of course, omit to register the debating point that such conditions would have been unthinkable in the Middle Ages, when "the existence of an abbey on any spot, with a large staff of clergy and ample revenues, would have sufficed to create around it a little paradise of comfort, cheerfulness and ease": and, characterizing the Westminster of 1850 as a city "in which the very grandeur of its public edifices is as a shadow to screen from the public eye sin and misery the most appalling", he concluded: "If the wealth of the Abbey be stagnant and not diffusive, if it in no way rescues the neighbouring population from the depths in which it is sunk, let there be no jealousy of anyone, who, by whatever name, is ready to make the latter his care, without interfering with the former."

But this indictment was already out of date: if the Abbey clergy were no longer living in the Middle Ages, neither were they living in the eighteenth century: and Wiseman's clever emotional histrionics were answered quietly and effectively by Mr Page Wood, M.P., who, writing over the signature of "A

Westminster Layman", pointed out that the Cardinal-Archbishop "really at present knows nothing of Westminster", or he would have known that the Dean and Chapter had no concern with "palaces and parks". Nor, as a corporation, did they have any spiritual charge outside the Precincts, although by a recent Act of Parliament the rectories of the two parishes of St Margaret and St John were respectively attached to Westminster Canonries. The Dean and Chapter had, however, for the past ten years, contributed nearly £8000 a year to further the work of the Church in the surrounding district; in addition, they had made a corporate donation of £1000 to the Spiritual Aid Fund which one of the Canons had personally originated and for which he had raised nearly £20,000, to provide grants for assistant curates and church schools; while another of the Canons was building a new church, which was expected to cost £6000, at his sole expense. "Twenty years ago there were two parish churches and one chapel without cure of souls . . . a mean brick building in a ruinous condition": but now there were already six churches, and would soon be nine; "and of these, five will be in the midst of the very slums to which Dr Wiseman so graphically refers". "Twenty years ago we had but six clergymen; we now have twenty hard-working, zealous men, whose week-day labours are incessant in the same slums. . . ." In addition to the four ancient charity schools—all of them endowed since the Reformation—and one large workhouse school, there were now nine Church schools, educating between them more than 2500 of the poorest children. "It is true, there are many Roman Catholics among us, nearly all Irish, who form the most wretched portion of the poorer inhabitants. . . . Well, Dr Wiseman's Church has provided them with one small school for boys, and one other for girls. Fifty of each, I believe, would be the largest number ever found there. The other Dissenters have, together with some Churchmen, established three ragged schools; and the Independents have one free school, of much larger dimensions than that of the Romanists. But, sir, the matter does not rest here. The miserable condition of the Irish, in temporal as well as spiritual matters, has occa-

sioned our clergy twice to call the attention of some wealthy
Romanists to the fact; but they remain as squalid and miserable
as ever, in spite of the contributions cheerfully made to their
relief by those who differ from them in creed, but regard them
as their brethren. . . ." If Dr Wiseman really wishes to
ameliorate the condition of these poor Irish Roman Catholics
in Westminster, "I have no objection to give him any information he may require . . . and for that purpose I enclose my name
and address."[22]

The writer of this letter—a future Lord Chancellor—was
himself for upwards of forty years a Sunday School teacher[23] at
St John's, which had awoken to new and vigorous parochial
life under the long incumbency (1832-83) of Archdeacon Jennings, a stalwart Evangelical. The revival of St Margaret's came
later in time, but, partly from the more conspicuous and more
commanding position of the church, it was far more spectacular
and more resounding.

It was in 1876 that Frederic William Farrar, at that time
Headmaster of Marlborough, was appointed Rector of St Margaret's and Canon of Westminster on the recommendation of
the then Prime Minister, Mr Disraeli, and he remained there
for nearly twenty years. In 1883 he succeeded Jennings as Archdeacon of Westminster, a purely titular office. To-day he is
seldom remembered except as the grandfather of Field-Marshal
Lord Montgomery of Alamein, or as the author of a powerful
if melodramatic story of school life entitled *Eric; or, Little by
Little* (1858). But he was one of the great parish priests of the
Victorian era.

In later life he recalled how, a few years before his appointment to St Margaret's, he had been invited by Dean Stanley to
preach at one of the popular nave services in the Abbey church.
"As I passed through our churchyard, not, as now, a space of
pleasant green with daisies growing on it, but a chaos of broken,
unsightly, half-sunken and obliterated tombstones, forming
the most neglected approach to any Cathedral in the world,
I saw rejoicing crowds thronging in one continuous stream

into the glorious Abbey, and I noticed one solitary old woman on crutches tottering languidly into St Margaret's. I still retain a vivid impression of the thought which crossed my mind, that the Rector of St Margaret's must be a person profoundly to be pitied. How could he hope that many could be drawn to go to a church under the shadow of the 'great Temple of silence and reconciliation', with its famous preachers, its heroic memories, its entrancing music? How little did I then dream that God's unseen Providence would for so long a period link the destiny of my own little life with this corner of God's vineyard."[24] At the time of which he spoke, the incumbent, Canon Conway, was in enfeebled health, and the parish and the fabric were alike going to rack and ruin.

Farrar never forgot how his heart sank within him when in 1876 he entered for the first time the parish church of St Margaret, Westminster, as it then was, and observed its eighteenth-century defacements; the huge unsightly galleries, "like the receding forehead of a gorilla", running round three sides of the building, and blocking the windows; the cumbrous two-decker pulpit with its dirty velvet cushion in the very centre of the edifice; the false Gothic apse of lath and plaster painted blue with yellow stars; the general air of squalor and depression, the mean seats and dusty furnishings and dingy paint, and the fat and frowsy pew-opener, a living symbol of the old regime.

But the herculean energies of the new Rector were adequate to his herculean task.[25] First, he restored and refurnished the dilapidated interior, raising for this purpose the astonishing sum of £30,000 (including a grant of £1500 from the House of Commons). He turfed the derelict churchyard where the poet Cowper, as a Westminster School boy, had received one of his earliest religious impressions from being struck on the leg by a skull thrown up by the spade of a grave-digger working late in the evening;[26] and where the Abbey choirboys used to spend their time between services in sailing their toy boats in puddles made by the sinking of the gravestones, or, if it were dry weather, in playing marbles on the flat slabs of the mouldering altar-tombs.[27] Within the church, galleries and apse were cleared away, and once again it was possible to see the true proportions of the building. By making use of every opportunity, Farrar found donors to fill the windows one by one with stained glass, for which he prevailed upon contemporary poets —Tennyson, Browning, Whittier—to compose appropriate mottoes. The inscription which Browning wrote for the window erected to commemorate the first Jubilee of Queen Victoria, was received, with a certain levity on the part of the Press, as one of his obscurer compositions:

> *Fifty years flight! Wherein should he rejoice*
> *Who hailed their birth, who as they die decays?*
> *This—England echoes his attesting voice:*
> *Wondrous and well!—thanks, Ancient Thou of days.*

But even this was good publicity for St Margaret's. More memorable, however, was the address delivered by Matthew Arnold—the last he ever gave—on 13 February 1888, at the dedication of the Milton window, presented by the munificence of Mr George W. Childs, proprietor of the *Philadelphia Ledger*.[28] We need not altogether regret that most of these windows were blown out by bombing during the war of 1939-45, since they made the church very dark: for Farrar's almost Oriental passion for colour was not an unmixed blessing. Architecturally, the restoration of St Margaret's was the last and best work of Sir Gilbert Scott. Again, it was fortunate that money began to run short before the end, which prevented all the architect's designs—especially a chancel screen—from being carried out.[29]

To this church, as restored and beautified, the Rector attracted crowded and admiring congregations. Distinguished ecclesiastics were glad to occupy the pulpit, from which, as we are proud to remember, some of the *Sermons preached in English Churches* by Bishop Phillips Brooks of Massachusetts were delivered. Farrar was himself a popular preacher of outstanding celebrity in a generation which made something of a cult of popular preachers. ("I remember clearly", wrote Thomas Burke in his reminiscences of *London in my time*, "how they were discussed and weighed and compared, and how Aunts would come with news of a wonderful preacher heard at some outlying church, in the manner of an impresario reporting to the opera-directors on a new Wotan. Parties would be made up to visit this discovery, and on return they would sit about criticising his matter, his delivery, his gestures, and how far he surpassed or fell short of their particular standards of unction and oratory."[30] This quotation is significantly taken from the chapter headed "*Entertainment*".) The vogue of a popular preacher may be superficial and ephemeral. But, as Rector of St Margaret's, Canon Farrar was always far more than a popular preacher. His work was constructed upon more solid foundations, because he never regarded himself primarily as a pulpit orator, but as a parish priest. It is understandable that both as a preacher and as a personality he had his detractors as well as his admirers. But there could be no denying that under his imaginative direction St Margaret's became, in organization and equipment, one of the "star" parishes in the diocese of London: and Farrar not only built up an enormous following —which can mean either much or little—but also exhibited a truly admirable pastoral zeal. When he was promoted to the Deanery of Canterbury in 1895, he invited all the young people whom he had prepared for Confirmation to communicate with him in the Lord's Supper after evening prayer on the last Sunday of his ministry as Rector of St Margaret's. It happened to be a night of torrential rain: but there were nearly six hundred young men and young women present in the congregation.

What now remains to show for Farrar's long, laborious, and spectacularly fruitful ministry? This is the kind of problem that is constantly confronting the ecclesiastical historian: and it is also, in a different way, at the back of the mind of every parish priest, although, if he is a good priest, it should seldom rise to the level of consciousness. Yet it is natural to a man to desire to be remembered: it is natural to an administrator to hope that his policy will be maintained: it is natural to a parish priest to pray that something of his pastoral ministry may survive and continue to bear fruit. And it is hard to say that any of these three desires, although in differing degrees they emanate from the frailty of our mortal nature, is intrinsically sinful.

The memory of Farrar at St Margaret's is in fact more vivid and historic than that of any of his successors, except Hensley Henson. Architecturally, both within and without, the church is very much as it was at the end of his incumbency: there have been certain alterations, but it is unquestionably more as he left it in 1895 than as he found it in 1876. The congregation, of course, is very different: although our senior sidesman was actually a boy in the choir in Dr Farrar's time, and (I am glad to say) measures all subsequent Rectors by that exacting standard. The main thing is that the neighbourhood has changed almost out of recognition: the poverty and overcrowding are a thing of the past, and office blocks and business premises have engulfed not only the slums but also the private houses of the upper classes: the parish has virtually ceased to be a residential district, and therefore not only are the problems different from what they were, but also there is no means of telling how much of Farrar's pastoral work has stood the test of time. "The secret things belong unto the Lord our God" (Deut. 29. 29): and to recognize this humbly and without question is a part of the mysterious discipline of the priestly life. A priest must never want to be appreciated, and he must never ask to see results.

We have of course the highest authority for saying that the wisdom of the children of this world in their generation is something that the children of light can always study with advantage. The Church has no business to be inefficient or amateur: and our debt to Sir Robert Peel, the creator of the Ecclesiastical Commission which reformed the medieval administrative system or lack of system of the Established Church, and to Bishop Samuel Wilberforce, who remodelled the office and work of the Episcopate, is indeed incalculable. Yet woe betide the spiritual society that relies too much on organization or on organizations. It is at its peril that the Church models itself upon the streamlined efficiency of a big business corporation. There is a story of a shrewd and saintly bishop at the beginning of this century who paid a pastoral visit of inspection to a parish in his diocese. The clergy proudly took him round the various parochial organizations—the Sunday School, the Mothers' Meeting, the Youth Club, the Boy Scouts, the Girl Guides, and so forth. It seemed that every possible activity was represented. At last, when they returned to the Vicarage, the bishop said: "Thank you very much for showing me all that. It was most interesting and impressive. But I have only half an hour before I have to catch my train: and before I go, will you not tell me a little about your work?"[31]

It is a truism that much of the social and philanthropic activity formerly undertaken by the Church is now done (rather more expensively) by the Welfare State. The resultant danger that the religion of the Church may become narrowed to a religion of the sacristy is, I think, more abstract than the practical dilemma in which the Church finds itself burdened with a dead weight of societies and organizations which once were flourishing but which have long since outlived their usefulness, and are kept in being only from a vague sense of duty.

There is indeed a sense in which the Church in its activities in the world is for ever sawing off the branch on which it is sitting. This is conspicuously true of what may be called its secular activities: but it is true not only of them. Consider, for example, the analogous case of the Salvation Army. Its official historian, Colonel Robert Sandall, regards the period 1878-86 as the Heroic Age of the Army. "During 1882, it was reported that soldiers and officers had been knocked down, kicked or otherwise brutally assaulted, 251 of them being women. . . . No fewer than 56 of the buildings used by the Army had been seriously damaged." But "in the course of the five years 1881-85, 250,000 persons knelt at Army penitent-forms." With this compare the passage in *Bishoprick Papers* in which Hensley Henson gives a dispassionate analysis of the reasons why, in his judgement, the Salvation Army has no future:

The conditions indispensable to the Army's success are rapidly disappearing. England to-day [1935] presents an aspect very different from the England of seventy years ago into which [General] Booth introduced his novel venture. There no longer exists a section of the community neglected, largely unknown, destitute, and almost incredibly debased. . . . In fact the Salvation Army has to work on an ever-shrinking area of suitable material. Booth may fairly claim to have taken some part in the process of waking the public conscience as to the social enormities within the national life, but the fact remains that his distinctive device for remedying them loses worth and relevance with their disappearance.[32]

To this we may retort: Which, after all, is more important—the cure of the disease, or the perpetuation of the remedy? It is not a corruptible crown for which we strive. "Except a corn of wheat fall into the ground and die, it abideth alone: but if it die, it beareth forth much fruit." It is only because, and in so far as, the Church is prepared to die as its Master died, that the gates of hell shall not prevail against it.

There stood in the midst of the throne of God "a Lamb as it had been slain". In the words of one of our younger theologians, the Reverend H. A. Williams: "The resurrection of Christ thus shows us temporal good as something which can be eternally possessed, earthly experience and achievement as something which can be given permanence in Heaven. Those things which time appears to kill and throw away are in fact being kept safe in God's eternity that we may possess them for ever. This may be comforting. But it is also extremely challenging. For it invests the historical order with an almost terrifying significance. It means that what we are and do here on earth is of supreme importance. For out of this material God is building His eternal city. Not for one moment can we abandon the attempt to make the world a better place, to contribute to its store of beauty and truth and goodness. For however ephemeral our efforts may be, however here and now they may fail or be superseded, it is with them that God has willed to weave a tapestry which will be for ever His possession and ours. 'Gather up the fragments that remain, that nothing be lost.' "[33]

This is a great mystery: but almost equally mysterious is the way in which the work of the Church militant here in earth seems to be at the mercy of external circumstances that it can neither anticipate nor control. Within an easy walk from St Margaret's, Westminster, the visitor will pass the haggard skeletons of several churches gutted by incendiary bombs and mutely awaiting demolition. Most, though not all, of these were among the new churches to which in 1850 Mr Page Wood, M.P., in the character of "A Westminster Layman", had pointed with legitimate pride as a visible, not to say obvious, refutation of the strictures passed by Cardinal Wiseman on the alleged pastoral indifference of the Dean and Chapter in His Eminence's letter to *The Times*. There are moreover many other churches in London and also in the Provinces—among them St Alban's, Holborn; St Jude's, Whitechapel; All Saints', Lambeth; St Peter's, Plymouth; St Agatha's, Landport—which, within living memory, were widely celebrated as centres of flourishing religious life, but which, for the same or for other reasons, are now derelict or ruined, like wells that have suddenly dried up. And so the sorrowful question arises: Why (if we may so express it) does God allow the work of his servants to be squandered in this way? Must we not say of Providence what Tennyson said of Nature?—

> So careful of the type she seems,
> So careless of the single life.[34]

Here is a real problem, and one that admits of no facile ready-made solution. Yet there are certain other considerations which must not be overlooked.

The first is that, to our finite understanding, the Carefulness of God is no less arbitrary than his Prodigality. For example, I am bound constantly to remember that it is only by a succession of miracles that St Margaret's still stands. Twice in the centuries before the Reformation—in the reign of Edward III, and again in the reign of Henry VII—it became ruinous, but

was rebuilt. Under Edward VI, in 1549, the Lord Protector
Somerset designed to pull it down in order to obtain more stone
for the building of his palace in the Strand, proposing (as
Heylyn tells us in his *Ecclesia Restaurata*) to turn the
parishioners,

> for the celebrating of all divine offices, into some part of the
> nave or main body of the abbey-church, which would be
> marked out for that purpose. But the workmen had no
> sooner advanced their scaffolds, when the parishioners
> gathered together in great multitudes, with bows and arrows,
> staves and clubs, and other such offensive weapons; which so
> terrified the workmen, that they ran away in great amaze-
> ment, and never could be brought again upon that
> employment.[35]

Throughout the seventeenth and eighteenth centuries,
repeated financial applications to the House of Commons were
necessary to keep the fabric in structural repair. Between 1734
and 1814, Parliamentary grants totalling £25,370 were expended for this purpose: and in the ensuing thirty years an
additional £10,855 was also spent upon repairs. In July 1844
a Select Committee of the House of Commons reported unani-
mously in favour of removing St Margaret's from its present
site, in order to improve the vista of Mr Barry's new Palace of
Westminster.[36]

> ... The incongruity of this Church in its style of architec-
> ture, and its close proximity to Westminster Abbey, have
> been frequently noticed and lamented. The incongruity,
> great as it is at present, will undoubtedly appear much
> greater when the New Houses of Parliament shall be
> completed.
>
> An opinion is indeed maintained by several persons, that
> it might be possible to remove this great architectural
> anomaly by improvements in St Margaret's as it stands at
> present—that it might be enriched in design, and rendered
> more pure in detail. But while, on the one hand, the expenses

attending so extensive a change might perhaps be scarcely inferior to those required for complete re-construction, it seems to be far more generally considered, that the effect could not be compared to that of an open space clear of any buildings in front of the Abbey, and of the Houses of Parliament.

Your Committee have no hesitation in expressing their unanimous recommendation, that the Church of St Margaret's shall be removed from its present site, and they have reason to think that a new Churchyard or Cemetery, in some less populous situation, might be purchased at a very moderate expense, and that it might be possible to obtain a portion of land not far distant from the present site, where the Church could be rebuilt, in a great measure, from the present materials. Before, however, any conclusive opinion could be formed upon this part of the question, it would be proper to consider the most suitable position of the Church in reference to the Congregation, since the Church now stands at the extremity of an extensive Parish. . . .

The report was not, however, implemented. But, not long after (according to the *Church of England Magazine* of 3 April 1869), there was some talk of demolishing St Margaret's on purely utilitarian and not aesthetic grounds: "A while ago a project was announced for the removal of this church by some railway company . . . to gratify the morbid desire of the public to traverse the metropolis in a few minutes less time than is now practicable." Both these proposals, it may be noted, were put forward before Farrar became Rector, and at a time when it was not implausible to classify St Margaret's as "redundant". But that lethal epithet from the vocabulary of bureaucracy ceased to be applicable when first the fervent industry of Farrar, and then the more urbane and more sophisticated genius of Henson, had left their mark. Then, during the second World War, the church was repeatedly damaged by bombing, and had indeed to be closed from 26 September 1940 to June 1941: and to this day there is a derelict patch in the north aisle, displaying blackened walls and charred timbers and a notice saying: "Damage done by an Oil Bomb on the night of Wednesday, September 25th, 1940. Please help our Restoration Fund." Nevertheless, St Margaret's still stands, and carries on its work. The Providence of God preserves far more than it destroys.

But the final answer is surely that the children of light must resist the insidious temptation to apply carnal measurements to spiritual things. Whether in good or in evil days, the work of the Kingdom is being carried forward, and souls are being saved, and the faithful are being edified, not because of any virtue or merit or wisdom of our own, but by the Divine grace of which we are the faithful or the unfaithful ministers. Every parish priest knows this in the recesses of his heart: but never perhaps has it been more nobly expressed than in the hymn[37] by W. H. Draper, sometime Master of the Temple, which always moves me to the verge of tears:

In our day of thanksgiving one psalm let us offer
  For the saints who before us have found their reward;
When the shadow of death fell upon them, we sorrow'd,
  But now we rejoice that they rest in the Lord.

In the morning of life, and at noon, and at even
  He call'd them away from our worship below;
But not till His love, at the font and the altar,
  Had girt them with grace for the way they should go.

These stones that have echo'd their praises are holy,
  And dear is the ground where their feet have once trod;
Yet here they confess'd they were strangers and pilgrims
  And still they were seeking the city of God.

Sing praise, then, for all who here sought and here
    found Him,
  Whose journey is ended, whose perils are past;
They believed in the Light; and its glory is round them,
  Where the clouds of earth's sorrow are lifted at last.

Church Problems are always ultimately pastoral problems. The end of our Ministry towards the children of God is that they may be saved through Christ for ever. And that, as you will now recognize, has been the basic theme of this whole course of Bishop Paddock Lectures, delivered in the Chapel of the Good Shepherd.

> *In the morning of life, and at noon, and at even,*
> *He call'd them away from our worship below;*
> *But not till His love, at the font and the altar,*
> *Had girt them with grace for the way they should go.*

There is no greater privilege than to be used by God as his living instruments in such a ministry, chosen from all eternity to be Messengers, Watchmen, and Stewards of the Lord. But what we have always to remember is that what he requires of us is not "success", but fidelity. *"I think"*, wrote Bishop Hensley Henson in 1924, *"the longer I live, the more resigned I grow to being unable to explain the deep enigmas of life, and the more certain I am that whatever improvement is possible in the world, must grow, not from enthusiastic crusades, but from the steady courage and sacrifice of individuals who 'stick it' in the trenches of common duty."* But this is not to be confused with stoicism, which it superficially resembles. "I remember once that Bishop Chavasse [of Liverpool] said to me, when I had expressed myself rather despondently about my work, 'Do not forget that you are the servant of Another.' There is the sheet anchor of our confidence."[38] Nor can these lectures more fittingly conclude than with the prayer written for the clergy of St Margaret's[39] by Dr Armitage Robinson, sometime Rector of this Church (1899-1900), and afterwards Dean of Westminster:

> *Remember, O gracious Lord, for good these Thy ministering servants: pour out upon them evermore Thy Holy Spirit, to strengthen, deepen, chasten, purify them; that, giving themselves up to Thy service, they may do and suffer all that Thou willest, and finally may reign with Thee in life everlasting; through Jesus Christ our Lord.*

APPENDIX

IN HIS latter years, Bishop Hensley Henson was inclined to take a pessimistic view of the ministry of preaching and of its possible effectiveness for good under the changing conditions and conventions of the English way of life. Some acute and and disquieting reflections on this topic will be found in his *The Church of England* (1939), pp. 239-40; with which it is interesting to compare his remarks in vol. i (1942) of the *Retrospect of an Unimportant Life*, p. 57 ("Sermons counted for much in English life forty years ago. Congregations were larger, more intelligent, and theologically better educated, and also far less shifting, than they are now"), and his description of the policy which he followed at St Margaret's (ibid., pp. 132-4), with its melancholy epilogue: "Yet I am bound to acknowledge that, as I review my career, I am sometimes disposed to think that I should have made a better use of my time if I had not devoted so much of it to the composition and delivery of sermons. The modern world seems to have outgrown preaching, and there is no sign that its tendency will alter. At least it is consoling to know that, in acting as I did, I was honestly trying to fulfil my duty as then I understood it." This is a repetition of what he had written in his private Journal (1 December 1934) on being complimented by a brother bishop on the immense trouble that he took over his sermons: ". . . It is the fact that I squander a prodigious amount of time and energy on the preparation of sermons and addresses, which have no real importance. Had my lot been cast in the age when sermons were appreciated, I might have effected something, but in this age? Reviewing my life, I find it difficult to avoid the conclusion that I have gravely blundered in taking my work as a preacher so seriously. . . ." (*Retrospect*, vol. ii, p. 356.)

No doubt a feeling of discouragement is natural at the conclusion of a preaching ministry: in part this is an emotional reaction (common also to veteran actors and political orators): in part it is due to the unpriestly craving to see results which assails even those who are perfectly sensible that their work has been to cast bread upon the waters. But I suspect that Henson was also troubled in conscience by a passage which he quotes in his introduction to *Selected English Sermons, Sixteenth to Nineteenth Centuries* (1939), p. x, from *The Naked Truth* (1675), a pamphlet by Herbert Croft, Bishop of Hereford, which he himself had edited in 1919:

> I am no enemy to true Apostolical preaching, God forbid I should; but to vain Scholastical useless preaching: to have the Pastor, who should daily watch over his Flock, sit in his study all the week long, picking from that or this quaint Author a few beautiful flowers, and then come on *Sunday* with his Nosegay in his hand to entertain Ladies and Courtiers: for my part I count this far more sinful laziness, than to read a pious Homily on *Sunday,* and all the week after go up and down from house to house, taking pains to instruct and exhort such as I mentioned [the common people . . . those poor souls that know nothing]. But these shall be called dumb dogs, yet surely by none but barking Currs, who are wholly ignorant in true Apostolick Preaching.

It is a constant difficulty for a parish priest, amid the miscellaneous cares and manifold opportunities of his ministry, to know how best to manage his time and to apply his talents in his Master's service. But that Hensley Henson's preaching at St Margaret's, however "Scholastical", was neither vain nor useless, can be illustrated by two spontaneous tributes which have been paid to it since his death, and which deserve quotation.

In her autobiography, *Return Passage* (Oxford University Press, 1953: pp. 90-1), Miss Violet R. Markham, C.H., formerly Chairman of the Central Committee on Women's Training and Employment, whose varied and responsible activities in the public service are succinctly enumerated in *Who's Who,* writes of her life in London between 1905 and 1914:

Events of great moment to oneself may hinge on trifles. An active agnostic with a haughty contempt for creeds and parsons, I never went to church in those days. But it happened one Sunday morning that I was dragged under protest to St Margaret's when Hensley Henson was preaching. What I heard startled and impressed me. I returned the following Sunday, then again and again. His teaching worked by degrees a revolution in my own ideas. In my arrogance I had regarded Christianity as a system based on sentiment and the miraculous bolstered by tradition. I had agreed heartily with the alleged remark that faith was the frame of mind which enabled you to believe to be true that which you otherwise knew to be false. Admirable the Christian ethic might be, but it was mixed up with a series of impossible stories that no person who thought at all could accept. Yet the Christian minister to whom I listened with growing bewilderment and admiration had not only a mind of his own but a mind of first-rate quality. How to account for such a discrepancy? I began to take my ideas to pieces and look at them afresh. As time went on I found that Canon Henson expounded a reasonable faith that could be accepted without capitulations. . . .

It was a long and difficult inner struggle, but in me, as in millions before me, the Word little by little worked its ageless miracle. I surrendered to its compelling force; I accepted its mystery and power as transcending ordinary human experience—the "good man" theory was not good enough to fit the facts—and I became, what I have since remained, a most imperfect Christian. There are, of course, many other paths besides the one I trod; in later years I have had other teachers whose view of Christianity was warmer and of wider vision. But it was primarily the tough intellectual quality of Hensley Henson's teaching that broke down my barriers of scepticism and revealed a new world of experience and belief. To him my debt remains supreme.

Hardly less arresting is the testimony of Mr Eric Bligh in his autobiography, *Tooting Corner* (Secker and Warburg, 1946: pp. 204-6):

I have already mentioned my father's Edinburgh friend, Dr Palm, who came to stay with us when I was about fifteen. He was deeply interested in what was then referred to as the Higher Criticism. . . . On Sunday evenings he liked to go to London to hear some famous preacher, and one day he expressed a wish to go to St Margaret's, Westminster, to hear Canon Hensley Henson, who stood for the new and liberal spirit in biblical scholarship and thought. I had heard a good deal of Canon Henson, because he held out the hand of friendship to Nonconformists, and he took a place unique in my eyes.

. . . We had a good seat to the left of the middle aisle. I was, of course, acutely interested in the details of the service, and I liked the austerity of the two candles alight above the altar. The music was of the congregational magnificence that has long characterised St Margaret's. The incredibly young-looking dark rector (so different from my anticipation of an older man) bowed each time he passed the altar. He was a direct descendant of the old high churchmen.

This tall figure, in whom I seemed to detect a sense of loneliness and isolation, at once in some way I cannot explain, called forth my admiration. It was a minor point of interest with me, but he pronounced the "t" in the words "epistle" and "apostle". In his sermon he referred to Jeremy Taylor, and spoke of a reference of his to duelling. I had not hitherto been accustomed to listen to sermons in which Jeremy Taylor was quoted. I was young and ignorant, and it had probably never occurred to me that a modern clergyman would quote him (which, if you think of the clergy, was not really so foolish on my part), or, in fact, that he might be quotable. This man was familiar with him, and alluded to him casually, as anyone else, the then Bishop of London, for instance, might refer to the writings of Guy Thorne. I remember the musical timbre of the voice as the easy antique

English name came out. The candles shone in the darkened church, and had I known it, I had been introduced to something for me new and important. I daresay by that time I had heard of the Caroline divines, and now did I not hear one of their great successors quoting from one of them?

I was here made vaguely conscious of a high churchmanship of which I had never dreamed, a spirit of religion which has always since attracted me, here, at last, pure, learned, and English.

The final hymn was sung with a sense of triumph and mounting faith that indeed has echoed in my mind ever since, though the plain and unaccompanied words, if I set them down here, will hardly interpret that feeling of the communion of saints which did come to me for a few moments:

> Angels of Jesus, Angels of light,
> Singing to welcome the pilgrims of the night!

I strained my eyes to have a last sight of that tall and solitary figure, and passed out into my own particular species of night. How often has the thought of this great man saved me from harsh judgement and a too great leaning to the prejudices and confined views of my Dissenting ancestors.

It is also interesting and significant that, on a riding expedition with a friend in the Easter Vacation of 1912, Maynard Keynes, who was an agnostic, had the curiosity to attend the Sunday morning service at Wells Cathedral and to hear a sermon by Canon Hensley Henson, who happened to be preaching there (*The Life of John Maynard Keynes* by R. F. Harrod, 1951: p. 160).

The conditions which made possible these three personal experiences are no longer applicable. The era of "sermon-tasting" is past: there are no more "famous preachers", in the traditional meaning of the phrase; and even if there were, it is unlikely that intelligent agnostics would have the curiosity to go to church to hear them. Nevertheless, these three examples show that what Henson's ministry as a preacher effected under the more favourable conditions of his time was infinitely worth while. Whether that type of pulpit discourse is ultimately as valuable as the plain and parochial preaching in which the Church of England is so strong even in these days of discouragingly meagre congregations (although that is not an universal phenomenon) is another question, and one which is perhaps both unanswerable and irrelevant. It is sufficient to observe that the particular and exceptional talent which God in his inscrutable providence had committed to Herbert Hensley Henson was not wasted.

NOTES

CHAPTER 1

1. T. S. Eliot, *East Coker* (1940).

2. Cf. Lawrence Tanner, art., "Westminster Topography" (in *Transactions of the London and Middlesex Archaeological Society*, vol. X, n.s., 1951, p. 241): ". . . it must be remembered that until the sixteenth century Westminster *as a town* consisted for all practical purposes simply of the Abbey and the Palace and their precincts and of the two streets, Tothill Street and King Street. Beyond these lay the open fields with a few scattered manor houses and farms."

3. John Stow, *A Survey of London* (1603 edtn., ed. C. L. Kingsford, 1908, vol. ii, p. 106). His account of the early history of the parish church of St Margaret (pp. 106, 112) is obviously derived from the *Liber Niger Quaternus* in the Abbey muniments: see App. A.—For the alleged date, I can find no earlier authority than *The History and Survey of London from its Foundation to the Present Times*, by William Maitland, F.R.S. and Others (1756), vol. ii, p. 1339: "about the Year 1064". Cf. the title (1847) of the invaluable pioneer *History of the Parish Church of Saint Margaret, in Westminster; from its foundation, A.D. 1064* [*sic*], by the Rev. Mackenzie E. C. Walcott, who was Milman's curate.

4. H. F. Westlake (*St Margaret's Westminster*, 1914, p. 4) objects: "So far as can be ascertained the name and fame of St Margaret of Antioch were unknown in England before the time of the Crusades." Yet among the relics presented by Edward the Confessor to Westminster Abbey were "the head of St Margaret, with other bones, and portions of her clothes"; and it is also noteworthy that St Margaret of Scotland, the daughter of his nephew, Edward the Ætheling, had her upbringing at his Court.

5. Richard Widmore, *An History of the Church of St. Peter, Westminster, commonly called Westminster Abbey* (1751), p. 12; Dom David Knowles, *The Monastic Order in England* (1940), p. 603 and n.; *Acta Stephani Langton, Cantuariensis Archiepiscopi*, ed. Kathleen Major (Canterbury and York Society, 1950), pp. 69-73; Westlake, op. cit., p. 2.

6. J. Armitage Robinson, *A Commemoration of K. Edward the Confessor* (1901), p. 17.

7. First Report from His Majesty's Commissioners appointed to consider the State of the Established Church, with reference to Ecclesiastical Duties and Revenues (1835), p. 10.

8. The section headed "De ecclesia parochiali sanctae Margaritae primo fundata per sanctum Edwardum Confessorem" in the *Liber Niger Quaternus* (f. lxxvi. *b.*) reads: "Haec itaque eadem ecclesia usque ad tempora Regis Edwardi filii Regis Henrici tercii perstitit: quo tempore stapula lanarum erat apud Westmonasterium." But since the Wool Staple at Westminster was not established until 1353, it may be surmised that the words *"filii Regis Henrici"* are an interpolation by a late fifteenth-century scribe intending to be helpful.

9. *The Scrope and Grosvenor Controversy*, ed. Sir N. Harris Nicolas (1832), vol. i, p. 156 ff., vol. ii, p. 366 ff.

10. "Le Puez": 29 parishioners paid rents varying from 3d. to 20d., according to position, for pews or seats for their wives: cf. J. Charles Cox, *Churchwardens' Accounts* (1913), pp. 27, 186-94. —Our Churchwardens' Accounts, 1460-1847 (which are kept at the Westminster City Library, Archives Department, Buckingham Palace Road), have never been published in full, although copious extracts were printed by John Nichols in his *Illustrations of the Manners and Expences of Antient Times in England* (1797), pp. 1-76: they are catalogued in J. E. Smith, *Westminster Records* (1900), pp. 63-77. Unfortunately, six volumes (1610-11, 1614-15, 1618-19, 1693, 1694, 1695) were destroyed, and five volumes (1612-13, 1620-1, 1658, 1659, 1696) seriously damaged, during evacuation in the last war.

11. Dr J. H. Monk (1784-1856), Bishop of Gloucester and Bristol.—See *Leaves from the Note-Books of Lady Dorothy Nevill*, ed. Ralph Nevill (1907), p. 268.

12. W. Maitland, op. cit. (1756), vol. ii, p. 1339.—This appears to be the original source of the phrase repeated in italics, which Walcott (op. cit.) on his title-page mistakenly attributed to the Journals of the House of Commons, A.D.1735; an error that has since been constantly reiterated.

13. J. E. Neale, *The Elizabethan House of Commons* (1949), p. 368; art., "Parliament at Prayer", by the Editor [Sir Arnold Wilson, M.P.], in *The Nineteenth Century and after* (April 1937), pp. 1-37.

14. Maurice Hastings, *Parliament House* (1950), p. 81.

15. *De Republica Anglorum. The maner of Governement or policie of the Realme of England, compiled by the Honorable Sir Thomas Smyth . . . , ed. L. Alston (1906), p. 49.

16. J. E. Neale, op. cit., p. 350 ff.

17. *The Letters of John Chamberlain*, ed. N. E. McClure (1939), vol. i, p. 525.

18. See *D.N.B.*, art., "Perrot, Sir James (1571-1637)", by Thomas Seccombe.

19. *Commons Debates 1621*, ed. Wallace Notestein, F. H. Relf, and H. Simpson (1935), vol. iv, p. 19, vol. v, p. 3, and *passim*; *The Life of the Most Reverend Father in God*, James Usher, *late Lord Arch-Bishop of Armagh, Primate and Metropolitan of all Ireland*, by Richard Parr, D.D. (1686), p. 17; J. A. Carr, *The Life and Times of Archbishop Ussher* (1895), p. 120 ff.; *The Substance of that which was delivered in a sermon before the Commons House of Parliament, in St Margarets Church at Westminster, the 18 of February, 1620*, by James Ussher, *Professor of Divinity in the University of Dublin, in Ireland* (1621), In Dean Stanley's *Historical Memorials of Westminster Abbey* (8th edtn., p. 416 n.), "precentor" should read "preacher."— F. M. G. Higham, *Charles I* (1932), pp. 72-5, gives a brilliant imaginative description of Laud preaching before the House of Commons in St Margaret's in the spring of 1628: it has escaped her notice that Laud, as a Bishop, preached his sermon before the King and the House of Lords in the Abbey church.

20. William Haller, *Liberty and Reformation in the Puritan Revolution* (1955), p. 68.

21. Historical Manuscripts Commission: Appendix to Fifth Report (1876), p. 160.

22. A. J. Eagleston, *The Channel Islands under Tudor Government* (1949), p. 57 ff.

23. H. Montgomery Hyde, *John Law* (1948), p. 121.

24. Michael Oakeshott, *The Social and Political Doctrines of Contemporary Europe* (1939); Alvin W. Johnson and Frank H. Yost, *Separation of Church and State in the United States* (1948), pp. 9, 262.

25. W. R. W. Stephens, *A Memoir of the Right Hon. William Page Wood, Baron Hatherley* (1883), vol. ii, p. 91.

26. It was not, however, automatic: e.g., when Dr Thomas Sprat (Minister of St Margaret's, 1679-83; author of the first History of the Royal Society) and Dr Gilbert Burnet preached before the House on the Fast-day appointed by His Majesty's Proclamation, 22 Dec., 1680, the customary vote of thanks was given to Burnet for his sermon ("and likewise for his Book, intituled, 'The History of the Reformation of the Church of England' "), but was tacitly withheld from Sprat: this "raised his

merit at Court", and the King rewarded him with a canonry of Windsor.

27. John Evelyn's *Diary*. Cf. art., "The Rise and Fall of a Martyrology: Sermons on Charles I", by Helen W. Randall, in the *Huntington Library Quarterly* (Feb. 1947), vol. x, pp. 135-67, which however contains one error: the scandalous sermon preached by Dr William Binckes on 30 Jan. 1702 was preached, not in St Margaret's before the House of Commons, but in King Henry VII's Chapel, Westminster Abbey, before the Lower House of Convocation.—It is a strange coincidence that 30 Jan. is also the date on which Adolf Hitler became Chancellor of the German Reich in 1933.

28. *Miscellaneous Works of Edward Gibbon, Esq.* (1814), vol. ii, p. 78. Cf. Boswell's *Life of Dr Johnson* (under 11 June 1784). *Parliamentary History of England* (1813), vol. xvii, p. 311 ff.— Dr Nowell is also remembered for his defence (*An Answer to "Pietas Oxoniensis"*, 1768) of the expulsion of the Six Students of St Edmund Hall.

29. Keith Feiling, *The Second Tory Party* (1938), p. 255.

30. Andrew Lang, *Life, Letters, and Diaries of Sir Stafford Northcote, first Earl of Iddesleigh* (1890), vol. i, p. 115. Cf., however, Sir Edward Russell, *That Reminds Me*—(1899), p. 153: "I was at St Margaret's, Westminster, when Melvill preached a wonderful sermon before the House of Commons on a Crimean fast-day, the church—galleried and stuffy, not the beautiful place it is now—full of aristocrats in black, whose relations had been killed in the trenches. Proud boy as I was, I touched my hat to Lord Palmerston afterwards in Parliament Street."—For Melvill's pulpit style, cf. the undergraduate recollections of Bishop Moule: ". . . the mighty master of a rhetoric which now probably would be thought too studied, but which was indeed a living force in his delivery. As each magnificent paragraph rolled to its close there came an audible sigh from the dense congregation, a sigh of tension relieved and attention renewed." (*Handley Carr Glyn Moule, Bishop of Durham: a biography*, by John Battersby Harford and F. C. Macdonald, 1922, p. 24.)

31. Thomas Archer, *Queen Victoria: her Life and Jubilee* (1888), vol. iv, pp. 219-25.

32. Dean Farrar's own copy of this historic address of thanks is preserved in the Vestry of St Margaret's, Westminster.

33. W. E. Henley, *London Voluntaries* (1892-3).

34. G. K. A. Bell, Bishop of Chichester, *Randall Davidson, Archbishop of Canterbury* (1935), vol. ii, p. 916.

35. Cyril Garbett, Archbishop of York, *Church and State in England* (1950), p. 122.

36. *Christian Life, its Course, its Hindrances, and its Helps. Sermons . . .* by Thomas Arnold, D.D., Head Master of Rugby School, and late Fellow of Oriel College, Oxford (1841: vol. iv of Arnold's *Sermons*), pp. 439 f., 450.—A. P. Stanley, *Historical Memorials of Westminster Abbey*, p. 92n.

CHAPTER 2

1. R. Porson, *Letters to Mr Archdeacon Travis, in answer to his defence of the Three Heavenly Witnesses, 1 John v. 7.* (1790), p. xxviii.

2. Introduction by Hilaire Belloc to *The Story of a Catholic Parish: S. James's, Farnham*, by Etienne Robo (1938), p. iii.

3. "However, he died in the same opinion he had embraced, few years after the Revolution, and edified much those that were about him": *Memoirs of Thomas, Earl of Ailesbury, written by himself,* ed. W. E. Buckley (Roxburghe Club, 1890), vol. i, p. 153.—Narcissus Luttrell's *A Brief Historical Relation of State Affairs from September 1678 to April 1714* (1857), vol. i, p. 398, gives the date of Peterborough's conversion as March 1687.

4. *The Auto-Biography of Symon Patrick, Bishop of Ely: now first printed from the original manuscript* (1839), p. 135. The "petty Canons" (now known as Minor Canons) were the priest-vicars whose duty is to sing the services in the Abbey church, The Broadway Chapel, founded in 1631 and opened in 1642, was a chapel of ease to St Margaret's (Walcott, *Memorials of Westminster*, 1851, p. 286 f.; Westlake, *St Margaret's Westminster*).—Cf. Stanley, *Historical Memorials of Westminster Abbey*, p. 447: "The Abbey was almost the only church in London where James II's Declaration of Indulgence was read. 'I was at Westminster School' (says Lord Dartmouth) 'at the time, and heard it read in the Abbey. As soon as Bishop Sprat (who was Dean) gave orders for reading it, there was so great a murmur and noise in the Church, that nobody could hear him; but before he had finished, there was none left but a few Prebends in their stalls, the choristers, and the Westminster scholars. The Bishop could hardly hold the proclamation in his hands for trembling, and everybody looked under a strange consternation.' (Note in Burnet's

Own Time, vol. i, p. 218.) 'He was surprised on the day when the Seven Bishops were dismissed from the King's Bench to hear the bells of his own Abbey joining in the many peals of the other London Churches, and promptly silenced them, not without angry murmurs.' (Macaulay, vol. ii, p. 368.)"

5. H. L. R. Edwards, *Skelton: The Life and Times of an Early Tudor Poet* (1949).

6. *The Diary of Henry Machyn, Citizen and Merchant-Taylor of London, 1550-1563,* ed. J. G. Nichols (Camden Society, 1848), p. 84 f.; J. F. Mozley, *John Foxe and his Book* (1940), p. 193; Thomas Fuller, *The History of the Worthies of England* (1662), part i, p. 151; Charles Smyth, art., "Sacrilege at St Margaret's", in the *Spectator,* 22 April 1955.

7. Peter Heylyn, *Cyprianus Anglicus: the Life of William [Laud], Lord Archbishop of Canterbury* (1668), p. 468.

8. Historical Manuscripts Commission: Report on MSS. in Various Collections, vol. ii (1903), p. 259; *The Knyvett Letters,* ed. Bertram Schofield (1949), p. 30.

9. Cf. "A Prayer to be used on the Sabbath day", in *Certaine Short Prayers and Meditations vpon the Lords Prayer and the Ten Commandements: with other particular Prayers for seuerall purposes: written by the right Worshipfull Sir* James Perrott, *Knight* (1630), p. 158: ". . . O Lord settle vs vnto [this day, which thou hast selected for thy seruice], fit vs for it, and grant grace not only vnto vs heere present, but to the publicke state, and to particular persons in other places: not only to rest from labours on this day, but to shun sinne, to communicate with thy seruants in thy seruice, to read thy Word, to heare it, *where it is preached;* to come vnto thy Congregations, and *where thy word is not preached,* to vse all the good meanes wee may for maintenance and increase of knowledge and of conscience; by praying, reading, meditating and conference. . . ." (Italics mine.)

10. John Edward Smith, *A Catalogue of Westminster Records* (1900), p. 66 n.; *D.N.B.,* art., "Stephen Marshall (1594?-1655)", by Alexander Gordon; E. Vaughan, *Stephen Marshall, a forgotten Essex Puritan* (1907); William Haller, *Liberty and Reformation in the Puritan Revolution,* pp. 35-7 and *passim.*

11. Venn, *Alumni Cantabrigienses; Memorials of the Family of Wimberley* (1893); John Nalson, *Impartial Collection* (1683), vol. ii, p. 202.

12. *D.N.B.,* art., "Bargrave, Isaac (1586-1643)", by Sidney Lee; David Lloyd, *Memoires* (1668), p. 687.

13. *Legenda Lignea: with . . . a Character of some hopefull Saints Revolted to the Church of Rome* (1653), chap. xxxviii: ". . . This drunken sot had the luck to reel out of *England* into *France,* and to stagger from *London* to *Paris,* there to guzzle as deeply in the juyce of the Grape, as he had swil'd himself in that of Good Ale. . . .This Buffoon is one of the common scorns of all Civil people, as carrying about him all the signes and tokens of a shameless Sot. . . . This debauched wretch is anxious to be accounted an example of piety, presumes to climb up into the Pulpits at *Paris,* and dispute before the Gates of the petty *Burbon,* commonly in the streets with simple weak Hugonots, and doth spit, and froath, and draffle as much nonsense, malice and vanity, as can be imagined . . .", etc., etc. Anthony Wood, *Athenae Oxonienses* (1691), vol. ii, p. 155: (2nd edtn., 1721), vol. ii, p. 241.

14. Robert S. Bosher, *The Making of the Restoration Settlement: the Influence of the Laudians, 1649-1662* (1951).

15. Thomas Hancock. "Disestablishment in Wales", in *Some Aspects of Disestablishment,* ed. H. C. Shuttleworth (1894), pp. 91-102.

16. *Mercurius Aulicus, a Diurnall, Communicating the intelligence, and affaires of the Court to the rest of the Kingdome*: Thursday 4 May 1643.

17. *Lives of the English Poets* by Samuel Johnson, LL.D. (ed. G. Birkbeck Hill, 1905, vol. i, p. 262).

18. *The Whole Works of the Rev. John Lightfoot, D.D., Master of Catharine Hall, Cambridge,* ed. J. R. Pitman (1824), vol. xiii, p. 15.

19. *Diary of Walter Yonge, Esq., Justice of the Peace, and M.P. for Honiton, 1604-1628,* ed. George Roberts (Camden Society, 1848), p. 86.—The problem "Why Puritanes make long Sermons?" had once aroused the curiosity of the young John Donne (*Paradoxes and Problems,* ed. Geoffrey Keynes, 1923, p. 42).

20. Cf. *The Life of the Rev. Philip Henry, A.M.,* by the Rev. Matthew Henry (ed. J. B. Williams, 1825), p. 6: ". . . On the Lord's day he sat under the powerful ministry of Mr Stephen Marshall, in the morning, at New-chapel; in the afternoon at St Margaret's, Westminster, which was their parish church. In the former place Mr Marshall preached long from Phil. ii, 5, 6, &c.; in the latter from John, viii, 36, of our freedom by Christ. This minister, and this ministry, he would, to his last, speak of with great respect, and thankfulness to God, as that by which he

was, through grace, in the beginning of his days, *begotten again to a lively hope* ... He also attended constantly upon the monthly fasts at St Margaret's, where the best and ablest ministers of England preached before the then House of Commons; and the service of the day was carried on with great strictness, from eight in the morning till four in the evening. He likewise frequented extraordinary fasts and thanksgivings. Here he used to sit always upon the pulpit stairs, and it was his constant practice, from eleven or twelve years old, to write, as he could, all the sermons he heard, which he kept very carefully, transcribed many of them fair over after, and, notwithstanding his many removes, they are yet forth-coming."

21. *The Life Records of John Milton*, ed. J. Milton French, vol. ii (1950), pp. 87-113; W. Haller, *Liberty and Reformation*, pp. 123-37.

22. 22 Dec. 1648 (being a "Day of Publick Humiliation"). This sermon was afterwards used in evidence against Peter at his trial for high treason. Raymond Phineas Stearns, *The Strenuous Puritan: Hugh Peter, 1598-1660* (1954), pp. 330-2; Haller, *Liberty and Reformation*, pp. 336, 383.

23. Robert S. Bosher, op. cit., p. 4; W. K. Jordan, *The Development of Religious Toleration in England*, vol. iii (1938), p. 195.

24. Geoffrey Soden, *Godfrey Goodman, Bishop of Gloucester, 1583-1656* (1953), pp. 442 f., 466.

25. Increase Mather, *Testimony against prophane customs* (ed. William Peden, 1953), p. 44.—The previous Christmas (1686), the Royal Governor, Andros, newly-arrived in Boston, had affronted Puritan opinion in Massachusetts by attending church services with his red-coated soldiers.—Cf. the entry under 25 Dec. 1669 in William Penn's *My Irish Journal, 1669-1670* (ed. Isabel Grubb, 1952, p. 31): "Was Pie Day, none could be got to work."

26. Arthur Bryant, *Samuel Pepys*, vol. i, *The Man in the Making* (1933), pp. 28, 198.

27. G. Kitson Clark, *Elizabeth by the Grace of God* (William Ainslie Memorial Lecture, 1953), p. 9.

28. William Perkins, *Works*, vol. i (1612), introduction ("To all ignorant people that desire to be instructed") to *The Foundation of Christian Religion*, p. A. 2; Joseph Addison, *The Freeholder*, No. 22 (1715).

29. But we are indebted to the Rev. J. C. S. Nias, *Gorham and the Bishop of Exeter* (1950), for a valuable and significant restatement of the issues at stake.

CHAPTER 3

1. Michael Joyce, *My friend H: John Cam Hobhouse, Baron Broughton* (1948), p. 267.

2. *The Times*, 20 Oct. 1834.

3. Cf. art., "Crisis in Education", by Dr Eric James, High Master of Manchester Grammar School (*Sunday Times*, 31 Jan. 1954): "There is no greater error than to regard the provision of educational opportunity as a kind of charity. The whole future of our kind of society is completely dependent on the full utilisation of its resources of ability and character. To provide the best possible education for its citizens is the most obvious form of communal self-interest."

4. H. C. Maxwell Lyte, *History of Eton College* (1875); Alec Macdonald, *Short History of Repton* (1929); W. H. D. Rouse, *History of Rugby School* (1898); Strype, *Life of Whitgift*; G. L. Hosking, *Life and Times of Edward Alleyn* (1952).

5. C. Wilfrid Scott-Giles, *The History of Emanuel School* (1935); 2nd Report of the Commissioners on the Education of the Poor (1819), pp. 69-72 and App., pp. 247-63.—The School removed from Westminster to Wandsworth Common in 1882.

6. Arthur F. Leach, *History of Winchester College* (1899); Lives of William of Wykeham by Mackenzie E. C. Walcott (1852), George Herbert Moberly (1887), G. C. Heseltine (1932).— The need of recruiting for the ministry (and also of raising the general tone of social life) was not less present to the minds of the Elizabethan hierarchy. Cf. Dr Kennedy on the Canons of 1571: "An interesting canon [headed *Ludimagistri*] . . . concerned the duties and aims of teaching . . . Schoolmasters were urged to give annual reports to the bishops of the progress of their pupils with the hope that parents would co-operate in preparing the most promising of them for public life or for the sacred ministry. Schoolmasters were also instructed to train the youthful tongues to speak clearly and distinctly, and to send or to accompany them to hear sermons, afterwards examining each of them as to what they had learned from the discourses. In this way it was hoped that the young might be drawn to virtue and industry, the evil and lazy reproved, and the diligent encouraged by praise." (W. P. M. Kennedy, *Elizabethan Episcopal Administration*, Alcuin Club, 1924, vol. i, p. cxlii; Edward Cardwell, *Synodalia*, 1842, vol. i, pp. 128-9.)

7. S.P. (Dom.) 1666-1667, vol. clxxxiii, p. 384 ("Dec. (?), 1666: Petition of the Churchwardens and Overseers of St Margaret's, Westminster, to the King, to continue his benevolence of 100 *l.* a year to the poor, but to settle half of it on the churchwardens for the poor of the parish, and half on King Charles's Hospital, formed by the late King for bringing up fatherless children, which has lost half its revenue in the late fire"). *United West-minster (Endowed) Schools: a brief account of the foundation and history of the Schools,* by Robert E. H. Goffin, Head Master (1894); *Westminster City School Magazine,* Nov. 1924, vol. x, no. 89; Walter Besant, *Westminster* (1895). The present West-minster City School had its first home in the buildings of the old St Margaret's Hospital, but was transferred in 1877 to new build-ings in Palace Street, at the back of the Emanuel Hospital site. These buildings are without aesthetic interest or merit: but in the forecourt there is a statue by Frank Taubman (erected 1901) of Sir Sydney Waterlow which is one of the curiosities of London, because it represents him carrying a soft hat and an umbrella. It is a replica of a statue erected by public subscription (1900) in Waterlow Park, Highgate. Sir Sydney Waterlow, sometime Lord Mayor of London, was the first Chairman (1873-1906) of the Governors of the United Westminster Schools.

8. For the Rev. James Palmer (1585-1660), see *D.N.B.* (art. by W. A. Shaw); Venn, *Alumni Cantab.,* pt. 1, vol. iii; Walker, *Sufferings,* pt. 2, p. 74; *Walker Revised,* ed. A. G. Matthews; D. Lloyd, *Memoires* (1668), p. 512; Fuller, *Worthies* (s.v. West-minster) and *History of the University of Cambridge* (s.v. Magd. Coll.); Newcourt, *Repertorium* (1708), vol. i, p. 317 (s.v. S. Brides); Walter H. Godfrey, *The Church of Saint Bride, Fleet Street* (Survey of London: 1944), pp. 13, 24-6; Guildhall Library Muniment Room, MS. 6554/1 (St Bride's, Vestry Minute Book); Westminster Abbey Muniments; Hatton, *New View of London* (1708), p. 339 and *passim;* E. B. Jupp and W. W. Pocock, *His-torical Account of the Worshipful Company of Carpenters of the City of London* (1887), pp. 416, 470, 552, 602; *The Endowed Charities of the City of London,* ed. Charles White (1829), p. 131; 1st Report of the Commissioners on the Education of the Poor (1819), p. 181 and App., pp. 287-92; Ernest H. Pearce, *The Sons of the Clergy,* 2nd edtn. 1928, pp. 97, 115-18.

9. G. F. Russell Barker, *Memoir of Richard Busby, D.D.* (1895); H. Hensley Henson, *Puritanism in England* (1912), pp. 243-66 ("Richard Busby"); Walcott, *St Margaret's Church,* p. 67; John Sargeaunt, *Annals of Westminster School* (1898); J. D. Carleton, *Westminster* (in *English Public Schools* series: 1938). Cf. also Edward C. Mack, *Public Schools and British Opinion,*

1780 to 1860 (1938), p. 18: of the seven English Public Schools at the end of the eighteenth century, "Westminster had both the most glorious and the most tragic career. Under the leadership of Richard Busby, probably the greatest schoolmaster before Arnold, it became, at the Restoration, England's foremost school, and educated a large percentage of the English aristocracy, as well as men like Dryden, Locke, Christopher Wren, Jeffreys, and Atterbury. After Busby's day his school continued to flourish, and attained another period of greatness under John Nicoll (1733-53); after mid-century, however, it began to decline before Eton's and Harrow's rising stars, and has never since recovered its early prestige."

10. "There was a Bishop, I think it was Sprat, who thanked God that, though he was not educated at Westminster, yet he became a Bishop. I, on the contrary, would not have been educated there for the best pair of lawn sleeves in the kingdom. But *de gustibus non est disputandum.*" Rev. William Mason to the Hon. Horace Walpole, 2 July 1782 (*Letters of Horace Walpole*, ed. Peter Cunningham, vol. viii, p. 240 n.).—Dr Thomas Sprat (1635-1713) was the second of eight successive Deans of Westminster to combine the deanery (in which he was installed in Sept. 1683) with the bishopric of Rochester (to which he was consecrated in Nov. 1684): an arrangement which, in the expressive phrase of Dean Stanley (*Memorials of Westminster Abbey*, 5th edtn., p. 446), "gave to that poor and neighbouring bishopric at once an income and a town residence." Sprat had previously been a Fellow (1657-70) of Wadham College, Oxford, under the Wardenship of Dr John Wilkins, and was elected a Fellow of the Royal Society in 1663. The son of a Puritan minister and author of a poem "upon the death of his late highness, Oliver, lord-protector", he revised his loyalties at the Restoration, and in 1661 was ordained priest. On the recommendation of his friend and fellow-poet, Abraham Cowley, he was appointed chaplain to the Duke of Buckingham. He became a Prebendary of Westminster (1669), Rector of Uffington in Lincolnshire (1670), Chaplain to Charles II (1676), Minister and Lecturer of St Margaret's, Westminster (1679) in succession to Dr Outram, and also Canon of Windsor (1681). John Evelyn, who on his sixtieth birthday (31 Oct. 1680) "heard Dr Sprat at St Margaret's, on *Acts* xvii.11.", thought highly of his talent as a preacher: but his standard of clerical duty as a parish priest seems to have left something to be desired (cf. Walcott, *St Margaret's Church*, p. 78). Sprat's principal literary work, and that by which he best deserves to be remembered, is *The History of the Royal-Society of London, for the Improving of Natural Knowledge* (1667): it

had a considerable influence upon the literary style of Anglican sermons (cf. Charles Smyth, *The Art of Preaching*, 1940, p. 135).

11. *Meet the British*, by Emily Hahn, Charles Roetter, and Harford Thomas (1953), p. 14.

12. C. K. Francis Brown, *The Church's Part in Education, 1833-1941, with special reference to the work of the National Society* (1942).

13. *The Love of Truth and Peace. A Sermon Preached before the Honourable House of Commons assembled in Parliament, Novemb. 29. 1640. By* John Gauden, *Bachelor in Divinity. Published by order of the house* (1641), pp. 41-3: "Here give me leave by way of short digression, in so great and publique an Assembly, to recommend to your favour, the noble endeavours of two *great* and *publique Spirits,* who have laboured much for *Truth and Peace,* I meane, *Commenius,* and *Duræus:* both famous for their learning, piety and integrity, and not unknowne, I am sure by the fame of their Works, to many of this Honorable, learned, and pious Assembly. . . . I leave it to your *Wisedomes,* at your leysure to consider, whether it were not worthy the name and honour of this State and Church, to invite these men to you, to see and weigh their noble and excellent designes; to give them all publike ayde and encouragement to goe on and perfect so happy Workes, which tend so much to the advancing of *Truth,* and *Peace.** [*Whereunto if it shall please God to encline any of your thoughts for the effectuall promoting of so commendable purposes, notwithstanding the distances whereat they now are the one being in *Poland,* the other in *Denmarke,* yet there is a faire, easie, and safe way of adresses to them both, opened by the Industry and fidelity of Mr *Hartlibe,* whose house is in Duksplace in *London,* a Gentleman who hath beene a constant furtherer, and great coadjuter with them both, in their Works: who hath correspondence with them; whose learning, piety, and unwearied industry towards the publike good, are so well knowne to the learned world, and many of your selves as well as to me, that he needs not the farther testimony of my Pen.]"—See also W. A. L. Vincent, *The State and School Education, 1640-1660, in England and Wales* (1950), pp. 23 ff., 37.

14. *John Knox's History of the Reformation in Scotland,* ed. William Croft Dickinson (1949), vol. i (Introd.), vol. ii, App. VIII (The Book of Discipline); H. M. Knox, *Two hundred and fifty years of Scottish Education, 1696-1946* (1953); W. J. Gibson, *Education in Scotland* (1912).—It may be remembered that James IV had attempted by an Act of the Parliament of 1496 to make education compulsory for the eldest sons and heirs of the

upper classes ("all barronis and frehaldaris that ar of substance"): from the age of 8 or 9 they were to be put to the
grammar schools till they had perfect Latin, and thereafter to
remain for three years "at the sculis of Art and Jure sua that thai
may have knawledge and understanding of the lawis.   Throw
the quhilkis Justice may reigne universalie throw all the realme.
Sua that thai that are Shereffis or Jugeis Ordinaris under the
Kingis hienes, may have knawledge to do Justice, that the pure
pepill suld have na neid to seik our soverane lordis principale
auditoris for ilk small Injure."   Any parent failing to comply
was to pay a fine of £20 to the King.   But this edict was incap-
able of enforcement: in 1545, of the Highland chieftains who
leagued with Henry VIII of England, not one could write.

15. For Emery Hill (1610-77), see Westminster Abbey Mun-
ments 34354 (copy of his Last Will); Guildhall Library Muniment Room MSS. 5444/xix-xxii (Court Minute Books of the
Brewers' Company); Stow's *Survey*, ed. John Strype (1720), vol.
ii, p. 45; 1st Report of the Commissioners on the Education of
the Poor (1819), p. 182 and App., pp 291-5; Further Report of
the Commissioners for inquiring concerning Charities (1824), pp.
278-81.—Emery Hill was twice married, but had no surviving
children of his own: his residuary legatee was his sister's second
son, Emery Argus (Churchwarden of St Margaret's, 1697-9). The
Will includes two personally revealing and suggestive items: a
bequest of two books ("One is Mr Allen upon the Doctrine of
the Bible or Gospell, and the other is Mr John Calven's Institutions of Christian Religion both in Folio"); and to Emery Argus
"my Bible that is in my Clossett with the Concordance in itt . . . .
and my best traineing Pike a Muskett and Carbine and my two
best Swords in my Clossett with two embroidered Belts and one
embroidered Hanger and Girdle and all my feathers and Rib-
bonds and Garters and also my Gloves plain and embroidered
except my two paires of best embroidered Gloves . . . and also
my Picture after the death of my Wife that is in my Chamber
. . . and all my Canes": the portrait here referred to eventually
came into the possession of St Margaret's Hospital, and now,
together with portraits of Charles I (attributed to Vandyke) and
of Charles II (by Lely), adorns the Board Room of the Governors of the United Westminster Schools.

16. Simon Patrick, *Auto-Biography*, p. 128; M. G. Jones, *The
Charity School Movement: a study of Eighteenth-Century Puri-
tanism in action* (1938); L.C.C. Survey of London, ed. Montagu
H. Cox and Philip Norman, vol. x, The Parish of St Margaret,
Westminster, pt. 1 (1926), p. 144 f.

17. E. S. Day (Head Mistress), *An Old Westminster Endowment: being a History of the Grey Coat Hospital as recorded in the Minute Books* (1902); D. F. Chetham-Strode, *Grey Coat Hospital, Westminster: a short history of the School* (1939).

18. The belief in the efficacy of religious instruction as a means of social reclamation and improvement is further reflected in 42 Geo. III, c. lxxiii. (An Act for the Preservation of the Health and Morals of Apprentices and others, employed in Cotton and other Mills, and in Cotton and other Factories: 22 June 1802), §8: "And be it further enacted, That every Apprentice, or (in case the Apprentices shall attend in Classes), every such Class shall, for the Space of one Hour at least every *Sunday*, be instructed and examined in the Principles of the Christian Religion, by some proper Person to be provided and paid by the Master or Mistress of such Apprentice; and in *England* and *Wales*, in case the Parents of such Apprentice shall be Members of the Church of *England*, then such Apprentice shall be taken, once at least in every Year during the Term of his or her Apprenticeship, to be examined by the Rector, Vicar, or Curate of the Parish in which such Mill or Factory shall be situate; and shall also after such Apprentice shall have attained the Age of fourteen Years, and before attaining the Age of eighteen Years, be duly instructed and prepared for Confirmation, and be brought or sent to the Bishop of the Diocese to be confirmed, in case any Confirmation shall, during such Period, take place in or for the said Parish"; and similar provisions are to apply in Scotland, when the parents are members of the Established Church; and all Apprentices are to be sent to church (Church of England or Church of Scotland) at least once a month, and if they cannot attend church every Sunday, then Divine Service must be performed in the Mill or Factory on every Sunday that they are unable to do so.—This Act was never effectively enforced: but the provision in regard to Confirmation is particularly interesting.

19. Printed in the *Gentleman's Magazine*, March 1789, vol. lix, pt. 1, pp. 203-4:

To his Excellency the Lord Lieutenant of Ireland.
March 14, 1786.

May it please your Excellency,
The humble Petition of the Inhabitants of Ayleston, Leicestershire, Old England.

If the High and Lofty One, that inhabiteth Eternity, waiting to be gracious, is accessible to the prayers of miserable sinners;

pattern, and be so godlike and condescending as to regard our petition, which affords you an opportunity to perform an act well-pleasing to God and man?

A charity-school at Ayleston, your Excellency's manor in Leicestershire, is an establishment highly necessary, to prevent barbarism: therefore, your Excellency's bounty in such a foundation is the favour we solicit at the hands of your humanity.

May Divine Providence incline you to supply our necessity, and repay the generous deed, by every needful blessing on your Excellency and your illustrious house!

There are, at this time, thirty children here, whose parents are unable to give them the least education; and the school-master of the town is declining his employment, for want of proper encouragement, by a competent number of scholars; and then the distress will extend to the whole community.

This is a true state of the case, as witness my hand,

WM. BICKERSTAFFE,

Curate of Ayleston.

⌈Signed by 58 house-dwellers in Ayleston.⌉

An obituary notice of the Rev. William Bickerstaffe will be found in *Gent. Mag.*, Feb. 1789, p. 182.

20. Robert Lowe, first Viscount Sherbrooke (1811-92): the east porch ("the House of Commons entrance") of St Margaret's, Westminster, with a portrait-bust and an inscription by Lord Selborne, is dedicated to his memory.

21. *Education, Religion, Learning and Research: an Inaugural Lecture* by the Rev. John Burnaby, Regius Professor of Divinity in the University of Cambridge (1953), p. 18 ff.

22. *Life and Letters of Fenton John Anthony Hort, D.D., sometime Hulsean Professor of Divinity in the University of Cambridge*, by A. F. Hort (1896), vol. ii, p. 435.

23. Quoted by Walter Bagehot, *Biographical Studies* (essay on Lord Brougham), p. 56.

24. Mandell Creighton, *Thoughts on Education: speeches and sermons*, ed. Louise Creighton (1902), p. 122.

25. Adolf Hitler, *Mein Kampf* (unexpurgated translation, 1939), p. 239.

CHAPTER 4

1. *Table Talk of John Selden*, newly edited for the Selden Society by Sir Frederick Pollock (1927), p. 71.—Cf. also p. 49 ("FRYERS"): "If there had been noe ffryers Christendome might have continued quiett and things remained att ye stay: If there had been no Lecturers (which succeeded ye ffryers in their way) the Church of England might have stood and flourished att this day."

2. Samuel Rawson Gardiner, *History of England from the Accession of James I to the Outbreak of the Civil War, 1603-1642*, vol. vii, (1884), p. 130.

3. Roland G. Usher, *The Reconstruction of the English Church* (1910), vol. ii, p. 356. This opinion is censured by the Canons of 1604 (Canon LVII: *The Sacraments not to be refused at the Hands of unpreaching Ministers*).—Cf. *The Second part of the Anatomie of Abuses, containing The display of Corruptions, with a perfect description of such imperfections, blemishes, and abuses as now reyning in euerie degree, require reformation for feare of Gods vengeance to be powred vpon the people and countrie, without speedie repentance and conuersion vnto God: made dialogwise* by Philip Stubbes (1583), ed. Frederick J. Furnivall for the New Shakspere Society, series VI, no. 12 (1882), p. 72: ("*The Corruptions and Abuses of the Spiritvalitie*") ". . . It is no good reason to say, bicause all [ministers] ought to be preachers, that therefore readers are not necessarie. But indeed I am of this iudgement with you, that whoso can but read onelie, and neither is able to interpret, preach, expound, nor explane the scriptures, nor yet to repell and conuince the aduersarie, nor to deliuer the true sense and meaning of the scriptures, ought not to occupie a place in the church of God, as pastor thereof. For God commandeth that the pastors be learned, saieng: *Labia sacerdotum custodiant veritatem, et edificant populi verbum dei ex ore eorum*, Let the lips of the priests preserue knowledge, and let the people learne the truth out of their mouthes. And therefore those that haue not this dexteritie in handling the worde of God, they are not sent of God, neither are they Christs vicegerents or pastors to instruct his flocke. . . . These are those idoll shepheards, and dumbe dogs, of whom speaketh the prophet, that are not able to barke against sinne. And therefore I beseech the Lord to remooue them, and place able and sufficient pastors ouer his church, that God may be glorified, and the church edified in the truth."

4. *An Impartial Collection of the Great Affairs of State from the Beginning of the Scotch Rebellion in the Year* MDCXXXIX *to the Murther of King Charles I* by John Nalson, LL.D., vol. ii (1683), p. 478: ". . . they were all the Parliaments, or rather the Presbyterian Factions Creatures, and were therefore ready in all places to Preach up their Votes and Orders, to Extol their Actions, and applaud their Intentions; these were the men that debauch'd the People with Principles of disloyalty, and taught them to Worship *Jeroboam's* Golden Calves, the pretended Liberty of the Subject, and the Glorious Reformation that was coming; which the Common People adored, even the Imaginary Idea of, like the wild *Ephesians*, as if it were a Government falling down from Heaven, and as they used to Cant it, the Pattern in the Mount, the New *Jerusalem*, and Mount *Zion.* . . ."

5. See *Dedham in History: Feudal, Industrial, and Ecclesiastical*, by Canon Gerald H. Rendall (Colchester: 1937), pt. iii, "Puritan Dedham". The lectureship, having been maintained by private contributions, fell into abeyance after the Restoration, but was revived and endowed by the Rev. William Burkitt (son of Miles Burkitt), Vicar of Dedham 1692-1703. "The long line of Lecturers remained unbroken till the retirement of the Rev. H. Ashwin in 1918, when, under a revised scheme of 1908, it was combined with the tenure of the living." (p. 150.)—The parish of St Antholin has been absorbed by St Mary Aldermary, but four lectureships still survive, although under altered conditions.

6. Strype, *Life of Bishop Aylmer* (1821 edtn.), p. 100. There is an attractive selection from *The Sermons of Henry Smith, the Silver-Tongued Preacher*, ed. John Brown, D.D. (1908).

7. William Haller, *The Rise of Puritanism* (1938), p. 52.

8. Cf. *Citt and Bumpkin. In a Dialogue over a Pot of Ale. Concerning Matters of Religion and Government.* By R[oger] L['Estrange]. 1680. Pt. 1, pp. 15-16:

Citt. You are to understand, that by the *Protestant Religion* is meant the *Religion* of the *Dissenters* in *England*, from the *Church* of *England*; As the First *Protestants* in *Germany* 1529 (from whom we denominate our Selves) were *Dissenters* from the Church of *Rome* . . .

Bum. So that I perceive We Set up *the* Protestant Religion: *we did not* Destroy *it: But they prest it Then, that the* Church *of* England *was a* Protestant Church, *and that the* Jesuites *had only* Design'd *the* Destruction *of it, where as* We *did* Actually Execute *it.*

Citt. Your Answer must be, that the *Church* of *England,* though it be a little *Protestantish*, is yet not directly Protestant: As on the Other side, it is not altogether the *Whore* of *Babilon*, though a good deal *Whorish*; and therefore the Reply to That must be, that we did not *Destroy*, but only *Reform* it.

Bum. *Why I have answer'd People out of my Own* Mother-Wit, *that we did but* Reform *it. And they told me again, the Cutting of it off* Root and Branch, *was a very Extraordinary way of* Reforming.

Citt. The Answer to That is Obvious, that the *Cutting Off Root and Branch*, is only a *Thorow*, or a *Higher degree* of *Reforming*. . .

9. The best account of this Trust is to be found in a valuable article by Professor Isabel M. Calder, "A Seventeenth Century Attempt to Purify the Anglican Church", in the *American Historical Review* (July 1948), vol. liii, pp. 760-75.

10. The four clergymen, as already mentioned, were Richard Stock (who was succeeded on his death in 1626 by William Gouge), Richard Sibbes, Charles Offspring, and John Davenport. The Rev. Hugh Peter, until he left England in 1629, was closely associated with the Trust and solicited gifts on its behalf, but was never actually a feoffee. The four lawyers were Christopher Sherland of Gray's Inn (succeeded on his death in 1632 by Sir Thomas Crew, also of Gray's Inn), Samuel Browne and Robert Eyre of Lincoln's Inn, and John White of the Middle Temple. The four merchants were Francis Bridges, salter; Richard Davis, vintner; John Gearing, grocer; and George Harwood, haberdasher. In order to procure a casting vote, the feoffees in 1626 elected as a thirteenth member Rowland Heylyn, ironmonger, alderman and sheriff of the City of London (succeeded on his death in Feb. 1632 by Nicholas Rainton, haberdasher, alderman and sheriff and in 1622-3 Lord Mayor of London).

Of these, the six adventurers in the Massachusetts Bay Company were Davenport, Browne, White, Bridges, Davis, and Harwood. Sherland was an original member of the Providence Island Company.

The Rev. John Davenport (1597-1670), before his election by the parishioners as Vicar of St Stephen, Coleman Street, on 5 Oct. 1624, had been for five years lecturer and curate of St Lawrence Jewry. Upon the advancement of Laud from the bishopric of London to the archbishopric of Canterbury in 1633, he became an Independent (= Congregationalist), and resigned his benefice. After a brief and stormy interlude in Holland, he returned to London, and in 1637, with a company of his former parishioners, sailed for New England. He was the first pastor of the church at Quinnipiac (New Haven), but after thirty years,

finding himself defeated in his opposition to the absorption of
the New Haven Colony by Connecticut, he accepted a call (unfortunately not unanimous) to the pastorate of the First Church,
Boston in Nov. 1668. There, on 15 March 1670, he died, as he
had lived, in the odour of controversy, and was buried in the
tomb of his friend, the Rev. John Cotton. (See the Biographical
Sketch in *Letters of John Davenport, Puritan Divine*, ed. Isabel
MacBeath Calder, 1937, pp. 1-12: also *A Puritan Church and its
relation to Community, State, and Nation*, by Oscar Edward
Maurer, D.D., 1938, pp. 1-46: both published for the First
Church of Christ in New Haven by Yale University Press.)

11. Heylyn, *Cyprianus Anglicus* (1668), pt. i, pp. 209-12. (Cf.
The Life of Dr Peter Heylyn by George Vernon, 1682, pp. 53-7.)
—"Great were the Sums of Money which the Piety of the Design,
and the Diligence of their Emissaries brought in from their
several Circuits; most men admiring, all men applauding the
nobleness of such a Popular and Religious Act. But so it
hapned, that one of the Fellows of *Magdalen Colledge*, resorting
frequently to a Town in *Glocestershire*, where one of these new
Lectures had been founded by them, observed these two things:
First, That the Impropriation of that place remained in the same
Lay-hands as before it did; and therefore that the *Lecturer* must
receive his Stipend from the Profits of some other Parish: And
secondly, he observed, That the man there planted in that *Lecture* was one of a notorious Inconformity, found upon further
search to have been hunted from one Diocess to another, till at
last he was Silenced upon that account by the *High-Commission*.
This gave him the first hint of making a more diligent Inquiry
into that Design; and the more he looked into it, the worse he
liked it."—When the feoffees were finally brought before the
Court of Exchequer to explain their activities, these were found
to include the maintenance of the curate of the church of St
John Baptist, Cirencester, Gloucestershire, which was not far
from Heylyn's native Burford. No other holding in that county
is mentioned in the list (cf. *A.H.R.*, vol. liii, p. 766 n.). "By
retaining possession of impropriations and other ecclesiastical
property which they had acquired and bestowing the revenue
upon ministers and schoolmasters who had their approval . . .
the feoffees could encourage godly, able, and fruitful preachers
of the word of God. By withholding any share in the revenue
of a parish from an incumbent of whom they disapproved, they
could force unsatisfactory ministers out of office. Indeed, the
feoffees occasionally went farther and paid a stubborn incumbent
to surrender his place. In 1627 they got rid of John Burgen or
Burgoyne, curate of the church of St John Baptist, Cirencester,

the impropriation of which was owned by the feoffees, by offering him the Easter-book, an official cure, and £30, and troubling and forcing him to agree with them.   After the departure of Burgen, the feoffees installed Alexander Gregory as curate, and over a five-year period paid him the profits of the living plus £60."   (Ibid., p. 765.)

Heylyn describes his namesake and relative, Alderman Rowland Heylyn, ironmonger, of London, as "Treasurer to the Company"; he was in fact President of the feoffees (since 13 Feb. 1630), although he had previously been Treasurer from 4 Jan. to 27 Dec. 1627, when he was succeeded by John Gearing.

12. S. R. Gardiner, vol. vii, p. 259.

13. William Carus, *Memoirs of the Life of the Rev. Charles Simeon, M.A., late Senior Fellow of King's College, and Minister of Trinity Church, Cambridge* (1847); Charles Smyth, *Simeon and Church Order* (1940); Arthur J. Tait, *Charles Simeon and his Trust* (1936); Herbert Hensley Henson, Bishop of Durham, *Sibbes and Simeon: An Essay on Patronage Trusts* (1932).

14. R. S. Bosher, *The Making of the Restoration Settlement* (1951), p. 12; J. H. Overton, *Life in the English Church, 1660-1714* (1885), p. 4; *D.N.B.*, art., "Warmestry, Thomas (1610-1665)"; A. G. Matthews, *Calamy Revised* (1934), p. 542.

15. Charles J. Abbey and John H. Overton, *The English Church in the Eighteenth Century* (1878), vol. ii, pp. 495-7; Overton, *Life in the English Church*, pp. 190-2.

16. In Appendix A. will be found extracts from George Whitefield's *Journal* for the period 2-21 Feb. 1739, which, viewed in retrospect, was probably the most critical passage in his life.— See also *Annals of a Clerical Family (Venn Family Annals)*, ed. John Venn (1904). pp. 50, 61 and n., 92; and L. Tyerman, *The Life of the Rev. George Whitefield* (1876), vol. i, p. 171 ff., vol. ii, p. 621 f.—It is noteworthy that both John and Charles Wesley had preached in St Antholin's on several mornings in 1738 (John Wesley on 21 April, 25 May, 6, 27 Oct., 3, 9 Nov., 15 Dec., but thereafter not again until 15 Nov. 1778); cf. also the following entries in *The Early Journal* (1736-1739) *of Charles Wesley, M.A., sometime Student of Christ Church, Oxford*, ed. John Telford (1910), pp. 206, 207, 216:

1738.   "*Friday, October* 20.—Seeing so few present at St Antholin's, I thought of preaching extempore: afraid; yet ventured on the promise, 'Lo, I am with you always'; and spake on justification from Rom. iii, for three quarters of an hour, without hesitation.   Glory be to God, who keepeth his promise for ever."

"*Thursday, December* 21.—At St Antholin's the clerk asked me my name, and said, 'Dr Venn has forbidden any Methodist to preach. Do you call yourself a Methodist?' 'I do not; the world may call me what they please.' 'Well, sir,' said he, 'it is a pity the people should go away without preaching. You may preach.' I did so, on good works."

Charles Wesley also records that on *Sunday, October* 1, "In the afternoon I read prayers, and preached at St Margaret's, Westminster."

17. Powel Mills Dawley, *John Whitgift and the English Reformation* (1954), p. 216; "The Church of England", by the Rev. H. Hensley Henson (editor), in *Church Problems: a View of Modern Anglicanism*, by various authors (1900), p. 5.

18. Izaak Walton, *Life of Mr George Herbert* (1670).

19. *The Real Christian, or a Treatise of Effectual Calling*, by Giles Firmin, sometime Minister of the Gospel in *Shalford* in *Essex* (1670), prefatory epistle "To the Christian Reader"; *Correspondence of John Evelyn, F.R.S.* (Jeremy Taylor to John Evelyn, 12 May 1658), quoted in *The Life and Writings of Jeremy Taylor* by C. J. Stranks (1952), p. 188.

20. John Edward Smith, *Local Government in Westminster* (1889), pp. 44-7: it may be noted that Dr Fynes, in his letter of 3 Nov. 1820, characteristically expressed a wish "to make it a condition with the Lecturer that he should read the Afternoon Prayers on Sunday as well as preach the Lecture", despite the fact that the Churchwardens had previously (Dec. 1801) taken legal opinion on this point, and had been advised verbally by the Commissary, Dr Swabey, that "the reading of the Evening Prayers did not form any part of the Lecturer's Duty" (p. 43). *Clinton v. Hatchard* (1822) 1 ADD. 96; *Annals of Our Ancestors: some records and recollections of the families of Fynes-Clinton and Mathews* [by Anna R. Craik], privately printed (1924); *Literary Remains of Henry Fynes Clinton, Esq., M.A.*, edited by the Rev. C. J. Fynes Clinton, Rector of Cromwell, Notts. (1854); *Gent. Mag.*, vol. xcvii, pt. 2, p. 570.—The Rev. Isaac Saunders, M.A., a graduate of St Edmund Hall, Oxford, was ordained in 1804 to the curacy of St Andrew by the Wardrobe with St Anne, Blackfriars (an Evangelical stronghold), during the incumbency of the Rev. W. Goode, whom he succeeded as Rector in July 1816: he also in 1809 succeeded the Rev. John Davies as Minister of the Broadway Chapel, Westminster, and was president of the Broadway Church Missionary Association: he died 1 Jan. 1836. See Charles Hole, *The Early History of the Church Missionary Society* (1896), p. 639.—The Rev. William Johnson Rodber (1790-1843), curate of St Margaret's, was also curate of St John's

Westminster, from 1818: he became Rector of St Mary at Hill, London, in 1825 (J. E. Smith, *St John the Evangelist, Smith Square: Parochial Memorials*, 1892, p. 114).—Maurice Swabey (1752-1826), D.C.L., Fellow of the College of Advocates, who delivered judgment in *Clinton* v. *Hatchard* (see Appendix B), had been Commissary for Westminster since 1782: he was also Chancellor of the Diocese of Rochester, and in 1790 had been one of the Commissioners to execute the Treaty with the U.S.A. (Barker and Stenning, *Record of Old Westminsters*, vol. ii, p. 897).

21. Hensley Henson, *Sibbes and Simeon*, p. 44.

22. William Crouch, *Bryan King and the Riots at St George's in-the-East* (1904); [Maria Trench,] *Charles Lowder: a biography* (1881); *The Ingoldsby Letters, 1858-1878*, by the Rev. James Hildyard, B.D., (collective edtn., 1879), letters lviii, lxiv-lxvi.

23. The successive editions, from 1549 to 1662, of "The Book of Common Prayer and Administration of the Sacraments and other Rites and Ceremonies of the Church according to the Use of the Church of England", rested upon statutory authority. King James' Bible of 1611, "Appointed to be read in Churches", and printed by the King's Printer, was never literally "authorized" (cf. Alfred W. Pollard, *Records of the English Bible*, 1911, p. 60), but it came to be known as "the Authorized Version" to distinguish it from the unauthorized Geneva Bible of 1560, which it was intended to supplant. The Geneva version was more popular, especially among the Puritans, and had enjoyed an unchallenged supremacy since the last edition of the Bishops' Bible in 1602: but it was distasteful to the ecclesiastical authorities and obnoxious to the King, who at the Hampton Court Conference (14 Jan. 1604) declared it to be in his opinion the worst of all translations of the Bible into English. This may seem surprising, for not only was it the first Bible ever published in Scotland (in 1579, with a dedication to himself), but it was also the translation on which he had himself been brought up, and from which he quoted in his own writings (J. Isaacs, in *The Bible in its Ancient and English Versions*, ed. H. Wheeler Robinson, 1940, p.197). King James' hostility is, however, explicable in the light of the caveat which he addressed to his translators "that no marginall notes should be added, hauing found in them which are annexed to the *Geneua* translation (which he sawe in a Bible giuen him by an English Lady) some notes very partiall, vntrue, seditious, and sauouring too much of daungerous, and trayterous conceites. As for example, *Exod.* 1, 19, where the marginal note alloweth *disobedience to Kings*. And 2 *Chron.* 15, 16, the note

taxeth *Asa* for deposing his mother, *onely* and *not killing her . . .*".

The authorized Catechism (before 1604) was the "Catechismus, sive prima Institutio Disciplinaque Pietatis Christianæ" (1570: Engl. tr., "A Catechism or first Instruction and Learning of Christian Religion", 1570) by Dr Alexander Nowell, Dean of St Paul's from 1560 to 1602 (cf. E. Basil Redlich, *The Church Catechism*, 1924). The authorized Latin Grammar (1st edtn., 1527) was that of William Lily, the first High Master of St Paul's School from 1512 until his death in 1522: he was assisted by Dean Colet (who submitted the manuscript to Erasmus for his criticisms), and by other scholars. The accidence is attributed to Colet: Lily wrote the syntax, including the mnemonic rhymes, "Propria quæ Maribus" and "As in Præsenti" known and distorted by so many generations of schoolboys. The new grammar was taken up by Cardinal Wolsey, and was authorized by King Henry VIII, who may have commissioned it in the first instance. Cf. *Liber quorundam Canonum disciplinæ ecclesiæ Anglicanæ* (1571): "Ludimagistri nullam doceant grammaticam, nisi eam, quam solam regia majestas per omne regnum in omnibus scholis legi mandavit; nec alium Latinum catechismum, quam qui anno editus est, MDLXX, quem etiam Anglice redditum, pueros, qui Latine nesciunt, docere volumus" (Edward Cardwell, *Synodalia*, 1842, vol. i, p. 128). Cf. also Archbishop Whitgift's Visitation Articles for the Diocese of Bath and Wells (1583): "Whether the schoolmasters which teach in your parish, either openly or privately in any gentleman's house, or in any other place there, be of good and sincere religion and conversation, and be diligent in teaching and bringing up of youth; . . . whether they teach the grammar set forth by King Henry the Eighth of noble memory and no other. . . ." (W. P. M. Kennedy, *Elizabethan Episcopal Administration*, Alcuin Club, 1924, vol. iii, p. 156). So late as 1736, S. Buckley and Thomas Longman combined to purchase from "the Family of the Nortons, the old Patentees, the Royal Grant and Privilege of Printing Lily's Grammar, which, from the time it was compiled, has by our several Kings and Queens successively been ordered generally to be used in Schools . . ." (Harold Cox and John E. Chandler, *The House of Longman*, pr., pr., 1925, pp. 7-10). But by that date Lily's Grammar no longer held an enforced monopoly of the scholastic curriculum: a Bill to make it compulsory had been read for the first time in the House of Lords on 26 May 1675, but had not been proceeded with.

24. *The Remains of Denis Granville, D.D., Dean and Archdeacon of Durham, &c.* (Surtees Society, 1865), pp. 101-7: Letter from a young Gentleman, Student in the Inns of Court, to a

Reverend Divine in the country, complaining of Ministers' irregularity in the City of London, &c., in point of conformity.

25. Cf. *An Admonition to the People of England* (1589) by T. C. [i.e., not Thomas Cartwright, but Thomas Cooper, Bishop of Winchester], ed. Edward Arber (1883), p. 119: "At the beginning, some learned and godly Preachers, for priuate respects in themselves, made strange to weare the *Surplesse, Cap*, or *Tippet*, but yet so, that they declared themselues to thinke the thing indifferent, and not iudge euil of such as did vse them. Shortly after rose vp other, defending that they were not thinges indifferent, but distayned with Antichristian idolatrie, and therefore not to bee suffered in the Church."

26. G. W. E. Russell, *Saint Alban the Martyr, Holborn: a history of fifty years* (1913), p. 49.

27. *Hymns and Spiritual Songs. In Three Books.* By I[saac] Watts, D.D. (1707). Bk. 1 (*Collected from the Scriptures*), lxxiv.

28. Preface to Cranmer's Bible (1540): ". . . And the old proverb affirmeth, that after tillage of corn was first found, many delighted more to feed of mast and acorns, wherewith they had been accustomed, than to eat bread made of good corn. Such is the nature of custom, that it causeth us to bear things well and easily, wherewith we have been accustomed, and to be offended with all things thereunto contrary. . . ." (*Works of Archbishop Cranmer: Remains and Letters*, ed. J. E. Cox: Parker Society, 1846: p. 118.)

CHAPTER 5

1. In *Tancred: or, the New Crusade*, by B. Disraeli, M.P., (1847), bk. II, ch. ix, Lady Constance introduces Tancred to "a startling work, just published", entitled "*The Revelations of Chaos*": "It is all science . . . Everything is proved—by geology, you know. You see exactly how everything is made; how many worlds there have been; how long they lasted; what went before, what comes next. We are a link in the chain, as inferior animals were that preceded us: we in turn shall be inferior; all that will remain of us will be some relics in a new red sandstone. This is development. We had fins—we may have wings."—It should, however, be admitted that the impact of "Darwinian wolution" (an impact brilliantly portrayed by Stephen Paget in *Have Reason To Believe*, 1921, p. 50 ff.) was more widely felt.

2. *Natural Religion and Christian Theology* (Gifford Lectures) by Charles E. Raven, D.D., D.Sc., F.B.A., Regius Professor Emeritus of Divinity, University of Cambridge: vol. i, *Science and Religion* (1953), ch. ix, "Darwin and the Century of Conflict", p. 170 and *passim*.

3. This paragraph is indebted to the series of lectures (1910-11) "On some Writers and Critics of the nineteenth century" in *On Writing and Writers* by Professor Sir Walter Raleigh, ed. George Gordon (1926), p. 190 and *passim*.

4. In 1710, the Rev. Dr Henry Sacheverell was suspended from preaching for three years. As soon as this period had elapsed (the Whig Ministry having fallen in the meantime), he preached before the House of Commons in St Margaret's, Westminster, on 29 May 1713, a sermon entitled *False Notions of Liberty in Religion and Government destructive of Both*, which immediately ran to four editions. Cf. F. Madan, *A Bibliography of Dr Henry Sacheverell* (1884).

5. A. W. Pickard-Cambridge, *Memoir of the Reverend Octavius Pickard-Cambridge, M.A., F.R.S.* (pr. pr., 1918), p. 8; Prof. T. G. Bonney, *Charles Lyell and Modern Geology* (1895), p. 59.

6. Leslie Stephen, *History of English Thought in the Eighteenth Century* (2nd edtn., 1881), vol. i, p. 80.—The Boyle Lectures began in 1692 (with Richard Bentley's *A Confutation of Atheism*): Collins' *Discourse of Freethinking* was published in 1713.

7. *The Works of the Reverend & Learned John Lightfoot D.D. late Master of Katherine Hall in Cambridge*, ed. John Strype (1684), vol. ii, pp. 1320-30.

8. Cowper, *The Task* (1785), bk. III, ll. 150 f.: *The Complete Poetical Works of William Cowper*, ed. H. S. Milford (1905), p. 167.

9. *The Minor Prophets*, by the Rev. E. B. Pusey, D.D., Regius Professor of Hebrew and Canon of Christ Church (1860), p. 510.

10. John Locke might speak of "the Spirit of God that dictated the sacred writings" without evaluating the precise implications of the phrase: on the other hand, Dr Pye Smith was able to quote an oracle of Robert Boyle—"We must carefully distinguish between what the Scripture says, and what is said *in* the Scriptures" (Crabb Robinson, *Diary*, vol. iii, p. 147).

11. Walter Bagehot, *Biographical Studies*, ed. R. H. Hutton (1895 edtn., p. 115), essay on "Mr. Gladstone" (1860).—The

reference is to Newman's University Sermon on "The Theory of Developments in Religious Doctrine" (preached on the Purification, 1843), § 40: ". . . but what if the whole series of impressions, made on us through the senses, be, as I have already hinted, but a Divine economy suited to our need, and the token of realities distinct from themselves, and such as might be revealed to us, nay, more perfectly, by other senses, different from our existing ones as they from each other? . . . Scripture, for instance, says that the sun moves and the earth is stationary; and science, that the earth moves, and the sun is comparatively at rest. How can we determine which of these opposite statements is the very truth, till we know what motion is? If our idea of motion be but an accidental result of our present senses, neither proposition is true, and both are true; neither true philosophically, both true for certain practical purposes in the system in which they are respectively found; and physical science will have no better meaning when it says that the earth moves, than plane astronomy when it says that the earth is still." (*Fifteen Sermons preached before the University of Oxford between A.D. 1826 and 1843*, by John Henry Newman, sometime Fellow of Oriel College, first published 1843: 1880 edtn., p. 347 f.)

12. Arthur C. Headlam, *History, Authority and Theology* (1909). p. 235; Edgar Vincent, art., "Some Aspects of the English Reformation, 1550-1660", in the *Church Quarterly Review* (Oct. 1929), vol. cix, pp. 68-89.

13. Charles Smyth, *Dean Milman* (1949); Arthur C. Headlam, D.D., Regius Professor of Divinity in the University of Oxford, art., "Hugh James Rose and the Oxford Movement", in the *Church Quarterly Review* (Oct. 1921), vol. xciii, p. 97. Newman's tribute to Rose is in pt. iv of the *Apologia*: ". . . he had been the first to give warning, I think from the University Pulpit at Cambridge, of the perils to England which lay in the biblical and theological speculations of Germany. The Reform agitation followed, and the Whig Government came into power; and he anticipated in their distribution of Church patronage the authoritative introduction of liberal opinions into the country . . .": cf. ibid., *Note A*, "Liberalism".—(Cf. *Letters Literary and Theological of Connop Thirlwall, late Lord Bishop of St David's*, ed. J. J. Stewart Perowne and Louis Stokes (1881), p. 349: ". . . Stanley informs me that he could not succeed in an attempt which he made to disabuse Newman of the illusion that 'he was driven from Oxford by the Liberals', as he asserts (*Apologia*, p. 329) . . .")

14. *Letters and Correspondence of John Henry Newman during his life in the English Church*, ed. Anne Mozley (1891), vol. II, p. 300 (Rev. J. H. Newman to Mrs J. Mozley).

15. Cf. Bishop Thirlwall's *Letters*, vol. i, ed. Perowne and Stokes, p. 260, letter dated 30 April 1867: ". . . It is necessary to be cautious in speculating on the character of another man's mind, especially for those who know nothing of him from personal acquaintance, which is my case as to Newman. But although it may be true that there was a want of balance and harmony in his nature, I doubt very much whether his secession was owing to the predominance of the imaginative element or to his proneness to the sensuous in religion. I see no reason for thinking that this was the attraction by which he was carried to Rome. My view of his character and internal history is, that his mind was essentially sceptical and sophistical, endowed with various talents in an eminent degree, but not with the power of taking firm hold on either speculative or historical truth. Yet his craving for truth was strong in proportion to the purity of his life and conscience. He felt that he was entirely unable to satisfy this craving by any mental operations of his own, and that if he was to depend on his own ability to arrive at any settled conclusion he should be for ever floating in a sea of doubt; therefore he was irresistibly impelled to take refuge under the wings of an infallible authority. No doubt this was an act of pure self-will. He bowed to an image which he had first himself set up. There was at once his strength and his weakness. He could deceive himself, and could not help letting himself be deceived. That is the impression which all I know of him has made on my mind . . ."

16 "Newman on the Development of Christian Doctrine", reprinted from the *Quarterly Review* (March 1846) in Milman's *Savonarola, Erasmus, and other essays* (1870), pp. 296-373; cf. G. M. Young, *Daylight and Champaign* (1937), p. 110 f.—What Fr Philip Hughes, L.S.H., in *The English Catholics, 1850-1950* (ed. George Andrew Beck, Co-adjutor Bishop of Brentwood: 1950), p. 10 n., describes as "Newman's profound analysis of Milman as a historian of Christianity", was published in the *British Critic* (Jan. 1841), vol. xxix, pp. 71-114, and reprinted (as usual, with innumerable verbal alterations) in Newman's *Essays Critical and Historical* (1871), vol. ii, pp. 186-248 ("Milman's View of Christianity").

17. Newman, *Apologia*, pt. v (Oxford edtn., 1913, pp. 211, 212, 235).

18. Duncan Forbes, *The Liberal Anglican Idea of History* (1952), p. 153.

19. *Westminster Review*, vol. xxxix (1843), p. 299: quoted by Sir A. W. Ward (ch. xiv, "Historians") in the *Cambridge History of English Literature*, vol. xii (1915), p. 318.

20. F. J. A. Hort, *The Way the Truth the Life* (Hulsean Lectures, 1871), 1922 edtn., p. 177.

21. Reginald Farrar, *The Life of Frederic William Farrar, sometime Dean of Canterbury* (1904), p. 113 f.

22. Edward C. Mack, *Public Schools and British Opinion since 1860* (1941), pp. 60-6; Farrar, *Life of F. W. Farrar*, p. 103 ff.

23. *The Letters of Queen Victoria*, 2nd Series, 1862-85, ed. G. E. Buckle, vol. iii (1928), p. 226 (Queen Victoria to Dean Wellesley, 22 July 1881).

24. *An Agnostic's Apology, and other Essays*, by Sir Leslie Stephen (2nd edtn., 1903), p. 95.—One of Farrar's less successful school stories, and the only one which he issued anonymously (*The Three Homes: A Tale for Fathers and Sons*), was written and published in 1873 under the pseudonym " F. T. L. HOPE", "which stood in my own mind for the words 'Faintly Trust the Larger Hope' " (preface to 1896 edtn.).—It is perhaps remarkable that the sermons on *Eternal Hope* should have occasioned so fierce an outcry more than ten years after the majority decision of the Judicial Committee of the Privy Council (Feb. 1864) in the *Essays and Reviews* case, commemorated in the mock epitaph on Lord Westbury (T. A. Nash, *Life of Lord Westbury*, 1888, vol. ii, p. 78 n.):

RICHARD BARON WESTBURY
Lord High Chancellor of England.
He was an eminent Christian,
An energetic and merciful Statesman,
And a still more eminent and merciful Judge,
During his three years' tenure of office
He abolished the ancient method of conveying land,
The time-honoured institution of the Insolvents' Court,
And
The Eternity of Punishment.
Towards the end of his earthly career,
In the Judicial Committee of the Privy Council,
He dismissed Hell with costs,
And took away from orthodox members of the
Church of England
Their last hope of everlasting damnation.

25. Father Furniss, a Redemptorist priest, whose *Books for Children* were published in Ireland *permissu superiorum* in the middle of the nineteenth century, and sold four million copies: according to the *Catholic Encyclopædia*, he "entered fully into the mode of thought of the child-mind". There is a classic passage in Book X, *The Sight of Hell*: "The Fifth Dungeon. *The Red-hot Oven.*" See Percy Dearmer, *The Legend of Hell* (2nd edtn., 1932), pp. 44, 141; G. G. Coulton, *Romanism and Truth* (1930), vol. i, pp. 74, 145-52, vol. ii, p. 306.

26. *Correspondence on Church and Religion of William Ewart Gladstone*, ed. D. C. Lathbury (1910), vol. ii, p. 108 (Gladstone to Sir Richard Owen, 23 Oct. 1885).

27. Cf. G. K. A. Bell, Bishop of Chichester, *Randall Davidson, Archbishop of Canterbury* (1935), vol. i, p. 179. See also the Farrar Scrapbooks (newspaper cuttings) in the Chapter Library, Canterbury Cathedral.

28. Herbert Hensley Henson, *Retrospect of an Unimportant Life*, vol. iii (1950), p. 359.

29. Quoted in *Six Liberal Thinkers* by A. M. Coleman (1936), p. 37.

30. Henson, *Retrospect*, vol. i (1942), p. 51.

31. C. A. Alington, *A Dean's Apology* (1952), pp. 53, 57. Chapters vi-viii of this book (pp. 42-58) are indispensable for the understanding of Hensley Henson's personality and character.

32. These lectures were delivered under the title, "Miracles and the Christian Faith", and were subsequently published as *Through Facts to Faith* (1912). Cf. J. M. T[hompson], *My Apologia* (printed for private circulation, 1940), p. 87.

33. Alington, op. cit., p. 47.

34. W. R. Inge, *Diary of a Dean: St Paul's, 1911-1934* (1949), p. 77.

35. Cf. Bishop Stubbs' second Oxford Visitation Charge (1893): "Certain great scholars and theologians are busy working at the higher criticism of the Old Testament, and at the reconciliation of our Lord's method of appeal to it with the truth of His Divine omniscience. It is not by any means necessary that either one or both of these subjects should be constantly ventilated in sermons on the elementary truths of the Gospel, or that every young clergyman should, in speaking to his people, be expected to make a general saving clause in favour of accepted verities that might be touched by such and such conclusions from these critical studies, or in demonstration of the fact that he holds himself in

suspense upon them. In nine cases out of ten the reference is unintelligible, in the tenth case it is suggestive only of misgiving. And, after all, no such expression of opinion is at all looked for from a preacher who is not supposed to have given special study to the subject." (*Visitation Charges delivered to the Clergy and Churchwardens of the Dioceses of Chester and Oxford* by William Stubbs, D.D. (ed. E. E. Holmes, 1904), p. 230.)

36. Quoted in *The Pentateuch and Book of Joshua critically examined*, by the Right Rev. John William Colenso, D.D., Bishop of Natal: pt. IV (2nd edtn. revised, 1864), preface, p. xvi n.—Cf. also the preface by the Rev. J. C. Ryle (afterwards Bishop of Liverpool) to *Moses, or the Zulu? A Detailed Reply to the Objections contained in Parts I and II of Bishop Colenso's Work*, by the Rev. W. Wickes (1863).

37. "Janus" [H. Wilson Harris] in the *Spectator*, 20 Feb. 1953. —Cf. the entry in Bishop Tait's diary (*Life of Archibald Campbell Tait, Archbishop of Canterbury*, by Randall Thomas Davidson and William Benham, 1891, vol. i, p. 347): "*5th March* 1863. —Yesterday I had a long conference with Bishop Colenso, from which I gained no hope. He seems fanatically convinced that he has a great mission to save the theology and religion of England from a great collision with Science. He seemed to me very wild, and to be likely to go very far in discarding the old faith."

38. Lord Courtney of Penwith, in *The Diary of a Church-goer* (1918), p. 15, recalled a Cambridge University Sermon by Colenso, then a parish priest in Norfolk, on the deception of Isaac by Rebecca and Jacob: "He suggested that most of us probably thought that Jacob was a mere stripling on the borders of manhood who might be excused if he could not withstand the authority of his mother; but he told us that if we examined the marginal figures in our Bibles we should find that Jacob was at least seventy years old. It was evident that no suspicion of Archbishop Ussher's chronology, still less of the punctual historical accuracy of the book of Genesis, had then entered Colenso's mind."

39. *Henry Hart Milman, D.D., Dean of St Paul's: a Biographical Sketch*, by Arthur Milman (1900), pp. 138-42; 3rd Report of the Commissioners appointed by Her Majesty to inquire into and consider the most effectual means of Improving the Metropolis (1845), Minutes of Evidence (the Rev. H. H. Milman examined, 1 May 1844), p. 12; *Carlyle and the London Library*, ed. Frederic Harrison (1907), pp. 62, 70, 83; J. E. Smith, *St John the Evangelist, Westminster* (1892), p. 508; John Langdon-Davies, *Westminster Hospital*, 1719-1948 (1952), p. 54; A Supplementary

Report on the Results of a Special Inquiry into the Practice of Interment in Towns, by Edwin Chadwick: extracts from a communication from the Rev. H. Milman (pp. 150-3): ". . . There always has been, and probably always will be, some distinction in the burial rites (I beg to say that to the credit of my curates, they refuse to make any differences between rich and poor in the services of the church) and in the humbler or more costly graves of rich and poor . . ."

40. H. Montagu Butler, *Ten Great and Good Men* (1910), p. 175.

41. Farrar, *Life of F. W. Farrar*, pp. 234-52.

42. Henson, *Retrospect*, vol. ii (1943), p. 362; *Coming of Age* (1947), reprinted in *More Letters of Herbert Hensley Henson*, ed. E. F. Braley (1954), pp. 151-8.

43. James Adderley, *In Slums and Society* (1916), p. 60.

44. Henson, *Ad Clerum*, p. 210.

CHAPTER 6

1. Sir Thomas Browne, *Hydriotaphia: Urn-Burial* (1658).

2. Bernard Lord Manning, *Essays in Orthodox Dissent* (1939), p. 14.

3. Henry Redeman, or Redman, was buried in St Lawrence's church, Brentford, where he was commemorated by a brass on the west wall, of which there is a drawing (from the Lysons collection at the British Museum) in W. R. Lethaby's *Westminster Abbey Re-examined* (1925), p. 153. "He appeared praying on the left; on the right were his wife and two daughters, and between them was a small plate, probably of the Virgin and Child. The inscription was: *Py for the Soule of Henry Redman sutyme chiefe M Mason of ye Kyngs works and Joha his wyf sp'all benefactors of this churche.'* It goes on to speak of lands and tenements, half stipend of a curate, and sufficient for a perpetual obit, and ends: *'deceased July 10, 1528. O' whos' soulle Jhu have M'cy.'* According to Lysons, he bequeathed the 'George' Inn and £3 6s. 8d. yearly for the curate; his will and that of his wife were still in the parish chest." (Ibid., p. 154.)

4. *St Margaret's, Westminster—the Story of the Fabric*: a Lecture, given in the Church on Saturday, 14 July 1906, by H. Hensley Henson, D.D., Canon of Westminster (*St Margaret's, Westminster, Parish Magazine*, Aug.-Sept. 1906).

5. Letter from the Rev. Mackenzie E. C. Walcott (*The Times*, 11 Oct. 1877).

6. *The COVENANT: with a Narrative of the Proceedings and Solemn Manner of Taking it by the Honourable House of Commons, and Reverent Assembly of Divines the 25th day of September, at Saint* Margarets *in* Westminster. *Also, Two Speeches Delivered at the same time; The one by Mr.* Philip Nye, *The other by Mr.* Alexander Hendersam [*sic*]. *Published by speciall Order of the House.* (London, 1643: pp. 11-25. The contemporary Edinburgh edtn. of the *Two Speeches* gives the names as "Naye" [*sic*] and "Henderson".)

7. Sheriff Robert Low Orr, *Alexander Henderson, Churchman and Statesman* (1919).

8. Vivian de Sola Pinto, *Peter Sterry, Platonist and Puritan, 1613-1672* (1934), pp. 23 ff., 230.—A stained-glass window in the Chapel of Emmanuel College, Cambridge, depicts Peter Sterry with St Margaret's church in the background.

9. *The Letters and Speeches of Oliver Cromwell with elucidations* by Thomas Carlyle, ed. S. C. Lomas (1904), vol. i, pp. 6-8.

10. G. Kitson Clark, *The English Inheritance: an Historical Essay* (1950), pp. 107-12.

11. Walcott, *Memorials of Westminster*, pp. 160-2; J. Armitage Robinson, "Westminster Abbey in the early part of the Seventeenth Century", in *Proc. Royal Institution*, vol. xvii, p. 519 f.

12. J. E. Smith, *Local Government in Westminster*, p. 168. These Royal Arms in a carved medallion may be seen above the west door inside the church.

13. Walcott, *St Margaret's Church, Westminster*, pp. 67, 77. We may note that the Vestry very soon requested that the "Singing Psalms" might be *read*, these having always been chanted since the erection of the new organ.—The predecessor of "Father" Smith was John Hilton, Mus. Bac. (Cantab.), who was both Organist and Parish Clerk: when the organ was taken down, pursuant to the Parliamentary ordinance of 1644, he continued to be Parish Clerk until his death (1657). In 1652 he published *Catch that Catch can, a Choice Collection of Catches, Rounds & Canons for 3 or 4 Voyces.* (Cf. Percy A. Scholes. *The Puritans and Music in England and New England*, 1934, p. 135 f.) He is especially remembered for the anthem, "Lord, for Thy tender mercies' sake", which is always sung at the Royal Maundy service in Westminster Abbey.—St Margaret's has a great musical tradition: our Organists have included Edward Purcell (1726), J. B. Sale, and, in more recent times, the almost legendary

Lemare, Goss Custard, Edwin Stephenson, Stanley Roper, and Herbert Dawson: and the present organ (Walker), which was installed in 1897, is reckoned the finest parish church organ in England.

14. *Cal.S.P. (Dom.) 1691-2,* p. 49.

15. Thomas Taylor, *A Life of John Taylor, LL.D.* (1910); Boswell's *Life of Johnson,* ed. Birbeck Hill, vol. iii, p. 181; *Boswell Papers,* ed. Geoffrey Scott and Frederick A. Pottle, vol. xiii, p. 47 n.; Sir John Hawkins, *The Life of Samuel Johnson LL.D.* (1787), p. 392 n. (Hawkins was himself a seat-holder at St Margaret's: cf. *Boswell Papers,* vol. xvi, p. 184.)—From 1760 to 1788, Dr Taylor occupied No. 20, Dean's Yard (assigned by Act of Parliament of May 1934 to be the Rectory of St Margaret's, Westminster), which, with its late fourteenth-century vaulted undercroft and early sixteenth-century Renaissance wall-paintings (illustrated in *The History and Treasures of Westminster Abbey* by Lawrence E. Tanner, 1953, p. 87), is the most beautiful and historic of the prebendal houses that survived the bombing in May 1941. Dr Johnson is known to have visited Taylor here on 18 March and 4 April 1778 (Boswell, vol. iii, pp. 222, 238-40): it was on the latter occasion that the memorable conversation took place as to what Johnson (who talked of going to Streatham that night) would or should do if he were to be held up by a highwayman.

16. *D.N.B.,* art., Wilson, Thomas (1703-1784)", by Alexander Gordon.—For the celebrated lawsuit (*Peirson* v. *Gell.* 1761-2) concerning the east window, see [Thomas Wilson and William Hole,] *The Ornaments of Churches Considered, with a particular View to the late Decoration of the Parish Church of St Margaret Westminster* (1761); Rothery's *Return of All Appeals in Causes of Doctrine or Discipline made to the High Court of Delegates* (House of Commons Accounts and Papers, vol. lvii, 1867-8, p. 85); J. E. Smith, *Local Government in Westminster,* pp. 64-7, and *Catalogue of Westminster Records,* pp. 195-6; Katharine A. Esdaile, art., "Changes at St Margaret's Westminster, in 1761", in the *Church Quarterly Review* (July-Sept. 1950), vol. cl, pp. 230-44.

17. A Tindal Hart, *William Lloyd, 1627-1717, Bishop, Politician, Author and Prophet* (1952), App. A, pp. 261-5.—In 1701 D'Emilliane migrated to America under the auspices of the Rev. Dr Bray, the Bishop of London's Commissary for Maryland (and founder of S.P.C.K. and S.P.G.), who made him a special grant of £133 12s. 10d. "for his own subsistance and to purchase two Negroes to stock his glebe he having a family" (H. P. Thompson, *Thomas Bray,* 1954, p. 63). He served Port Tobacco Parish,

Charles County, Md., for two years, and in 1703 was inducted
into Christ Church, Calvert County, where he died in 1714.—
Walcott, *Memorials of Westminster*, p. 121; H. C. Beeching,
Francis Atterbury (1909), pp. 201, 205.

18. J. E. Smith, *Local Government in Westminster*, p. 70.

19. W. E. Gladstone, *Gleanings of Past Years* (1879), vol. vii,
"The Evangelical Movement", p. 220.

20. A. P. Stanley, *The Life and Correspondence of Thomas
Arnold, D.D.* (1844), vol. i, p. 287.

21. Alfred Blomfield, *A Memoir of Charles James Blomfield,
D.D., Bishop of London* (2nd edtn. 1864), p. 41.—Cf. C. K.
Francis Brown, *A History of the English Clergy, 1800-1900*
(1953); A. Tindal Hart and Edward Carpenter, *The Nineteenth
Century Country Parson, circa 1832-1900* (1954).

22. Denis Gwynn, *Cardinal Wiseman* (1929), pp. 181-7;
W. R. W. Stephens, *Memoir of Lord Hatherley* (1883), vol. ii, pp.
33-41, 111 f.

23. It is memorable that three Victorian Lord Chancellors—
Lord Cairns, Lord Hatherley, and Lord Selborne—taught in
Sunday School.

24. "Last Words at St Margaret's", a sermon preached by
Dean Farrar on Sunday morning 21 July 1895 (*St Margaret's,
Westminster, Parish Magazine*, Augt. 1895).—"Private audiences
were given yesterday morning and evening, by invitation of the
Directors of the Electrophone Company, Gerrard-street, Soho, on
the occasions of the farewell addresses of Dean Farrar in St Margaret's, Westminster. The parties were small ones, as only fifteen instruments were available. The whole of the Church services were
listened to with great attention. The organ music, the singing, and
the various voices of the officiating clergy were clearly distinguish-
able. The Dean's morning sermon was received in absolute perfection. His voice was distinct and loud, and he was followed
through the instruments without the loss of a single word. The
evening sermon was also fully audible, although the preacher's
voice occasionally dropped." (*Daily Chronicle*, 22 July 1895.)
Was this the pioneer experiment in religious broadcasting?

25. Farrar, *Life of F. W. Farrar*, ch. ix.

26. *Notes of the early life of William Cowper, Esq, written by
himself, and never before published* (1816), pp. 4-5. "Here [at
Westminster School] occurred the second instance of serious
consideration. As I was crossing St Margaret's Church-yard,
late one evening, I saw a glimmering light in the midst of
it, which excited my curiosity. Just as I arrived at the spot, a
grave-digger, who was at work by the light of his lanthorn, threw

up a skull which struck me on the leg. This little accident was an alarm to my conscience; for that event may be numbered among the best religious documents which I received at Westminster. The impression, however, presently went off, and I became so forgetful of mortality that, strange as it may seem, surveying my activity and strength, and observing the evenness of my pulse, I began to entertain, with no small complacency, a notion, that perhaps I might never die! This notion was, however, very short-lived; for I was soon after struck with a lowness of spirits, uncommon at my age, and frequently had intimations of a consumptive habit . . .". (A more highly coloured version of this incident may be found in Lord David Cecil's *The Stricken Deer: the Life of Cowper*, 1929.)—Cowper entered Westminster School in April 1742, and left in 1749. "The most conspicuous event of his schooldays must have been the building and completion of the western towers of the Abbey, and it may well have been while watching their progress that his eye fell on a tombstone which almost within living memory still stood prominently in St Margaret's Churchyard and bore the immortal name 'Mr John Gilpin'." (Lawrence E. Tanner, "Some Literary Links with Westminster Abbey", in *Transactions of the Royal Society of Literature*, vol. xviii, n.s., 1950, p. 38.)

27. *The Life and Correspondence of William Buckland, D.D., F.R.S., sometime Dean of Westminster*, by his daughter, Mrs Gordon (1894), p. 239.

28. The inscription beneath the window (dedicated "to the glory of God and in memory of the immortal poet, John Milton, whose wife and child lie buried here") was contributed, at Farrar's request, by the American poet, J. G. Whittier:

> *The New World honours him whose lofty plea*
> *For England's freedom made her own more sure,*
> *Whose song, immortal as its theme, shall be*
> *Their common freehold while both worlds endure.*

Among those present at the unveiling of the window on 13 Feb. 1888, were Robert Browning, Lewis Morris, W. E. H. Lecky, the United States Minister (Mr Phelps), and the Baroness Burdett-Coutts. Matthew Arnold's address on "Milton" was published posthumously in his *Essays in Criticism* (2nd series: 1888).—The Milton Window was badly damaged during the second World War by a high explosive bomb. The broken lights were replaced by public subscription, and on 4 July 1949 a special service was held in St Margaret's to commemorate the restoration of the window: an address on "Arnold on Milton" was delivered by Dr E. M. W. Tillyard (and subsequently published in his *Studies in Milton*, 1951, pp. 1-7), and Dr T. S. Eliot read the sonnet, "Methought I saw my late espoused Saint".—John Milton was a parishioner of St Margaret's from 1651 to 1660, living in a house in Petty France. The Parish Registers record the publication (22 and 27 Oct. and 3 Nov. 1656) of the banns of his marriage to his second wife—

John Milton of this Parish Esq. &
Mrs Katherin Woodcock of the parish of Alderman-bury
Spinster

—and her burial in our churchyard on 10 Feb. 1658, followed a few weeks later (20 March) by that of their child.

29. *The Times*, 3 July 1878.

30. Thomas Burke, *London in my time* (1934), p. 146.

31. Especially revealing and significant are the reflections of the Very Rev. Dr A. V. Baillie, late Dean of Windsor, (in his autobiography, *My First Eighty Years*, 1951, pp. 148-9), on his work as Rector and Rural Dean of Rugby, 1898-1912. ". . . I risk being accused of egoism and conceit in saying all this about our work, but I have done so quite deliberately because our success failed to satisfy me. I had a feeling that somehow it was not producing in the people the kind of personal religion evident among the best Christians in my younger days. It certainly raised morality; it certainly turned people to Christian observances; it certainly made a great many people do what is called Christian work; it certainly made immense numbers listen to instruction. But were we giving our people the real thing and developing within them the power of true Christianity? . . . The weakness of which I was aware was not purely due to my individual faults —it was part of the weakness of the contemporary Church. I believe that the majority of the clergy were suffering from the same limitation as myself. We of the priesthood believed in the influence that can be brought to bear through organisation. We believed that a right theology was a very important thing, and that we must instruct the people in theology; we studied and acted accordingly. We believed in the education of the young in a high standard of morality, and we tried to give them this education. The Church was behind us in each of these respects. I am quite certain that there never has been a period in which the clergy were more conscientious and hard-working, and yet I felt there was something wanting with us all . . . I do not mean to imply that we did not achieve any good, for that would be absurd. Nor do I mean there were not people who had the vital religion which it seemed to me that our work lacked. It was, rather, that I felt such people derived it either from home

influences or from the teaching of my predecessors instead of from us."

32. Robert Sandall, *The History of the Salvation Army*, vol. ii (1950), pp. 181, 183; Hensley Henson, *Bishoprick Papers* (1946), pp. 194-5 ("General Booth and his Army").

33. From a broadcast sermon (Easter Day 1952). Mr Williams is a Fellow of Trinity College, Cambridge.

34. *In Memoriam* (1850), canto 55.

35. Peter Heylyn, *Ecclesia Restaurata; or, The History of the Reformation of the Church of England* (1661), ed. James Craigie Robertson (Ecclesiastical History Society, 1849), vol.i, p. 151.— Cf. Sir William Dugdale, *The Baronage of England*, vol. ii (1676), p. 363: Somerset "intended to have pull'd down St *Margarets* Church at *Westminster*, but that the standing thereof was preserved by his fall"; a pun which appears to be plagiarized from Sir John Hayward's *Life and Raigne of King Edward the Sixt* (1630).

36. Report from the Select Committee on St Margaret's Church, Westminster: with the Minutes of Evidence. Ordered to be printed, 10 July 1844.—Cf. Alex. James B. Beresford Hope, M.P., *Public Offices and Metropolitan Improvements* (1857), p. 26 ff.: "In connection with the arrangement of the space in front of the Houses of Parliament the retention of St Margaret's Church has been warmly canvassed. Upon this matter I desire to record not my own opinion, but that of two names most eminent respectively in England and France for their thorough acquaintance with the principles (practical and theoretical) of Gothic architecture. Both these distinguished architects have strongly expressed to me their aversion to its removal, grounding that feeling upon the consideration that the church in question, as it is, gives scale to the Abbey, while its removal would leave that pile to be dwarfed by the adjacent Palace. When I say that the English advocate for the retention of St Margaret's is Mr Scott, and the French, M. Viollet Le Duc, I shall have urged enough to suspend that unthinking fashion of reprobation with which that Church is too commonly visited. . . ."

37. *Hymns Ancient and Modern for use in the Services of the Church* (standard edtn.: 1916), no. 746.

38. *More Letters of Herbert Hensley Henson*, ed. E. F. Braley (1954), pp. 141, 85.

39. Included in *The Prayer Manual* compiled by Frederick B. Macnutt (1951), p. 157.

INDEX

A

Adderley, James, 182
Addison, Joseph, 67
Alington, C. A., 175, 249
Alleyn, Edward, 74
Aragon, Catherine of, 197
Arnold, Matthew, 88, 107, 204, 255
Arnold, Dr Thomas, 33, 104, 163, 199, 225, 231
Assheton, Sir Ralph, 18

B

Bagehot, Walter, 161, 245
Baillie, A. V., 256
Baillie, Robert, 193
Balfour, Arthur, 89
Bargrave, Isaac, 52-3
Barnes, Bishop, 178
Belloc, Hilaire, 38
Beresford Hope, A. J. B., 257
Bickerstaffe, William, 103, 235
Billing, Lady Mary, 185
Bilney, Thomas, 41
Blake, Robert, 4, 194
Blew Coat School, Westminster, 71, 79, 100
Bligh, Eric, 216-18
Booth, General, 181, 208
Bosher, R. S., 54, 59, 121
Boswell, James, 197
Brougham, Lord, 89, 104
Browning, Robert, 204, 255
Brummell, George Bryan ("Beau"), 4
Buckland, Dean, 158
Burke, Edmund, 20, 24, 25
Burnaby, Professor John, 105
Busby, Dr Richard, 55, 86-8, 98, 231

C

Canterbury, the Archbishop of (Dr Fisher), 73
Carlyle, Thomas, 163, 193-4
Castlemaine, Lady, 4
Caxton, William, 4
Chamberlain, John, 8, 14
Chaucer, Geoffrey, 4
Childs, George W., 204
Churchill, Sir Winston, 4
Clark, G. Kitson, 67, 194, 228, 252
Colenso, Bishop, 168, 178-9, 250
Collins, Anthony, 159
Comenius, 90, 232
Cooper, Bishop, 244
Cowper, William, 22, 157, 160, 203, 254-5
Cranmer, Archbishop, 139, 244
Creighton, Bishop, 109
Croft, Bishop, 215

D

Dacre, Lady, 71, 75, 79
Davenport, John, 118, 238-9
Davidson, Archbishop, 32
Dawley, Professor Powel M., 125
D'Emilliane, Gabriel, 198, 253-4
Disraeli, Benjamin, 28, 89, 104, 138, 157, 202, 244
Donne, John, 74, 227
Draper, W. H., 212
Dulwich College, 74
Dury, John, 90, 232

E

Edward the Confessor, King, 2, 35
Elstob, Elizabeth, 4
Emanuel Hospital, Westminster, 71, 75, 79, 229, 230
Eton College, 71, 88, 231
Evelyn, John, 128, 224, 231

M

Machyn, Henry, 42
Magee, Archbishop, 68
St Margaret's Church, Westminster, foundation of, 2, 35, 221 :
—— Churchwardens' Accounts, 5, 7, 43, 47, 64, 187-90, 222 :
—— Day, 20 July, 2, 187
—— Rectory, 253
Markham, Violet R., 215-16
Marshall, Stephen, 47-9, 60, 93, 121, 194, 227
Mather, Increase, 62
Maurice, F. D., xvi, 106
Melvill, Henry, 28, 224
Milman, Henry Hart, 3, 158, 162ff,. 179-80, 250, 251
Milton, John, 4, 59, 66, 255, 256
Montgomery, Field-Marshal Lord, 202

N

Nalson, John, 115, 237
Neale, Dr John Mason, 5
Nettleship, Henry, 174
Newman, John Henry, 161, 162ff., 246, 247
Northcote, Sir Stafford, 28
Nowell, Dr Thomas, 26ff., 224
Nye, Philip, 57, 190-2, 193, 194

O

Onely, Dr Nicholas, 198

P

Page Wood—see Hatherley
Palmer, Herbert, 59
Palmer, James, 79ff., 95ff., 112, 230
Parker, Sir Peter, 4
Patrick, Simon, 39, 99
Pattison, Mark, 174
Peel, Sir Robert, 3, 37, 163, 206
Penn, William, 228

Pepys, Samuel, 4, 18, 66, 80, 195
Perceval, Spencer, 28
Perkins, William, 67, 117
Perrott, Sir James, 8, 9ff. 33, 226
Peter, Hugh, 59, 228, 238
Peterborough, Earl of, 39, 225
Phillips Brooks, Bishop, 204
Pole, Cardinal, 22
Porson, Richard, 38
Port, Sir John, 72
Prynne, William, 18
Pusey, Professor E. B., 161, 171, 172
Pye Smith, John, 163, 245
Pym, John, 4, 13, 44, 57, 194

R

Ralegh, Sir Walter, 4, 102
Raleigh, Professor Sir Walter, 245
Raven, Professor Charles E., 157, 245
Redeman, Henry, 186, 251
Repton School, 72-4
Robinson, Henry Crabb, 163
Robinson, J. Armitage, 3, 213
Rodber, William Johnson, 149-54, 241-2
Rogers, John, 127
Rogers, Richard, 48, 116
Rose, Hugh James, 24, 163, 246
Rowland, William, 53-4, 227
Rugby School, 74
Rumsey, James, 4

S

Sacheverell, Henry, 158, 245
Salvation Army, 181, 207ff.
Saunders, Isaac, 129-32, 150-4, 241
Scott, Sir Gilbert, 204, 257
Selden, John, 113, 236
Shaftesbury, Lord, 180
Sibbes, Richard, 117, 118, 120
Simeon, Charles, 119-20, 133-5